AGN Wo3
3332700697049 3
Wood, Brian.
Fight for tomorrow [graphic
novel]

LIBRARY DISCARD
NON-RETURNABLE

戰勝明天

FIGHT FOR TOMORROW

D1314217

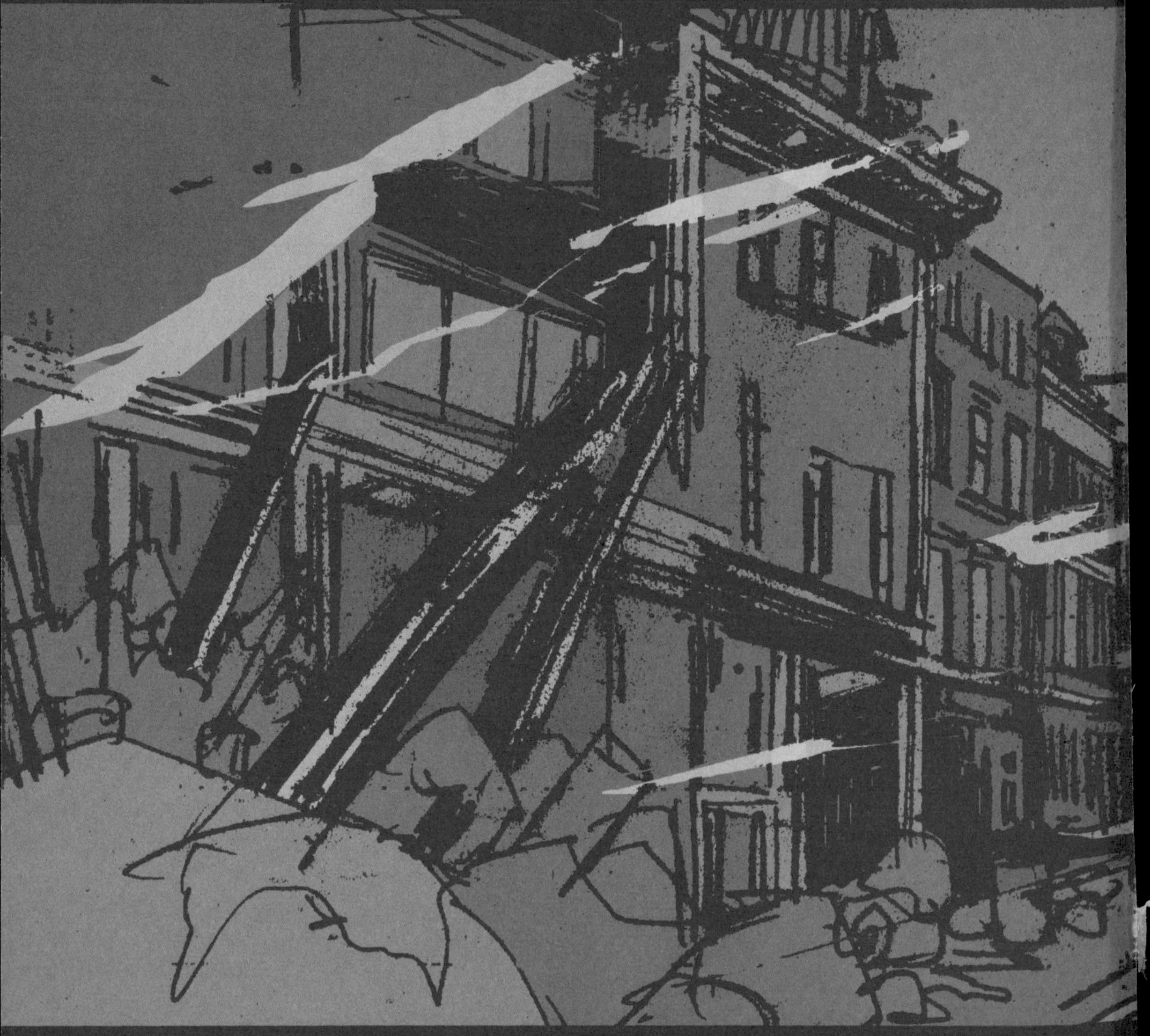

戰勝明天

FIGHT FOR TOMORROW

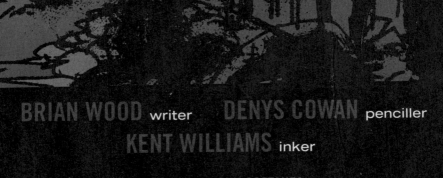

BRIAN WOOD writer   **DENYS COWAN** penciller

KENT WILLIAMS inker

LEE LOUGHRIDGE colorist   **JOHN COSTANZA** letterer

original series covers by **JIM LEE** (#1)   **KENT WILLIAMS** (#2)

DAVID CHOE (#3)   **NATHAN FOX** (#4)   **JO CHEN** (#5)   **CELIA CALLE** (#6)

KAREN BERGER Senior VP-Executive Editor
HEIDI MACDONALD ZACHARY RAU Editors-original series
SCOTT NYBAKKEN Editor-collected edition
ROBBIN BROSTERMAN Senior Art Director
PAUL LEVITZ President & Publisher
GEORG BREWER VP-Design & DC Direct Creative
RICHARD BRUNING Senior VP-Creative Director
PATRICK CALDON Executive VP-Finance & Operations
CHRIS CARAMALIS VP-Finance
JOHN CUNNINGHAM VP-Marketing
TERRI CUNNINGHAM VP-Managing Editor
ALISON GILL VP-Manufacturing
DAVID HYDE VP-Publicity
HANK KANALZ VP-General Manager, WildStorm
JIM LEE Editorial Director-WildStorm
PAULA LOWITT Senior VP-Business & Legal Affairs
MARYELLEN MCLAUGHLIN VP-Advertising & Custom Publishing
JOHN NEE Senior VP-Business Development
GREGORY NOVECK Senior VP-Creative Affairs
SUE POHJA VP-Book Trade Sales
STEVE ROTTERDAM Senior VP-Sales & Marketing
CHERYL RUBIN Senior VP-Brand Management
JEFF TROJAN VP-Business Development, DC Direct
BOB WAYNE VP-Sales

Cover illustration by Jo Chen.
Logo design by Brian Wood.
Publication design by Amelia Grohman.

FIGHT FOR TOMORROW
Published by DC Comics. Cover and compilation
copyright © 2008 DC Comics. All Rights Reserved.
Originally published in single magazine form as
FIGHT FOR TOMORROW 1-6. Copyright © 2002, 2003
Brian Wood and Denys Cowan. All Rights Reserved.
VERTIGO and all characters, their distinctive likenesses
and related elements featured in this publication
are trademarks of DC Comics. The stories, characters
and incidents featured in this publication are entirely fictional.
DC Comics does not read or accept unsolicited submissions
of ideas, stories or artwork.

DC Comics, 1700 Broadway, New York, NY 10019
A Warner Bros. Entertainment Company.
Printed in Canada. First Printing.
ISBN: 978-1-4012-1562-0

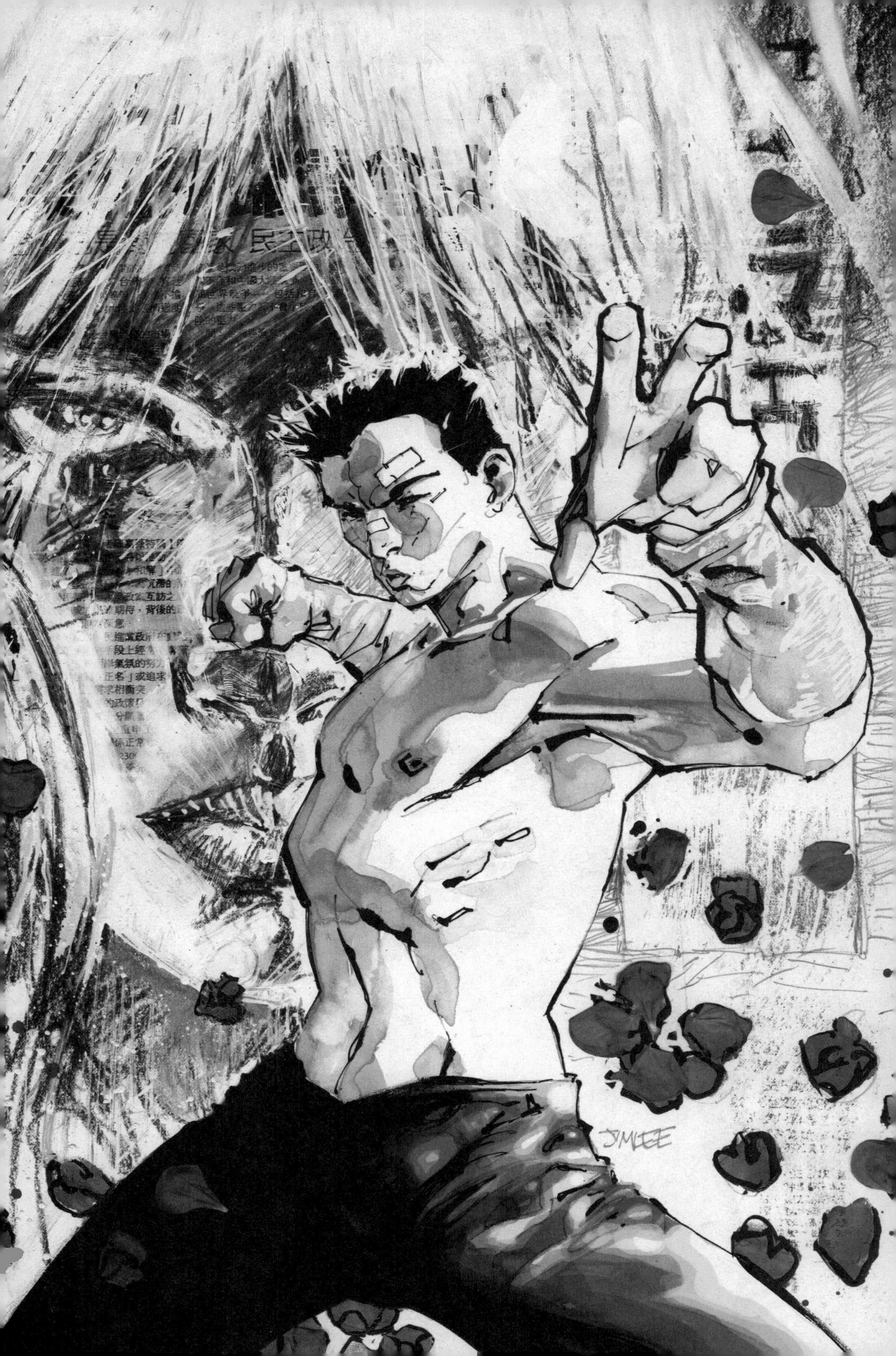

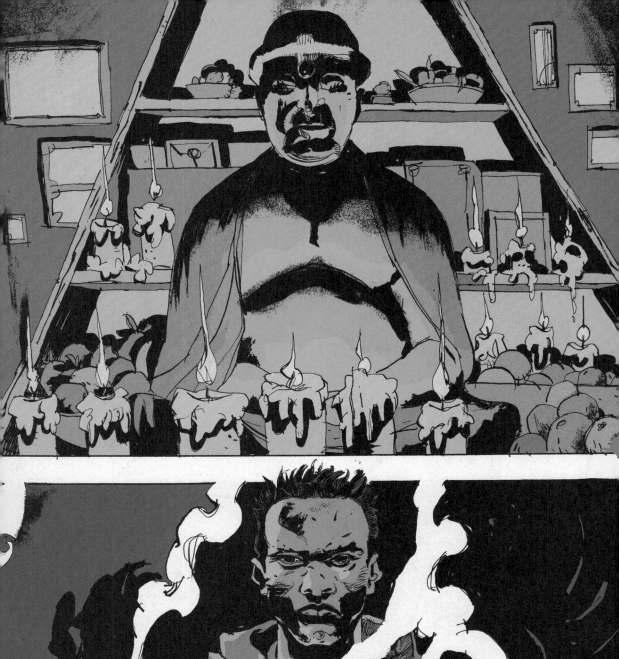

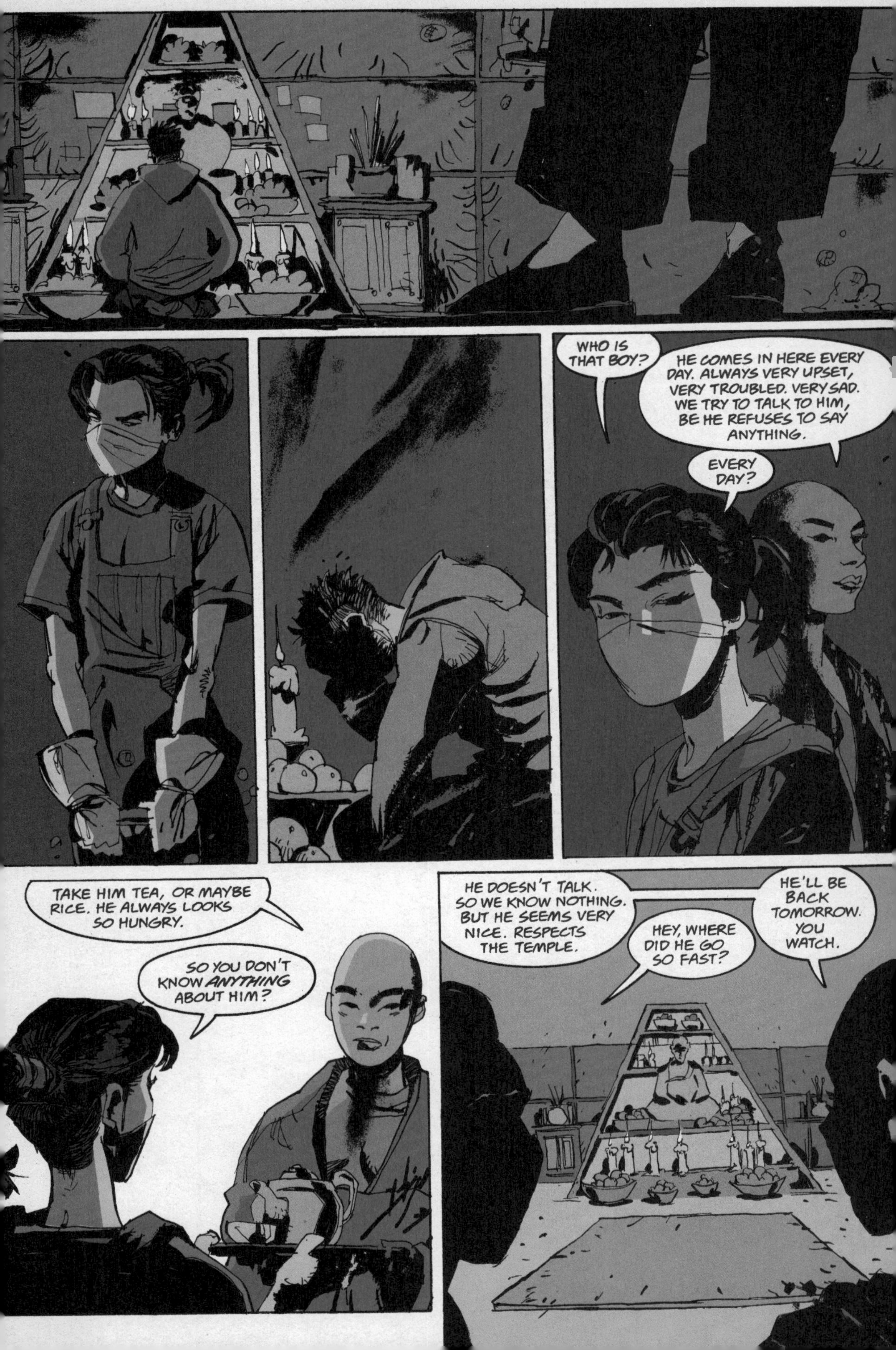
WHO IS THAT BOY?
HE COMES IN HERE EVERY DAY. ALWAYS VERY UPSET, VERY TROUBLED. VERY SAD. WE TRY TO TALK TO HIM, BE HE REFUSES TO SAY ANYTHING.
EVERY DAY?
TAKE HIM TEA, OR MAYBE RICE. HE ALWAYS LOOKS SO HUNGRY.
SO YOU DON'T KNOW *ANYTHING* ABOUT HIM?
HE DOESN'T TALK. SO WE KNOW NOTHING. BUT HE SEEMS VERY NICE. RESPECTS THE TEMPLE.
HEY, WHERE DID HE GO SO FAST?
HE'LL BE BACK TOMORROW. YOU WATCH.

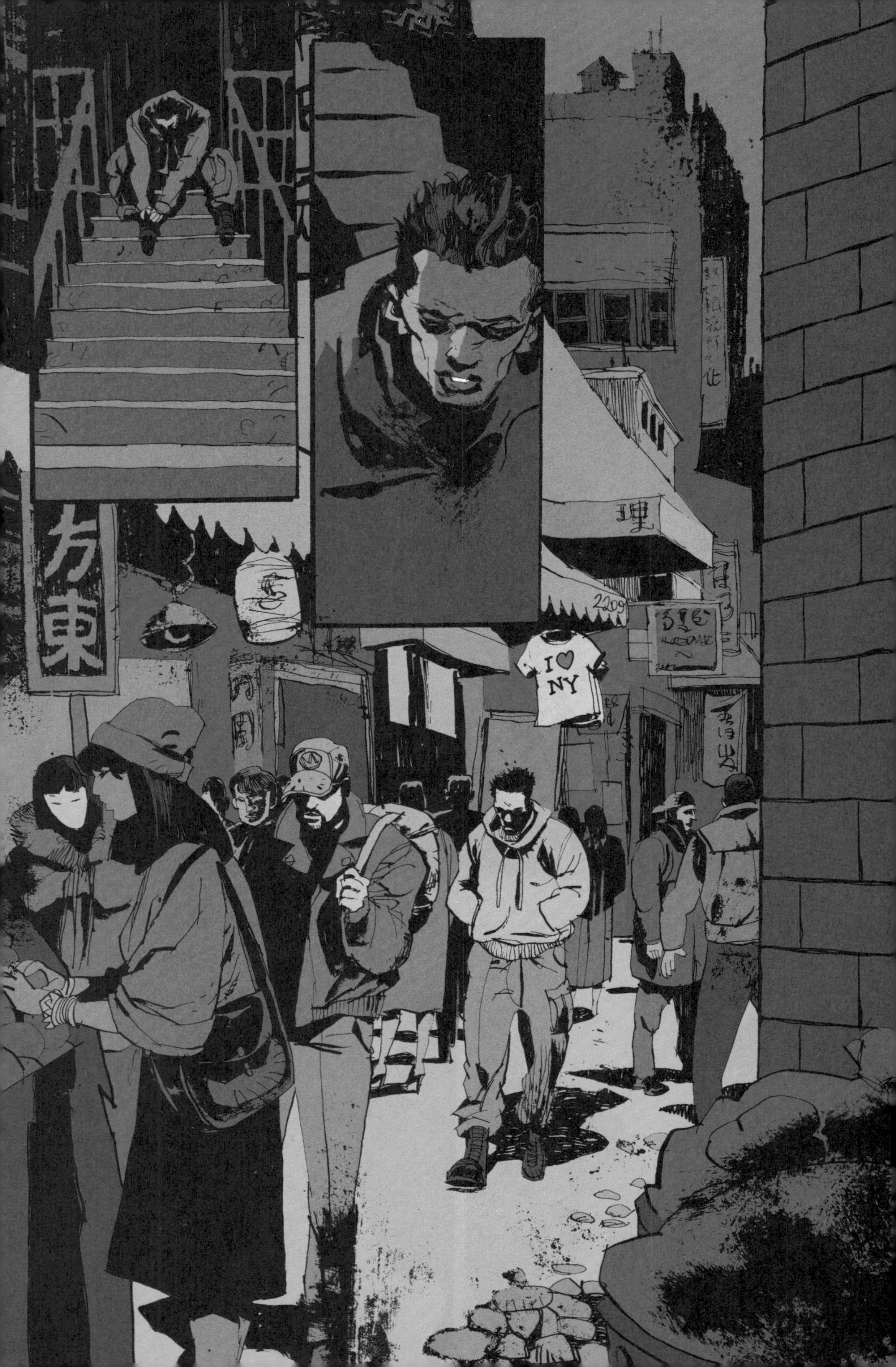
方東
理
2209
I ♥ NY

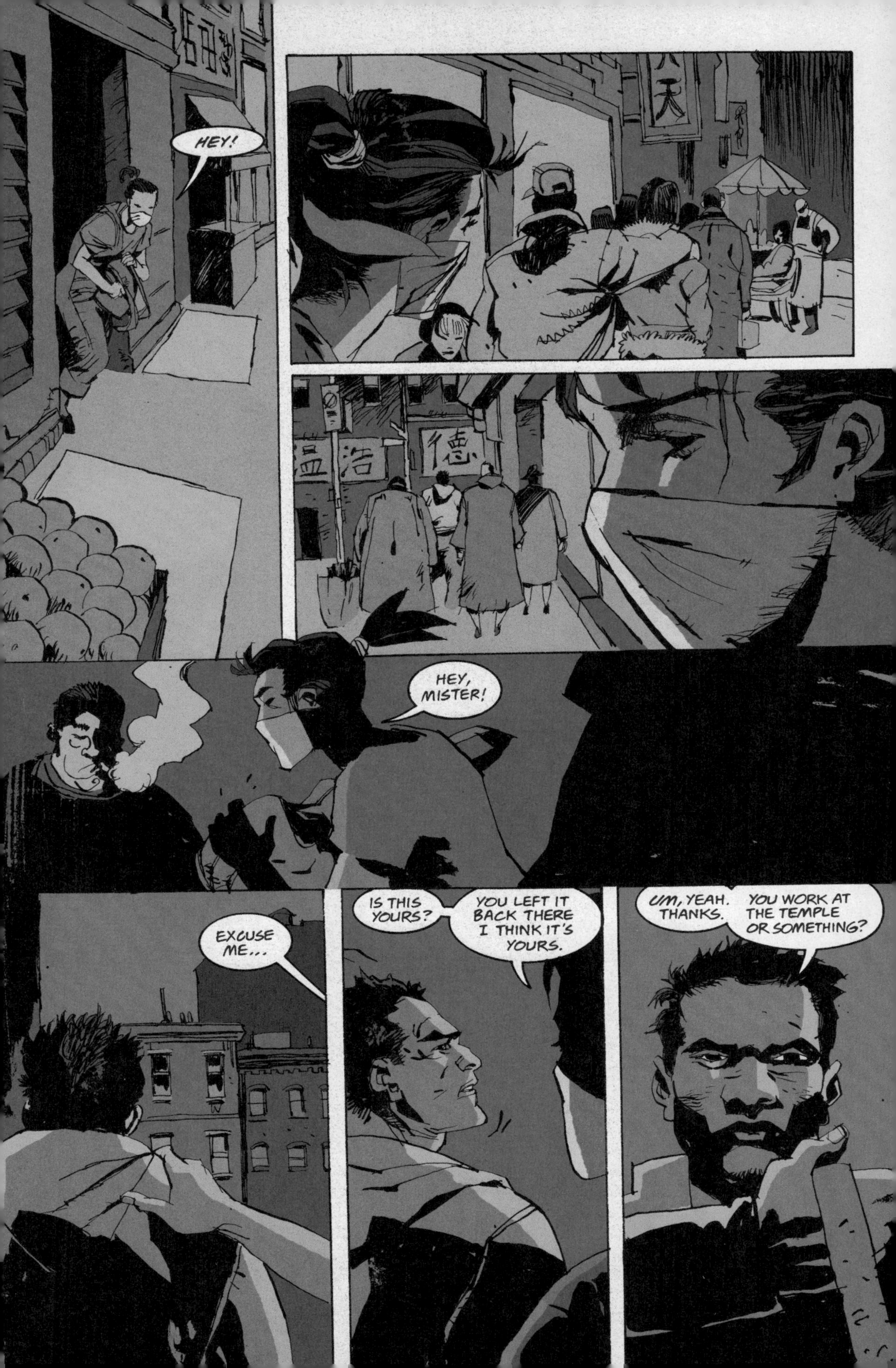
HEY!
HEY, MISTER!
EXCUSE ME...
IS THIS YOURS?
YOU LEFT IT BACK THERE I THINK IT'S YOURS.
UM, YEAH. THANKS.
YOU WORK AT THE TEMPLE OR SOMETHING?

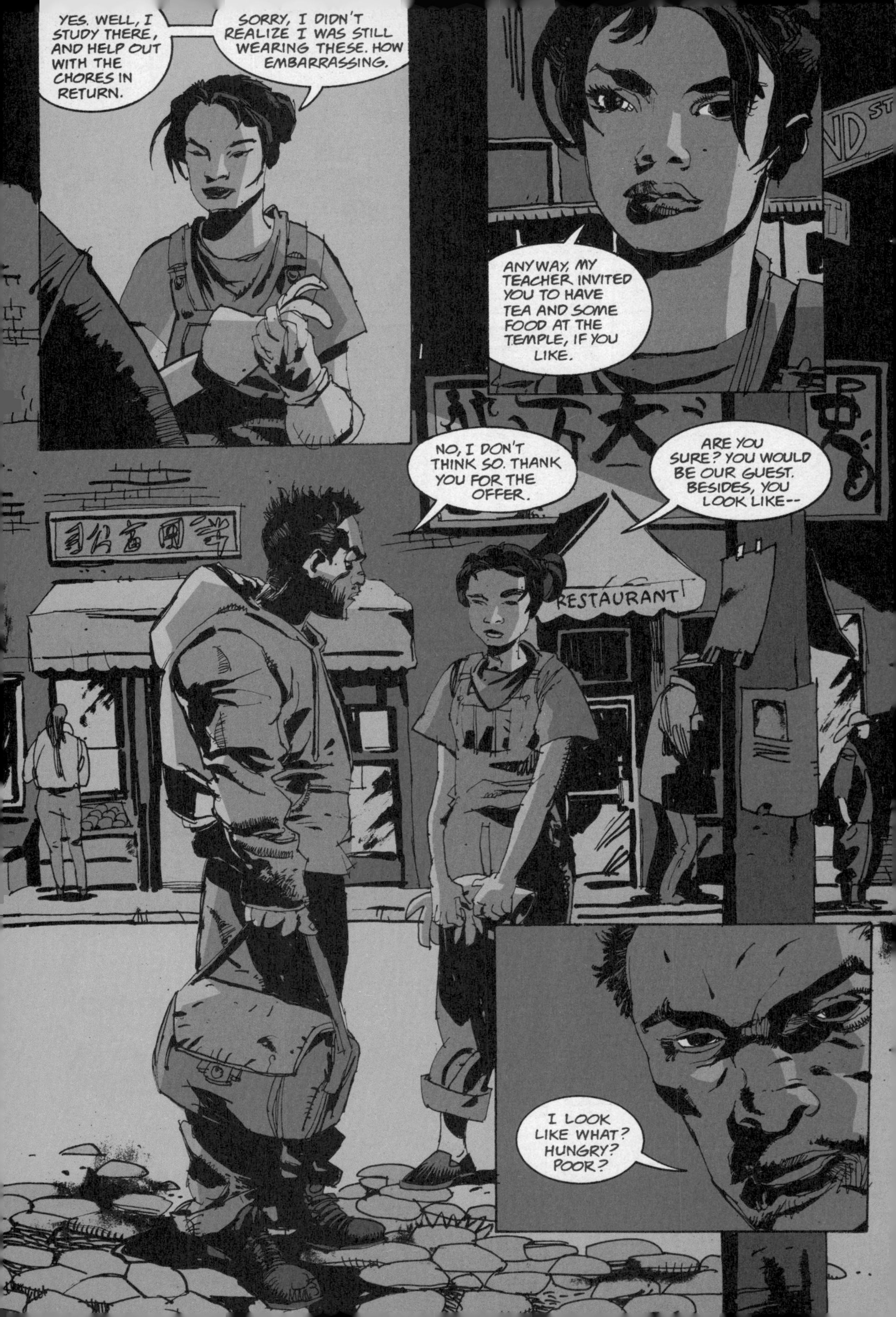
YES. WELL, I STUDY THERE, AND HELP OUT WITH THE CHORES IN RETURN.
SORRY, I DIDN'T REALIZE I WAS STILL WEARING THESE. HOW EMBARRASSING.
ANYWAY, MY TEACHER INVITED YOU TO HAVE TEA AND SOME FOOD AT THE TEMPLE, IF YOU LIKE.
NO, I DON'T THINK SO. THANK YOU FOR THE OFFER.
ARE YOU SURE? YOU WOULD BE OUR GUEST. BESIDES, YOU LOOK LIKE--
RESTAURANT
I LOOK LIKE WHAT? HUNGRY? POOR?

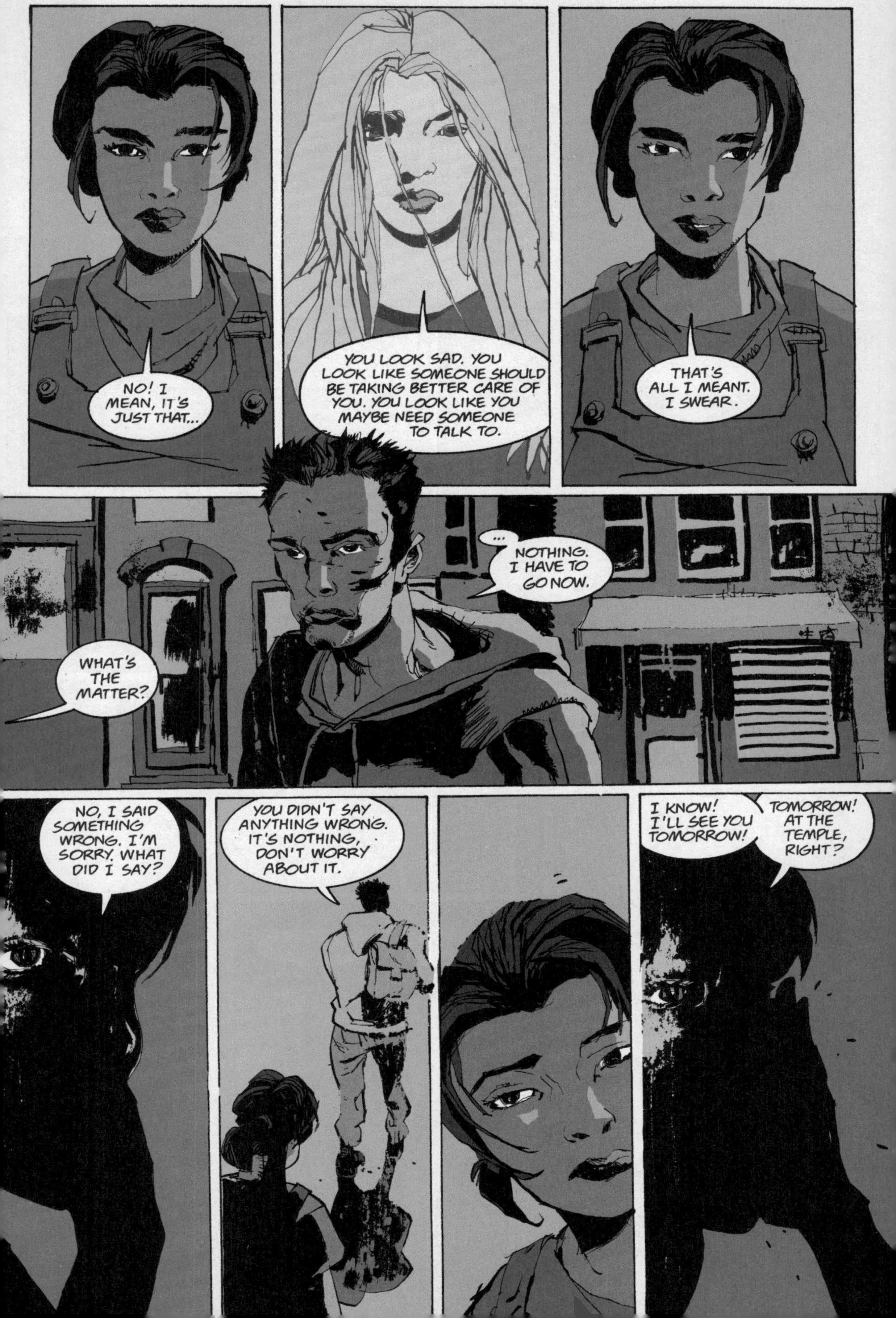
NO! I MEAN, IT'S JUST THAT...
YOU LOOK SAD. YOU LOOK LIKE SOMEONE SHOULD BE TAKING BETTER CARE OF YOU. YOU LOOK LIKE YOU MAYBE NEED SOMEONE TO TALK TO.
THAT'S ALL I MEANT. I SWEAR.
WHAT'S THE MATTER?
... NOTHING. I HAVE TO GO NOW.
NO, I SAID SOMETHING WRONG. I'M SORRY. WHAT DID I SAY?
YOU DIDN'T SAY ANYTHING WRONG. IT'S NOTHING, DON'T WORRY ABOUT IT.
TOMORROW! AT THE TEMPLE, RIGHT?
I KNOW! I'LL SEE YOU TOMORROW!

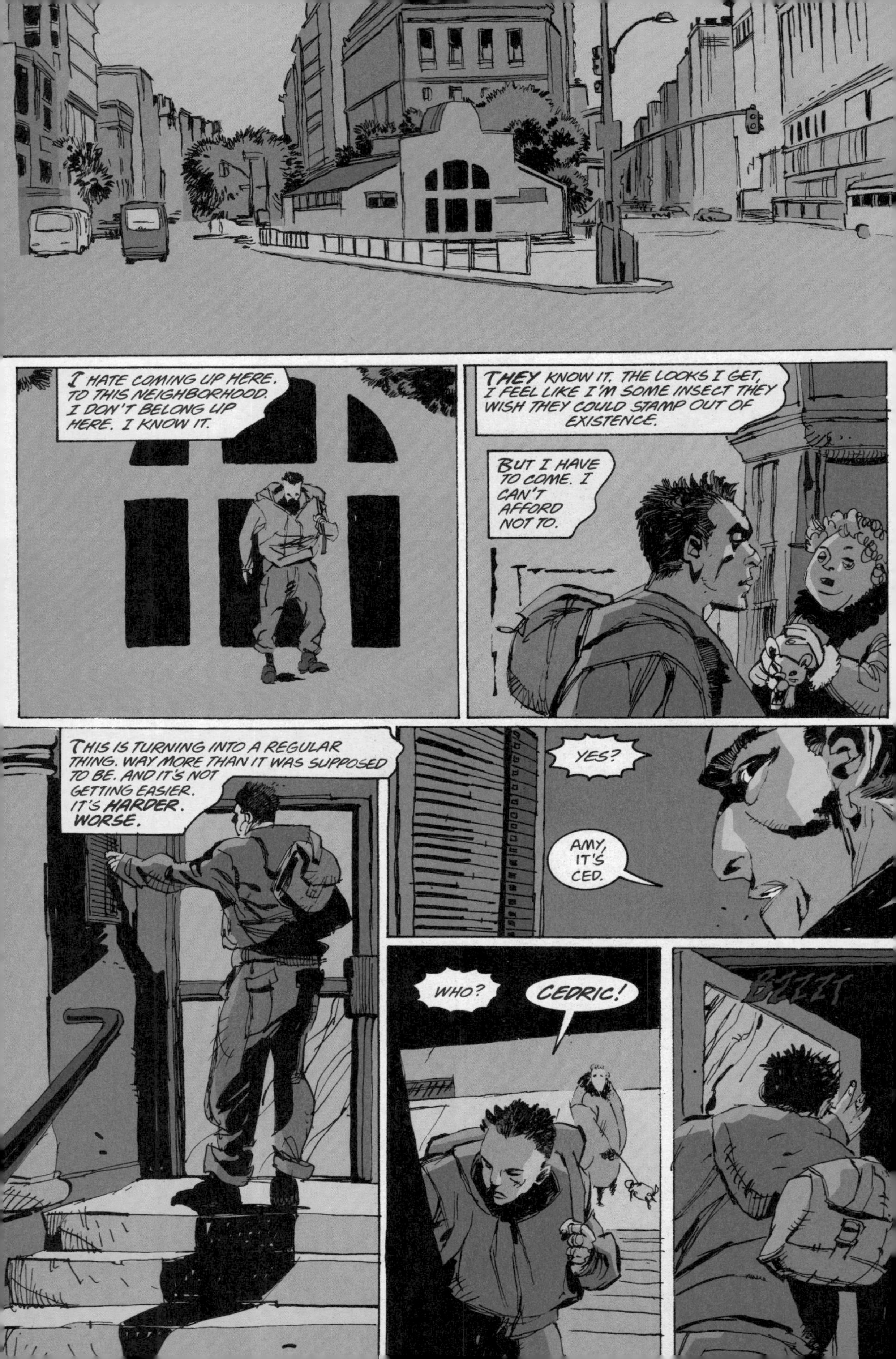
I HATE COMING UP HERE. TO THIS NEIGHBORHOOD. I DON'T BELONG UP HERE. I KNOW IT.
THEY KNOW IT. THE LOOKS I GET, I FEEL LIKE I'M SOME INSECT THEY WISH THEY COULD STAMP OUT OF EXISTENCE.
BUT I HAVE TO COME. I CAN'T AFFORD NOT TO.
THIS IS TURNING INTO A REGULAR THING. WAY MORE THAN IT WAS SUPPOSED TO BE. AND IT'S NOT GETTING EASIER. IT'S HARDER. WORSE.
YES?
AMY, IT'S CED.
WHO?
CEDRIC!
BZZZT

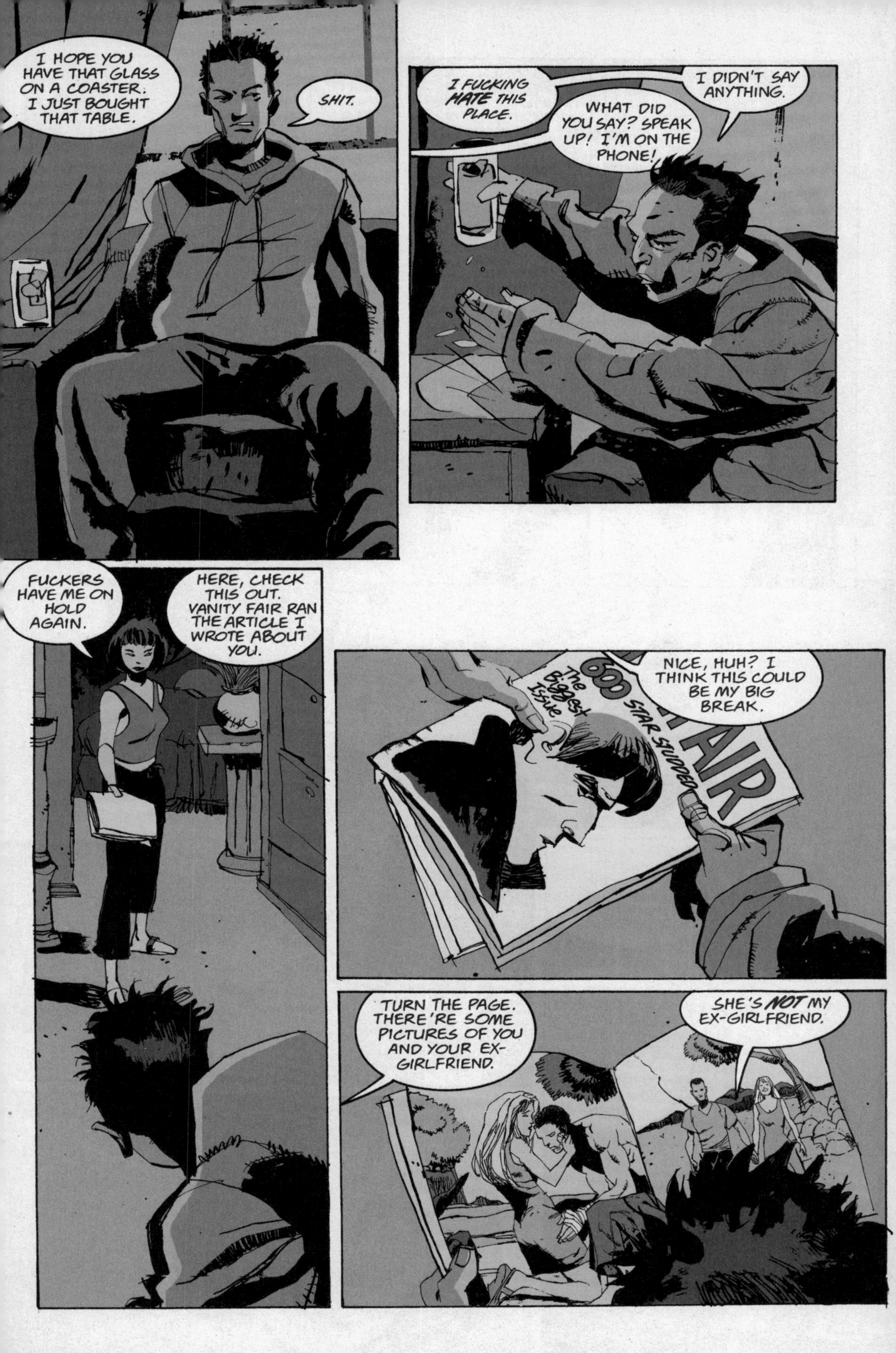
I HOPE YOU HAVE THAT GLASS ON A COASTER. I JUST BOUGHT THAT TABLE.
SHIT.
I FUCKING HATE THIS PLACE.
I DIDN'T SAY ANYTHING.
WHAT DID YOU SAY? SPEAK UP! I'M ON THE PHONE!
FUCKERS HAVE ME ON HOLD AGAIN.
HERE, CHECK THIS OUT. VANITY FAIR RAN THE ARTICLE I WROTE ABOUT YOU.
600 STAR STUDDED
The Biggest Issue
AIR
NICE, HUH? I THINK THIS COULD BE MY BIG BREAK.
TURN THE PAGE. THERE'RE SOME PICTURES OF YOU AND YOUR EX-GIRLFRIEND.
SHE'S NOT MY EX-GIRLFRIEND.

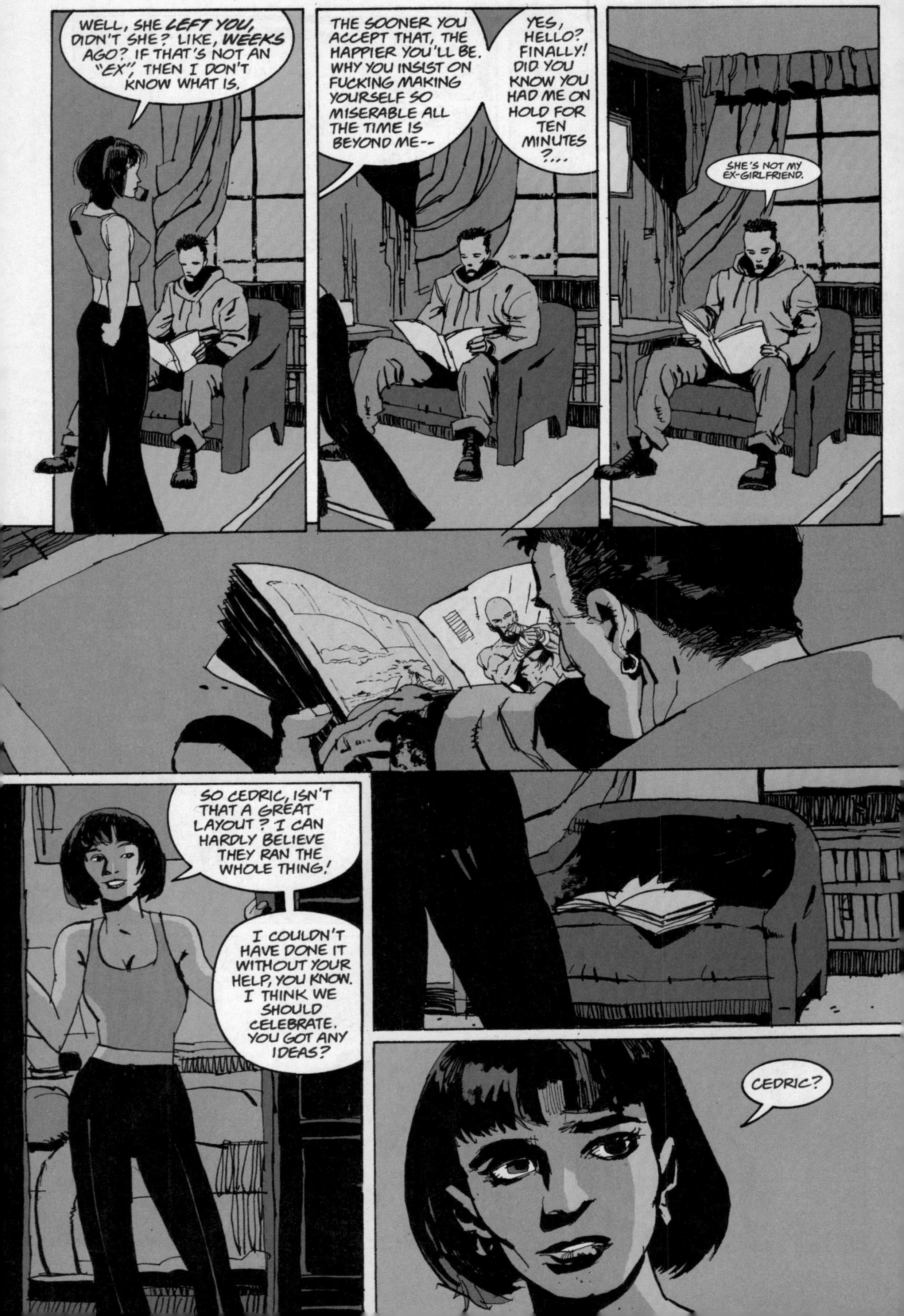
WELL, SHE LEFT YOU, DIDN'T SHE? LIKE, WEEKS AGO? IF THAT'S NOT AN "EX", THEN I DON'T KNOW WHAT IS.
THE SOONER YOU ACCEPT THAT, THE HAPPIER YOU'LL BE. WHY YOU INSIST ON FUCKING MAKING YOURSELF SO MISERABLE ALL THE TIME IS BEYOND ME--
YES, HELLO? FINALLY! DID YOU KNOW YOU HAD ME ON HOLD FOR TEN MINUTES ?...
SHE'S NOT MY EX-GIRLFRIEND.
SO CEDRIC, ISN'T THAT A GREAT LAYOUT? I CAN HARDLY BELIEVE THEY RAN THE WHOLE THING!
I COULDN'T HAVE DONE IT WITHOUT YOUR HELP, YOU KNOW. I THINK WE SHOULD CELEBRATE. YOU GOT ANY IDEAS?
CEDRIC?

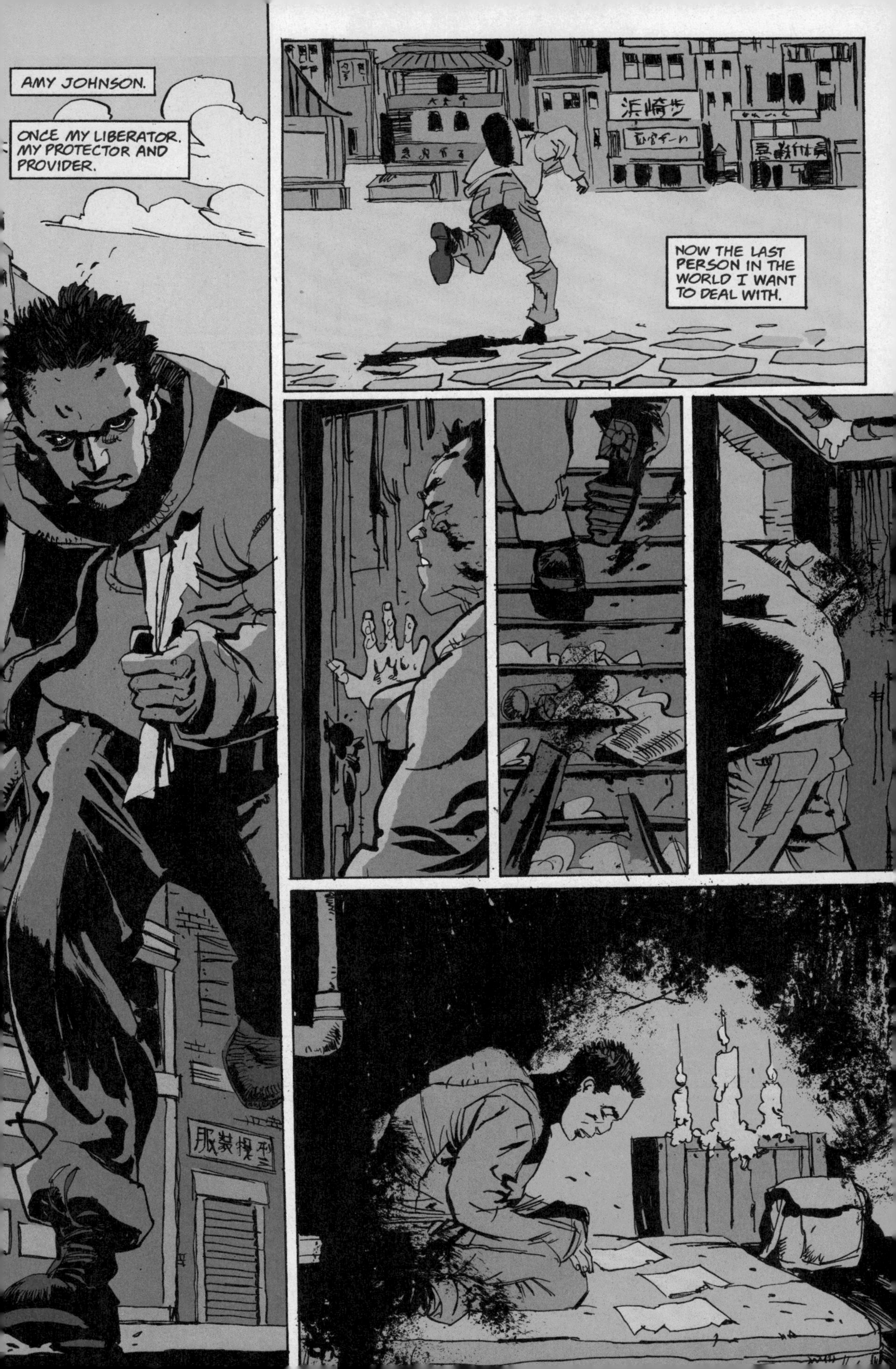
AMY JOHNSON.
ONCE MY LIBERATOR. MY PROTECTOR AND PROVIDER.
NOW THE LAST PERSON IN THE WORLD I WANT TO DEAL WITH.

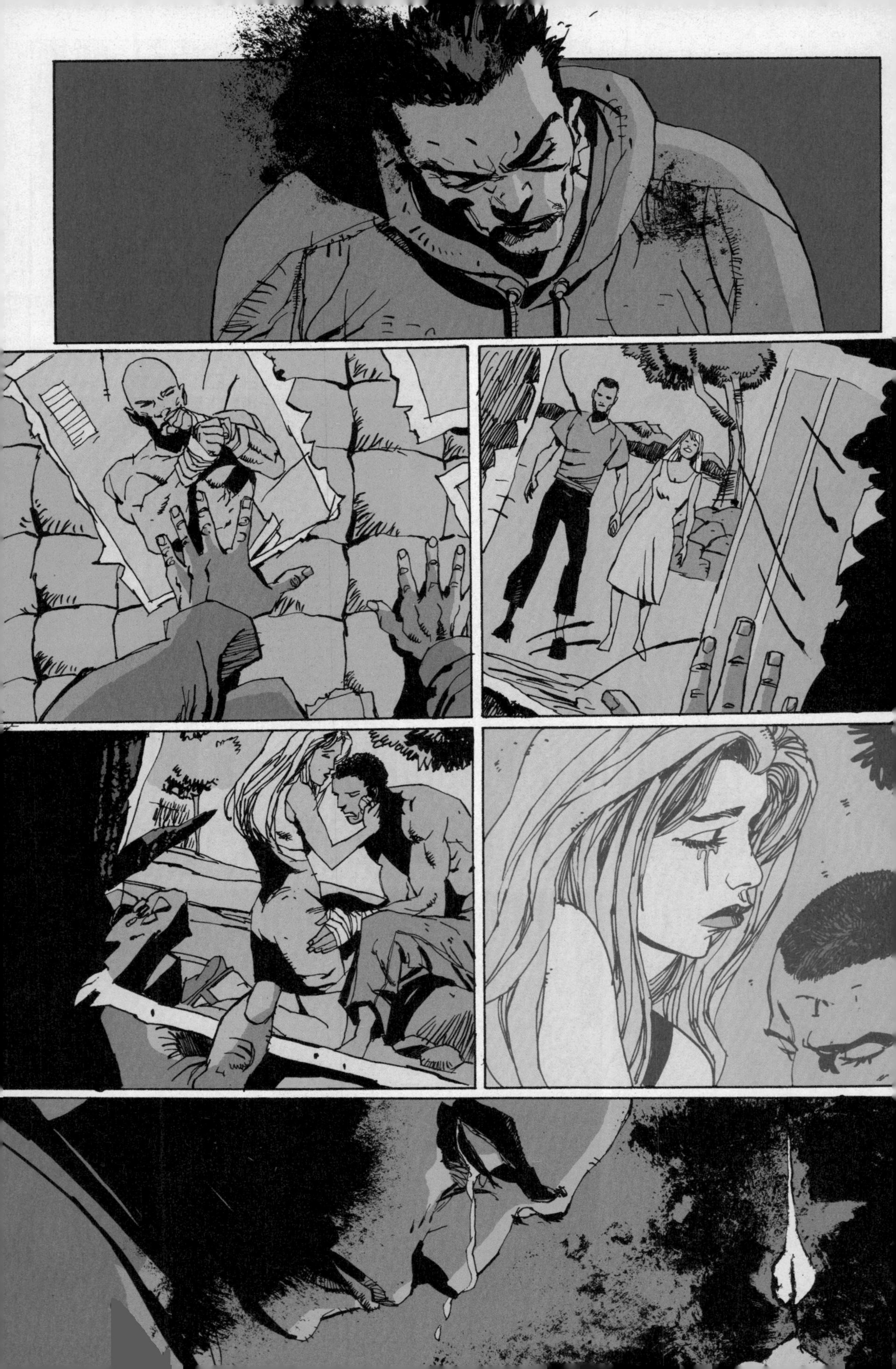

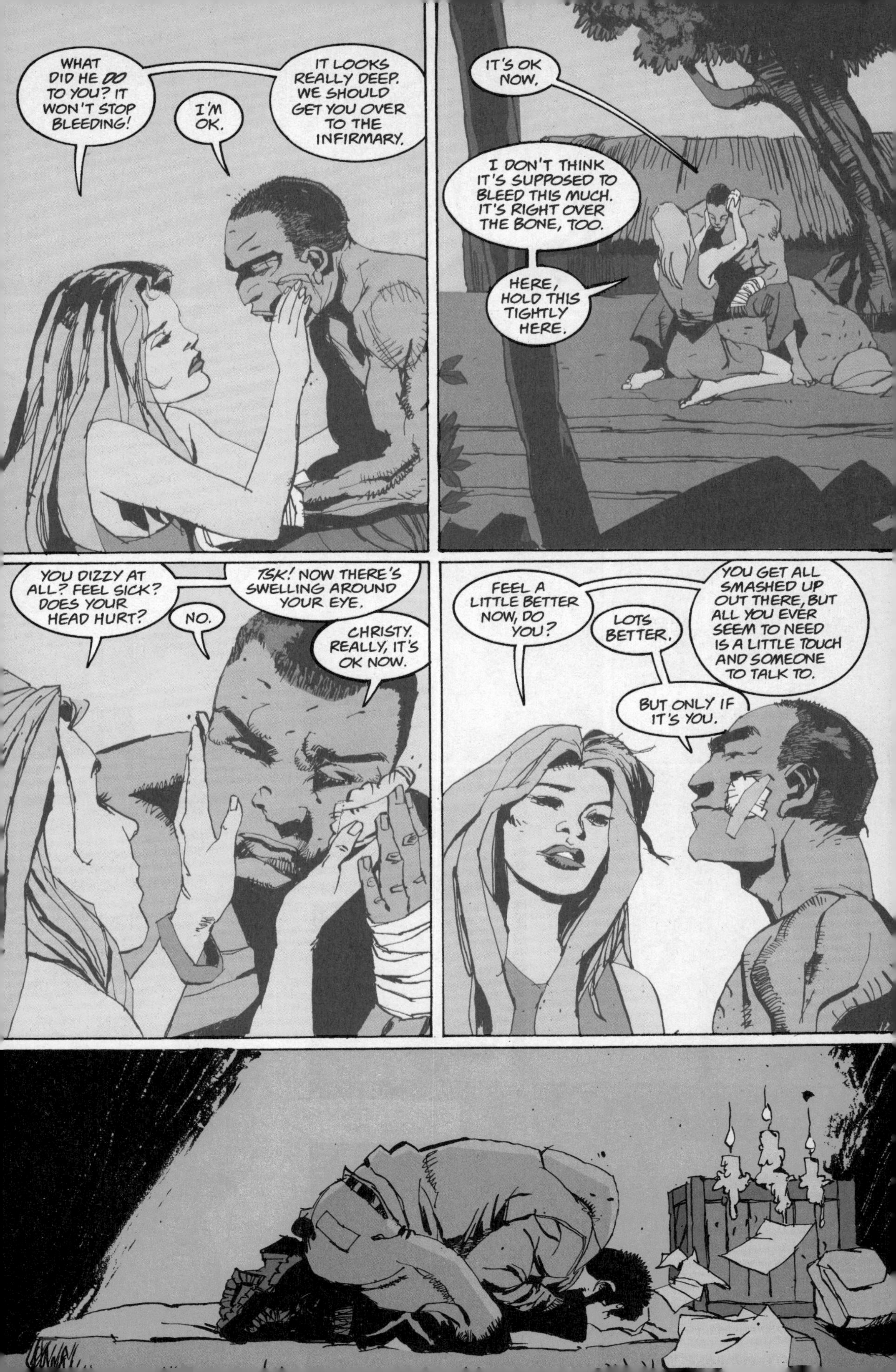

WHAT DID HE DO TO YOU? IT WON'T STOP BLEEDING!
I'M OK.
IT LOOKS REALLY DEEP. WE SHOULD GET YOU OVER TO THE INFIRMARY.
IT'S OK NOW.
I DON'T THINK IT'S SUPPOSED TO BLEED THIS MUCH. IT'S RIGHT OVER THE BONE, TOO.
HERE, HOLD THIS TIGHTLY HERE.
YOU DIZZY AT ALL? FEEL SICK? DOES YOUR HEAD HURT?
NO.
TSK! NOW THERE'S SWELLING AROUND YOUR EYE.
CHRISTY. REALLY, IT'S OK NOW.
FEEL A LITTLE BETTER NOW, DO YOU?
LOTS BETTER.
YOU GET ALL SMASHED UP OUT THERE, BUT ALL YOU EVER SEEM TO NEED IS A LITTLE TOUCH AND SOMEONE TO TALK TO.
BUT ONLY IF IT'S YOU.

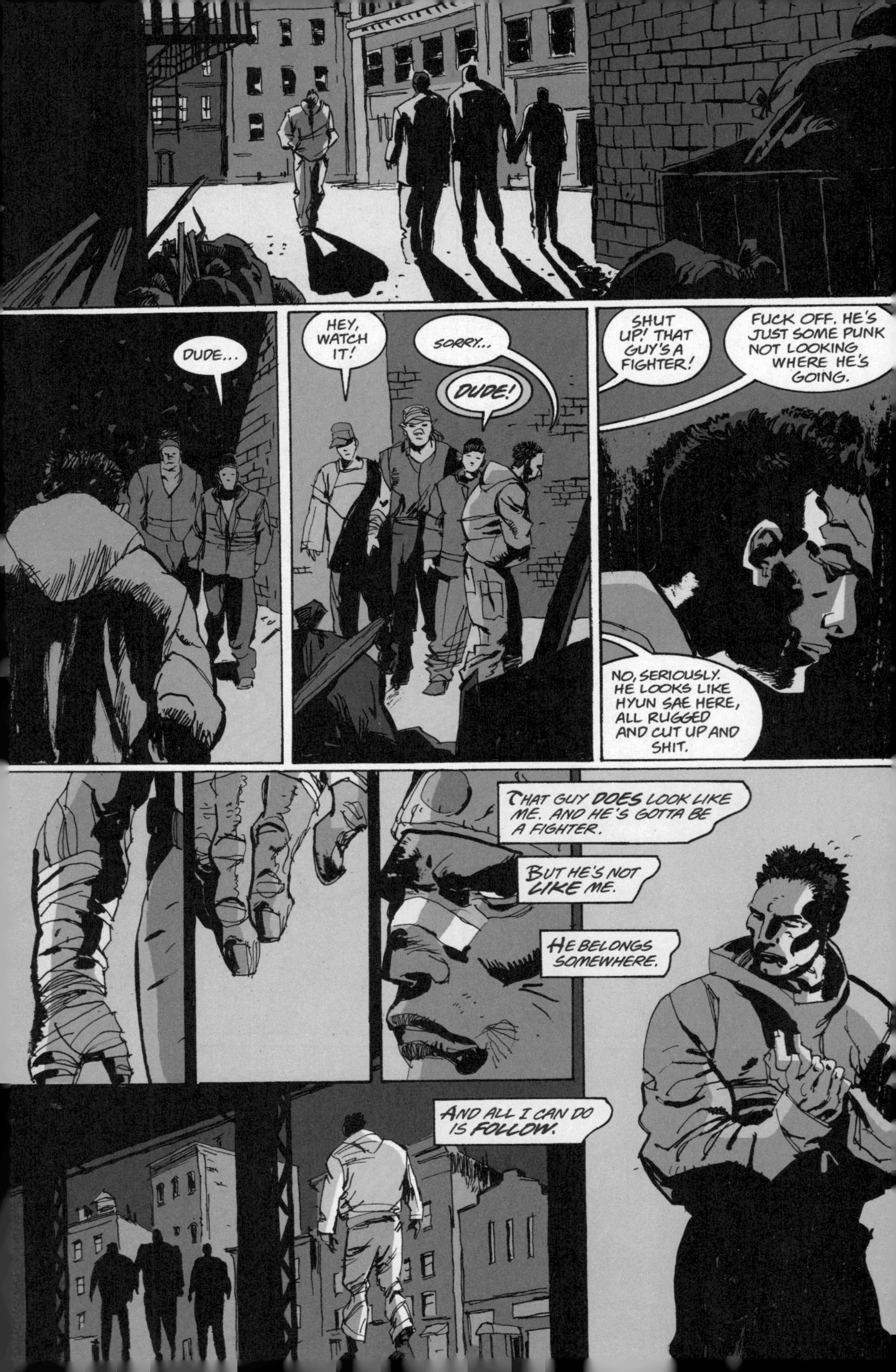
DUDE...
HEY, WATCH IT!
SORRY...
DUDE!
SHUT UP! THAT GUY'S A FIGHTER!
FUCK OFF. HE'S JUST SOME PUNK NOT LOOKING WHERE HE'S GOING.
NO, SERIOUSLY. HE LOOKS LIKE HYUN SAE HERE, ALL RUGGED AND CUT UP AND SHIT.
THAT GUY DOES LOOK LIKE ME. AND HE'S GOTTA BE A FIGHTER.
BUT HE'S NOT LIKE ME.
HE BELONGS SOMEWHERE.
AND ALL I CAN DO IS FOLLOW.

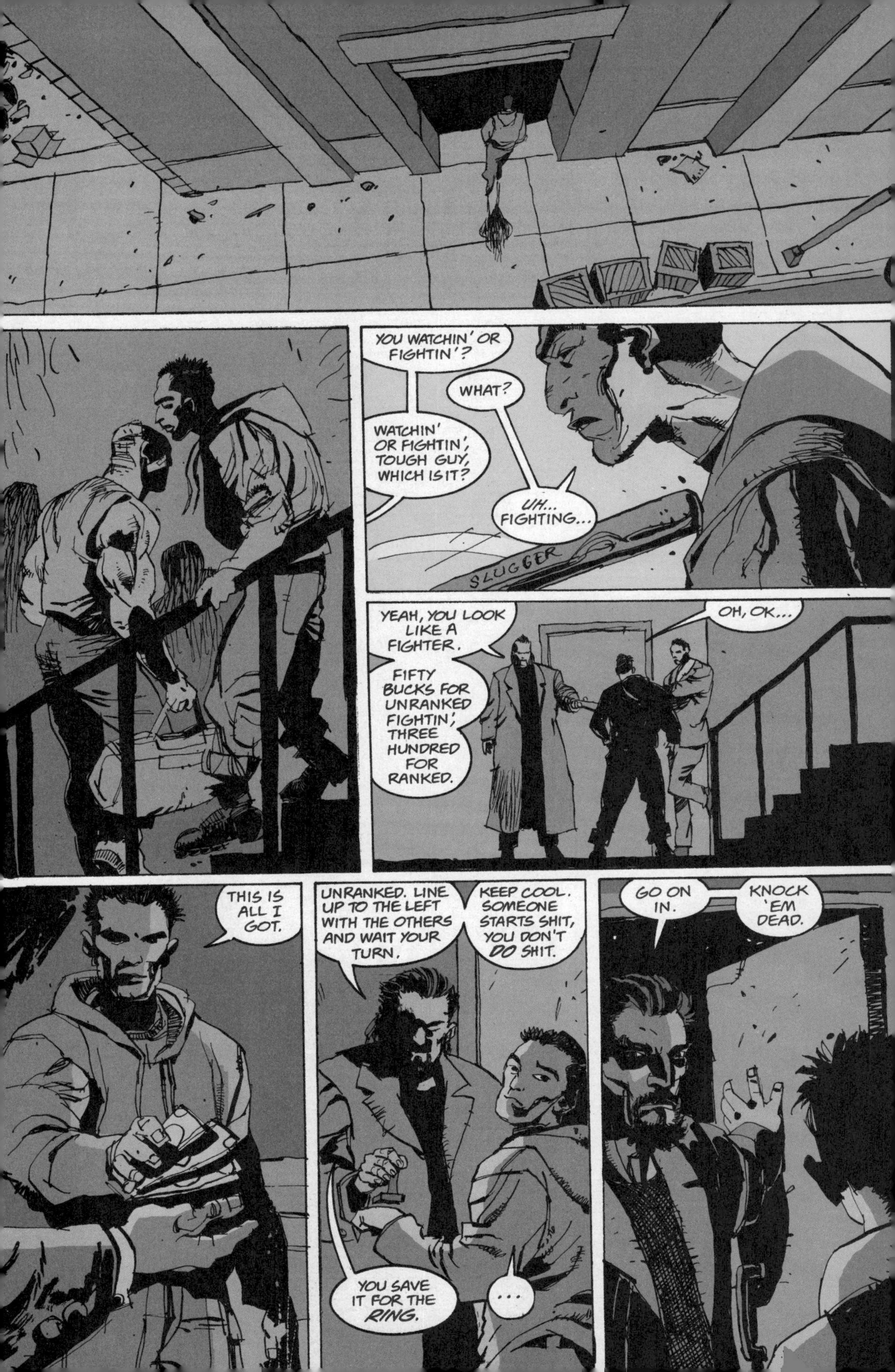
YOU WATCHIN' OR FIGHTIN'?
WHAT?
WATCHIN' OR FIGHTIN', TOUGH GUY, WHICH IS IT?
UH... FIGHTING...
SLUGGER
YEAH, YOU LOOK LIKE A FIGHTER.
FIFTY BUCKS FOR UNRANKED FIGHTIN', THREE HUNDRED FOR RANKED.
OH, OK...
THIS IS ALL I GOT.
UNRANKED. LINE UP TO THE LEFT WITH THE OTHERS AND WAIT YOUR TURN.
KEEP COOL. SOMEONE STARTS SHIT, YOU DON'T *DO* SHIT.
YOU SAVE IT FOR THE *RING*.
...
GO ON IN.
KNOCK 'EM DEAD.

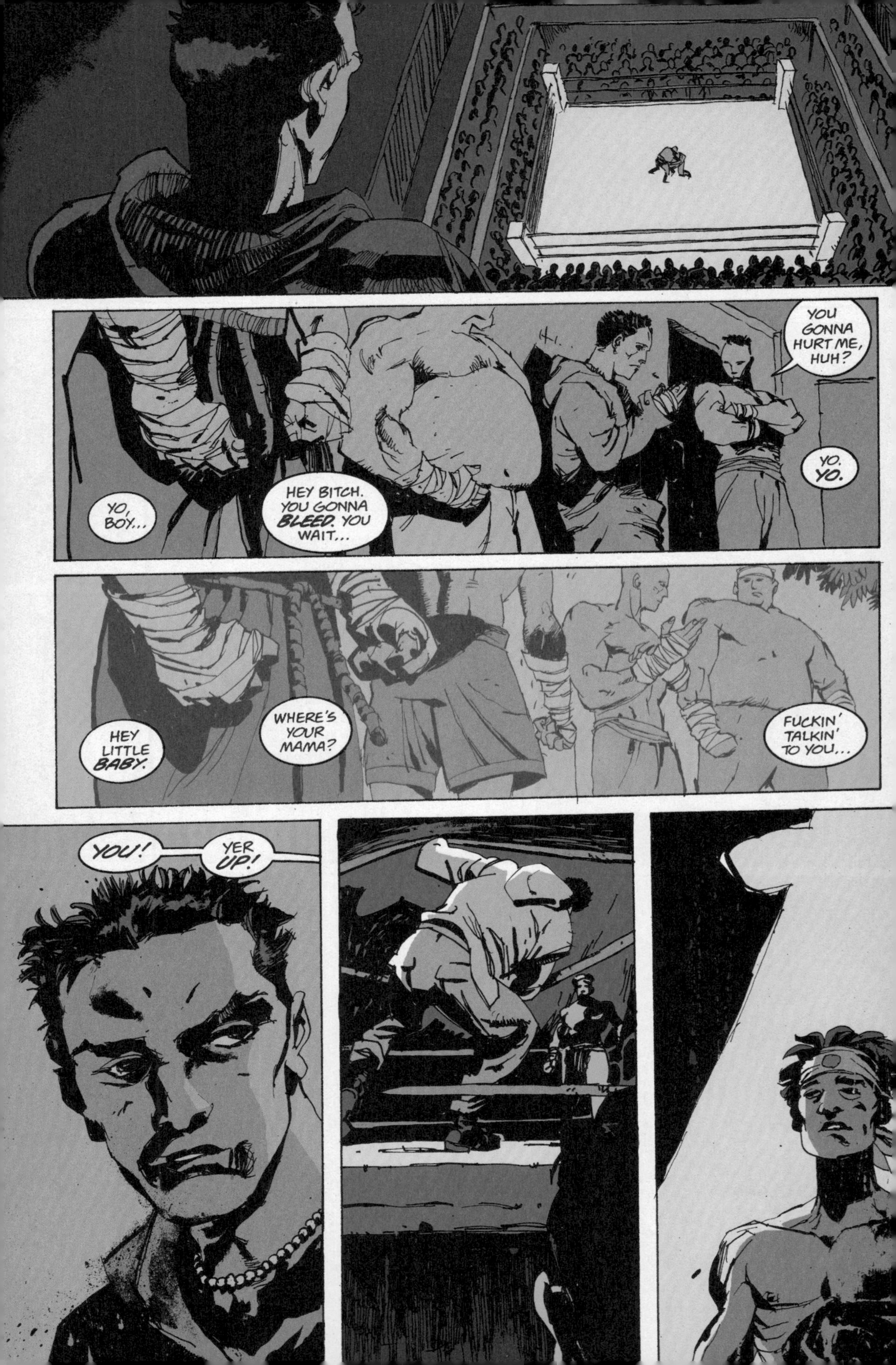
YOU GONNA HURT ME, HUH?
YO, BOY...
HEY BITCH. YOU GONNA BLEED. YOU WAIT...
YO. YO.
HEY LITTLE BABY.
WHERE'S YOUR MAMA?
FUCKIN' TALKIN' TO YOU...
YOU!
YER UP!

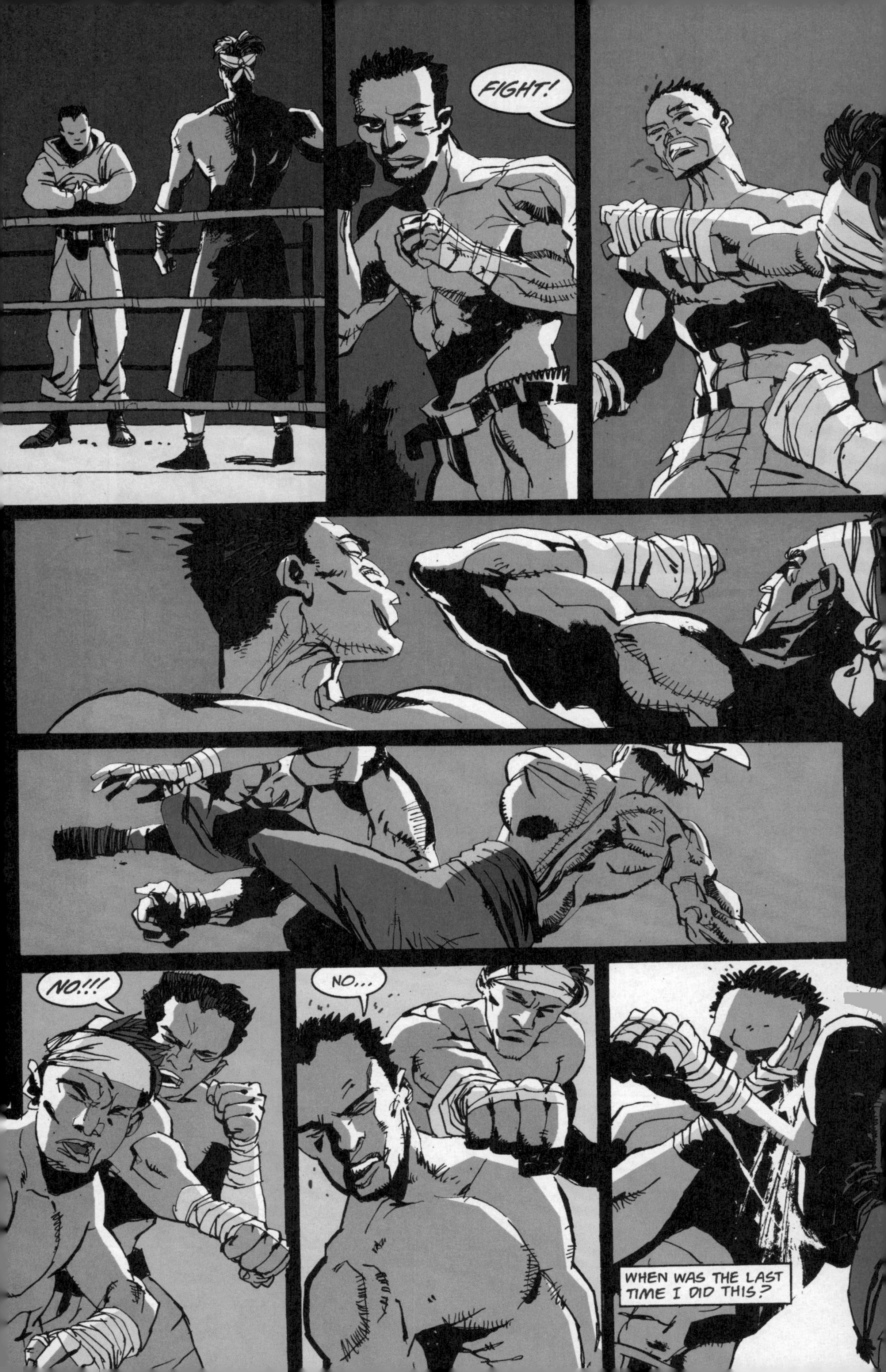
FIGHT!
NO!!!
NO...
WHEN WAS THE LAST TIME I DID THIS?

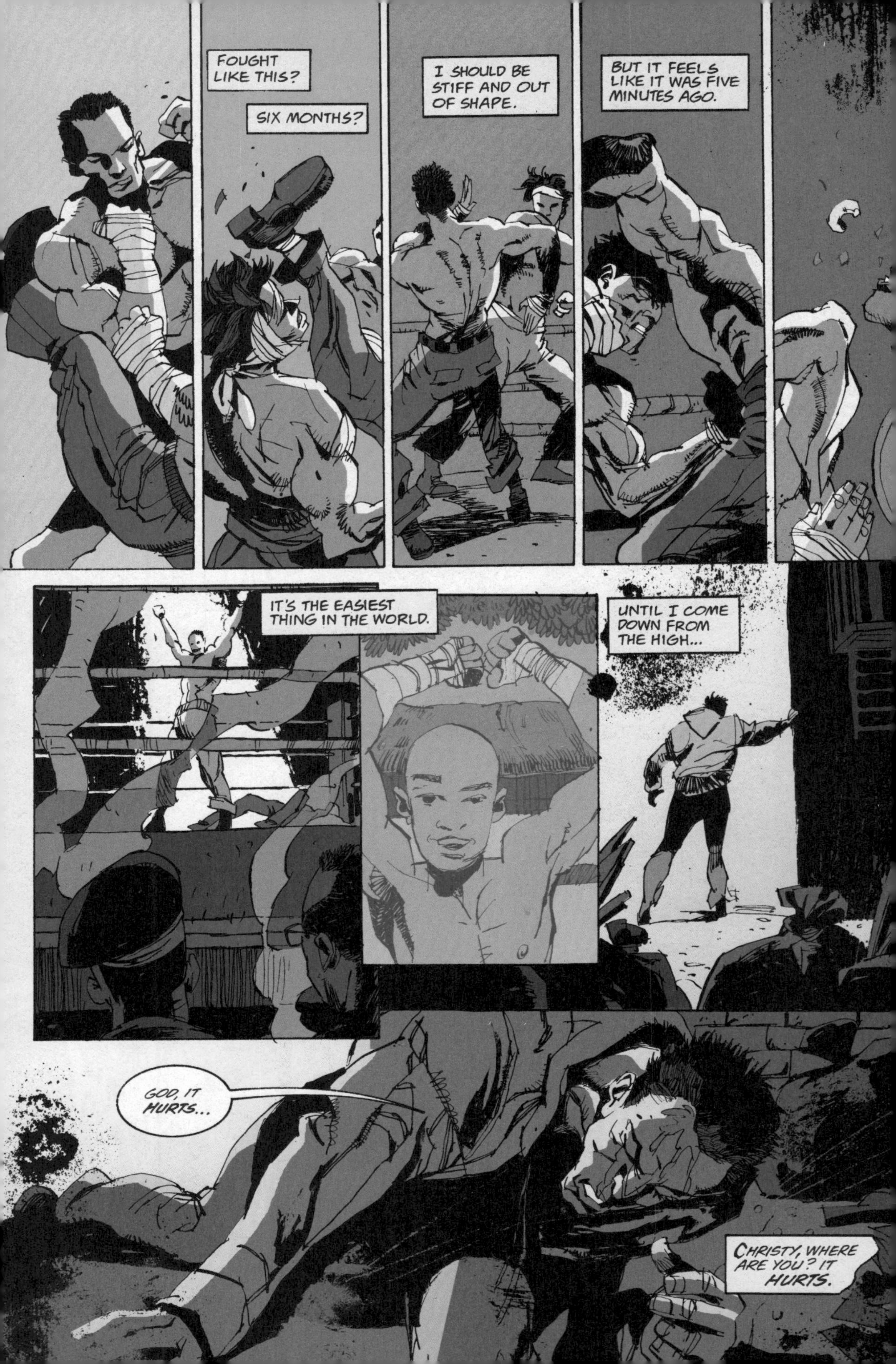
FOUGHT LIKE THIS?
SIX MONTHS?
I SHOULD BE STIFF AND OUT OF SHAPE.
BUT IT FEELS LIKE IT WAS FIVE MINUTES AGO.
IT'S THE EASIEST THING IN THE WORLD.
UNTIL I COME DOWN FROM THE HIGH...
GOD, IT HURTS...
CHRISTY, WHERE ARE YOU? IT HURTS.

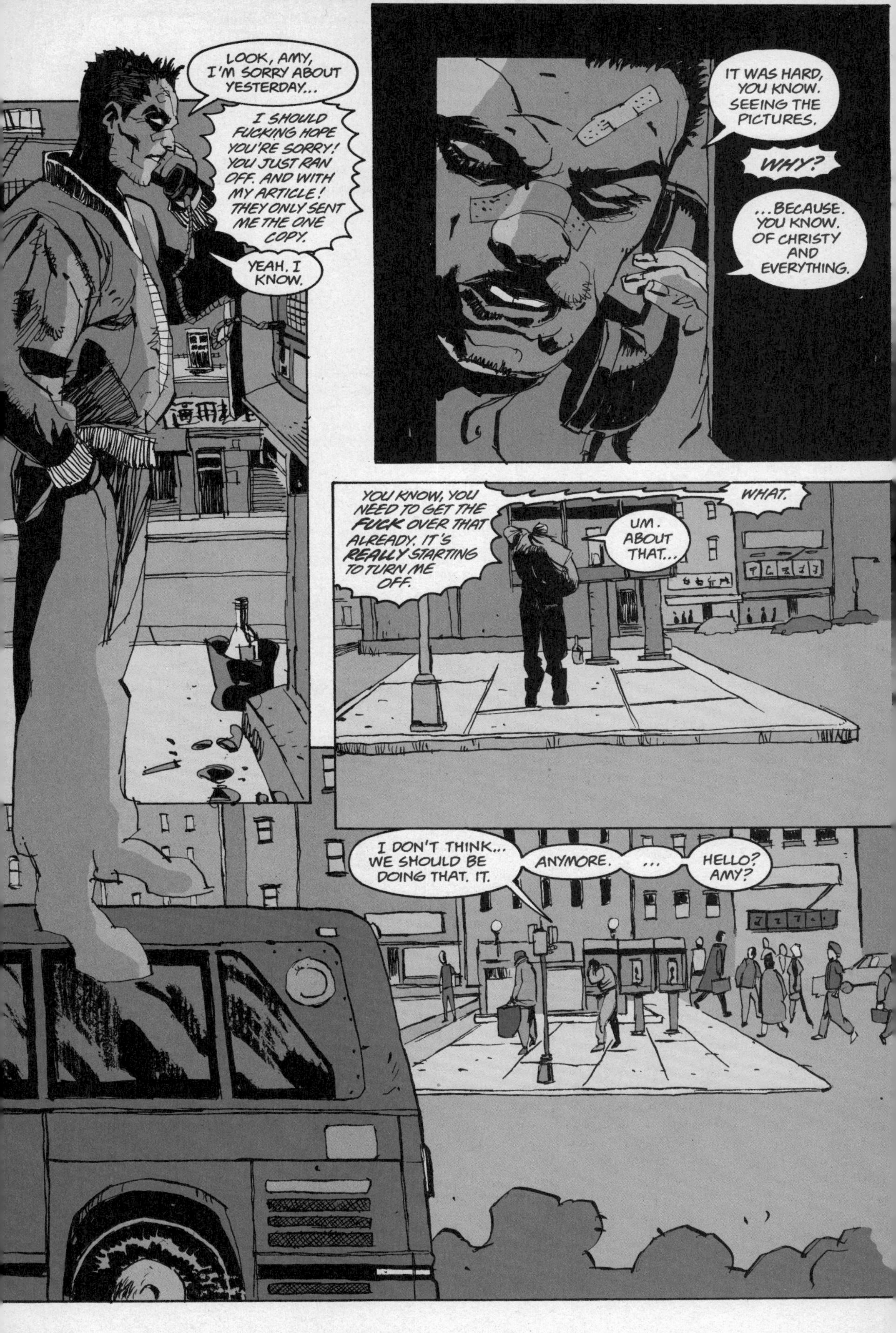
LOOK, AMY, I'M SORRY ABOUT YESTERDAY...
I SHOULD FUCKING HOPE YOU'RE SORRY! YOU JUST RAN OFF. AND WITH MY ARTICLE! THEY ONLY SENT ME THE ONE COPY.
YEAH. I KNOW.
IT WAS HARD, YOU KNOW. SEEING THE PICTURES.
WHY?
...BECAUSE. YOU KNOW. OF CHRISTY AND EVERYTHING.
YOU KNOW, YOU NEED TO GET THE FUCK OVER THAT ALREADY. IT'S REALLY STARTING TO TURN ME OFF.
WHAT.
UM. ABOUT THAT...
I DON'T THINK... WE SHOULD BE DOING THAT. IT.
ANYMORE.
...
HELLO? AMY?

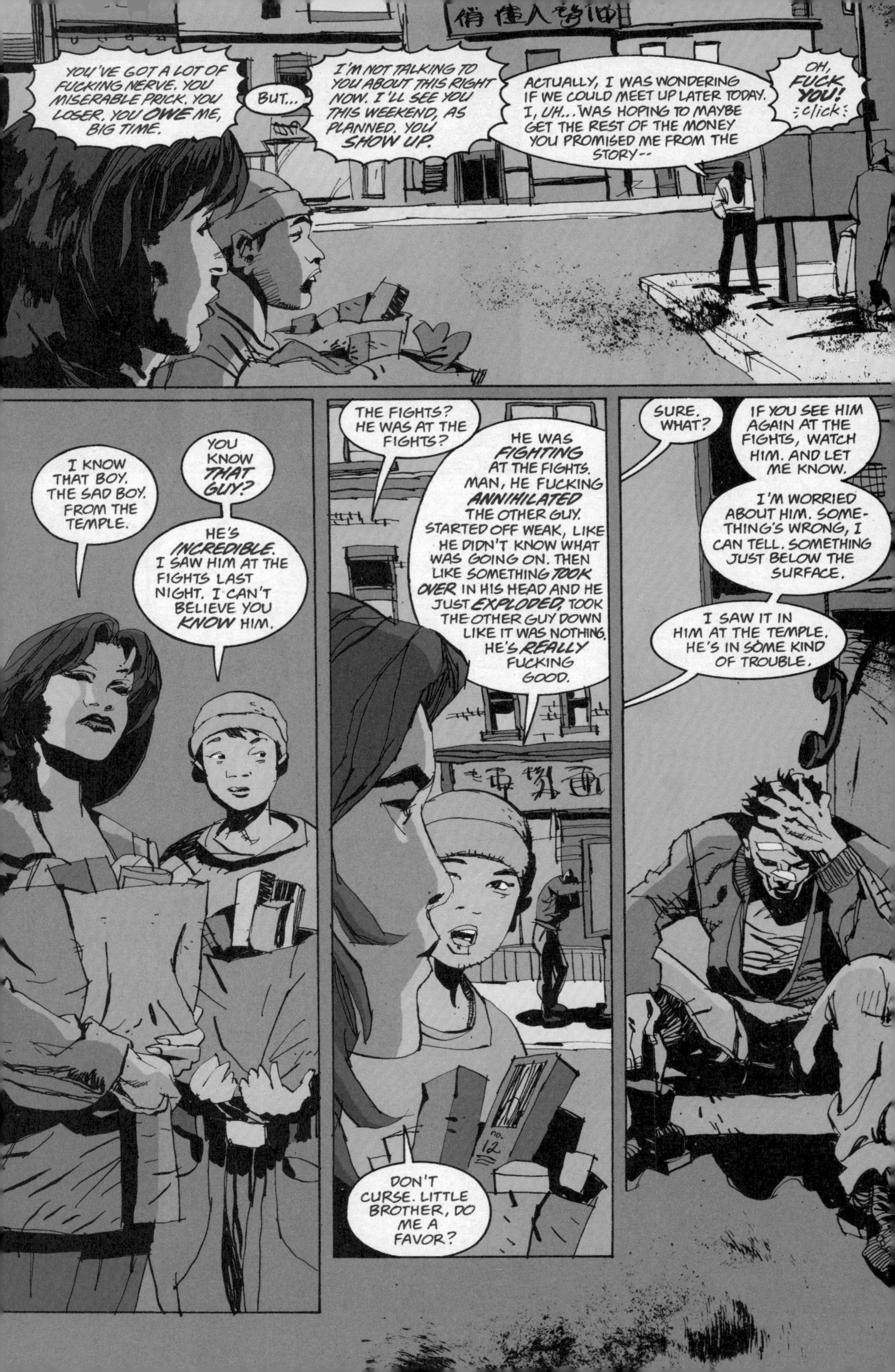
YOU'VE GOT A LOT OF FUCKING NERVE. YOU MISERABLE PRICK. YOU LOSER. YOU OWE ME, BIG TIME.
BUT...
I'M NOT TALKING TO YOU ABOUT THIS RIGHT NOW. I'LL SEE YOU THIS WEEKEND, AS PLANNED. YOU SHOW UP.
ACTUALLY, I WAS WONDERING IF WE COULD MEET UP LATER TODAY. I, UH...WAS HOPING TO MAYBE GET THE REST OF THE MONEY YOU PROMISED ME FROM THE STORY--
OH, FUCK YOU!
click
I KNOW THAT BOY. THE SAD BOY. FROM THE TEMPLE.
YOU KNOW THAT GUY?
HE'S INCREDIBLE. I SAW HIM AT THE FIGHTS LAST NIGHT. I CAN'T BELIEVE YOU KNOW HIM.
THE FIGHTS? HE WAS AT THE FIGHTS?
HE WAS FIGHTING AT THE FIGHTS. MAN, HE FUCKING ANNIHILATED THE OTHER GUY. STARTED OFF WEAK, LIKE HE DIDN'T KNOW WHAT WAS GOING ON. THEN LIKE SOMETHING TOOK OVER IN HIS HEAD AND HE JUST EXPLODED, TOOK THE OTHER GUY DOWN LIKE IT WAS NOTHING. HE'S REALLY FUCKING GOOD.
DON'T CURSE. LITTLE BROTHER, DO ME A FAVOR?
SURE. WHAT?
IF YOU SEE HIM AGAIN AT THE FIGHTS, WATCH HIM. AND LET ME KNOW.
I'M WORRIED ABOUT HIM. SOMETHING'S WRONG, I CAN TELL. SOMETHING JUST BELOW THE SURFACE.
I SAW IT IN HIM AT THE TEMPLE. HE'S IN SOME KIND OF TROUBLE.

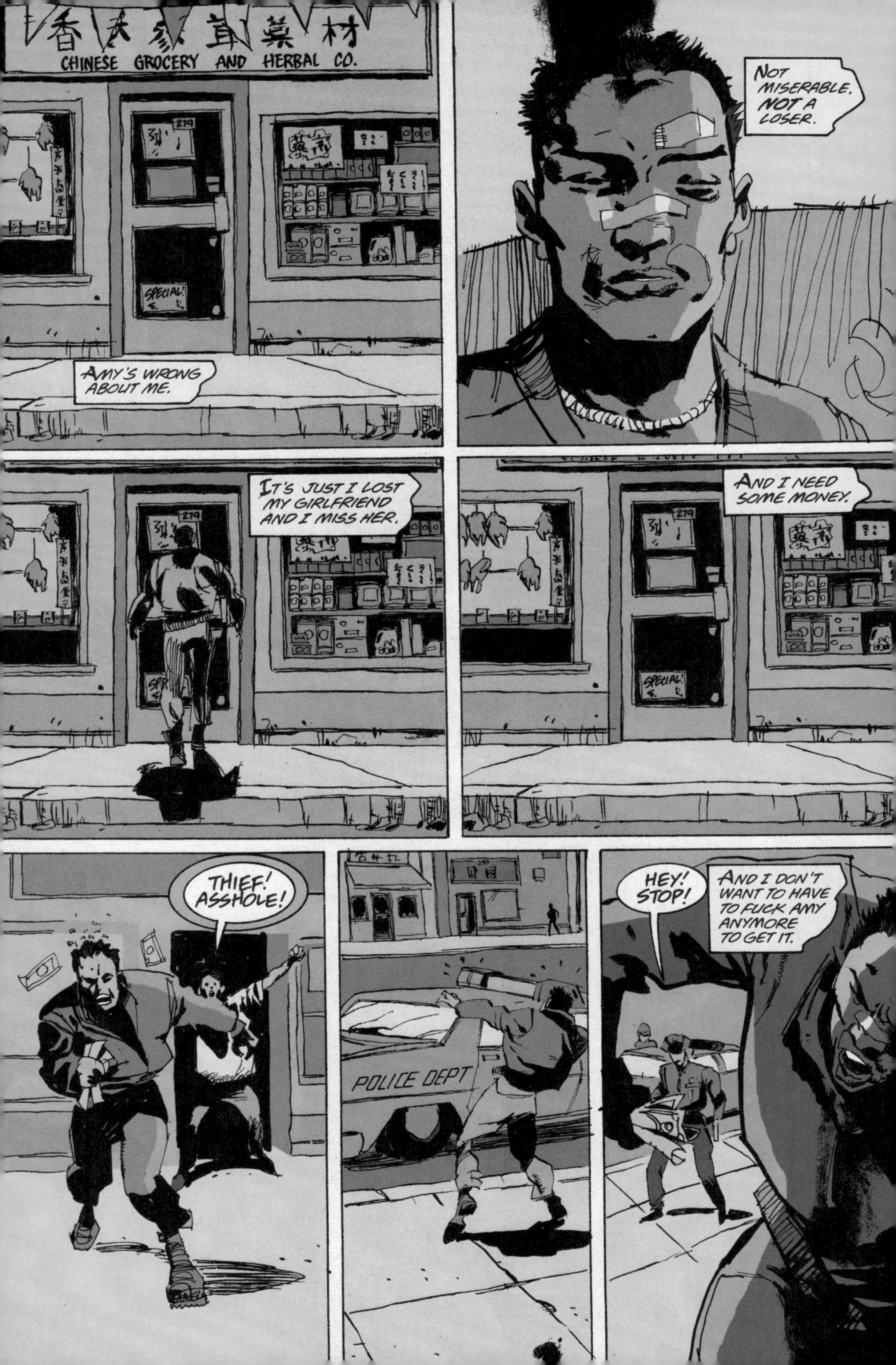
CHINESE GROCERY AND HERBAL CO.
AMY'S WRONG ABOUT ME.
NOT MISERABLE. NOT A LOSER.
IT'S JUST I LOST MY GIRLFRIEND AND I MISS HER.
AND I NEED SOME MONEY.
THIEF! ASSHOLE!
POLICE DEPT
HEY! STOP!
AND I DON'T WANT TO HAVE TO FUCK AMY ANYMORE TO GET IT.

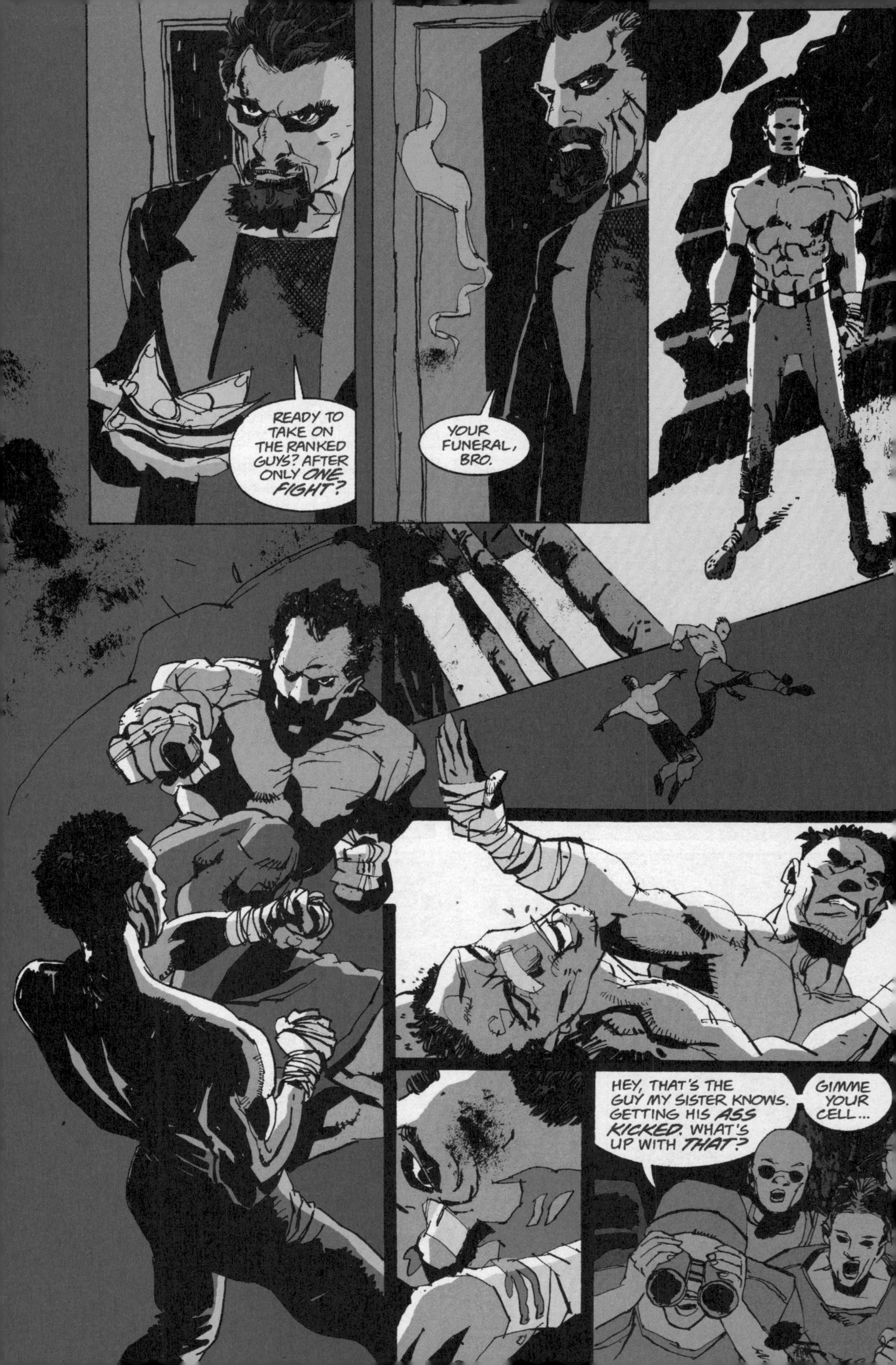
READY TO TAKE ON THE RANKED GUYS? AFTER ONLY ONE FIGHT?
YOUR FUNERAL, BRO.
HEY, THAT'S THE GUY MY SISTER KNOWS. GETTING HIS ASS KICKED. WHAT'S UP WITH THAT?
GIMME YOUR CELL...

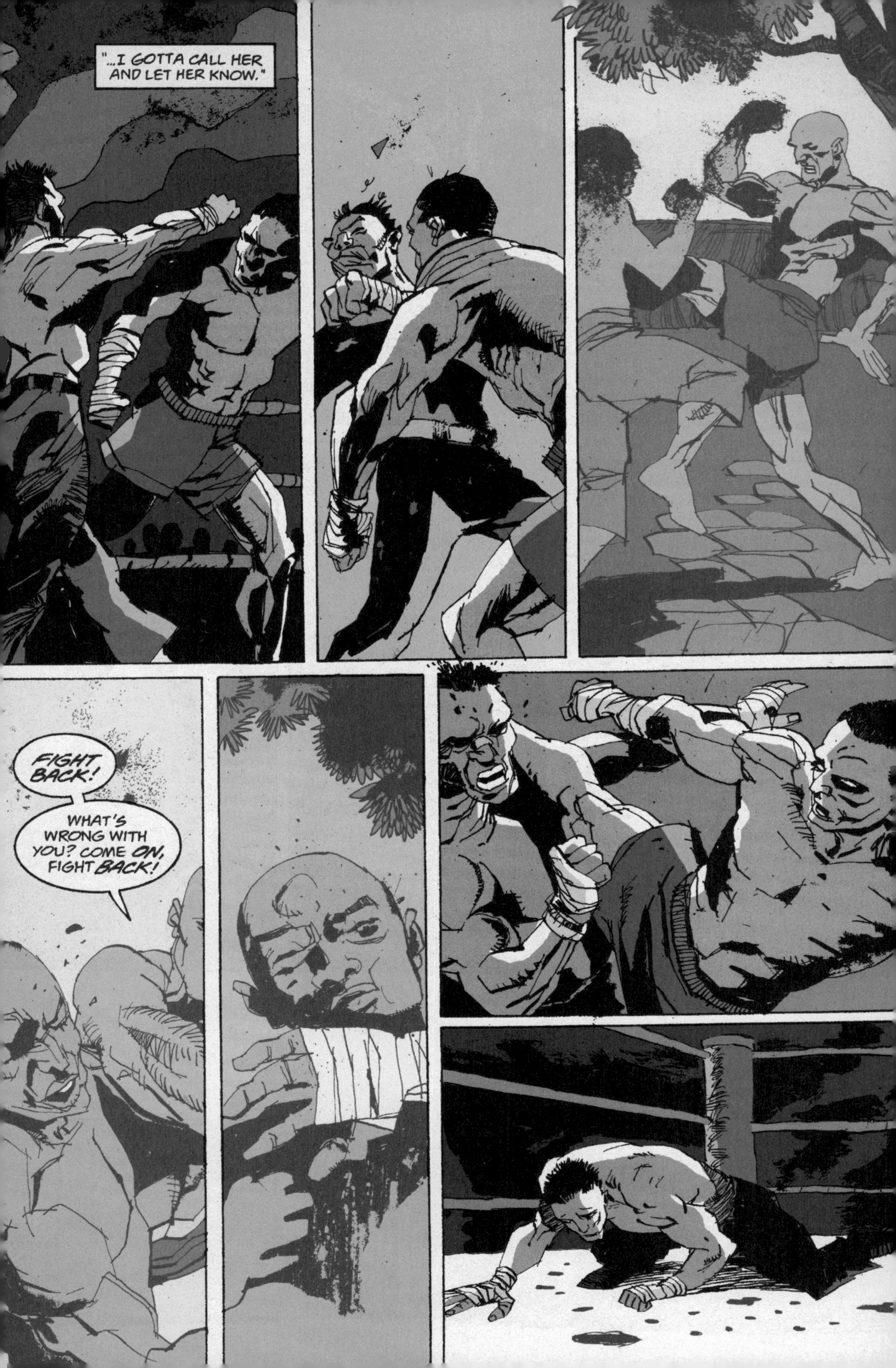
"...I GOTTA CALL HER AND LET HER KNOW."
FIGHT BACK!
WHAT'S WRONG WITH YOU? COME ON, FIGHT BACK!

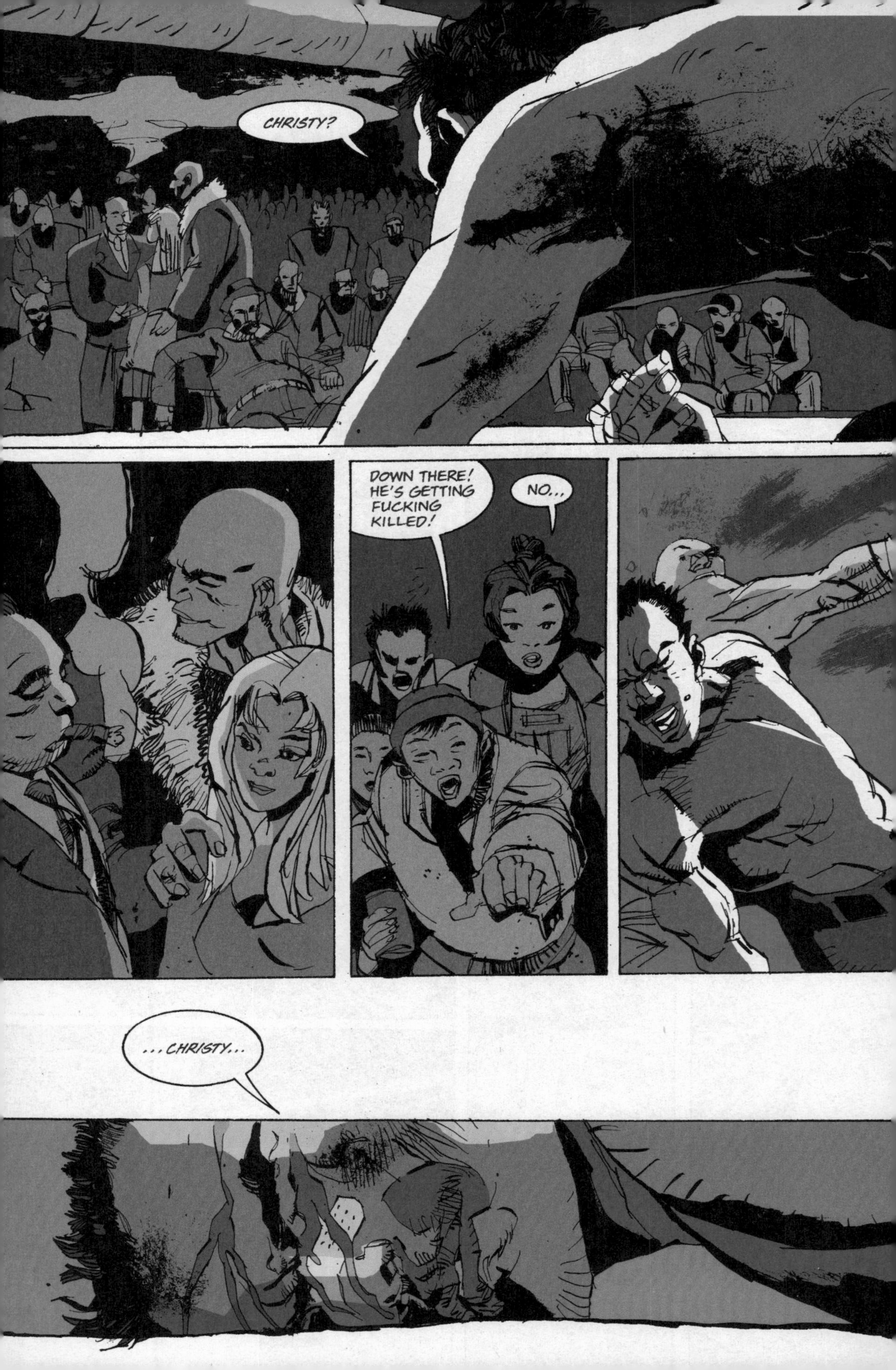
CHRISTY?
DOWN THERE! HE'S GETTING FUCKING KILLED!
NO...
...CHRISTY...

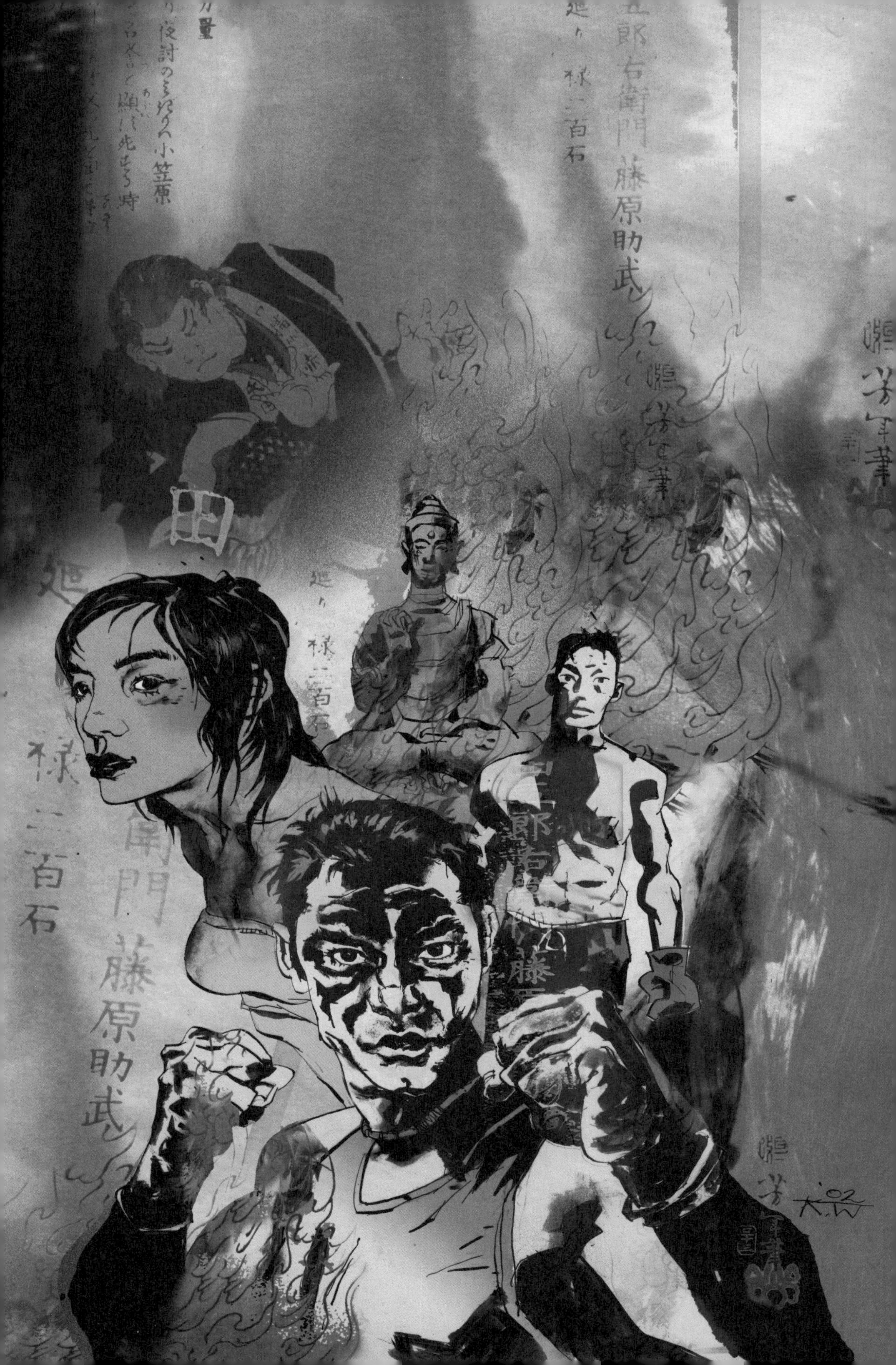
五郎右衛門藤原助武
廻り様二百石
嶋芳年筆
K.W. '02

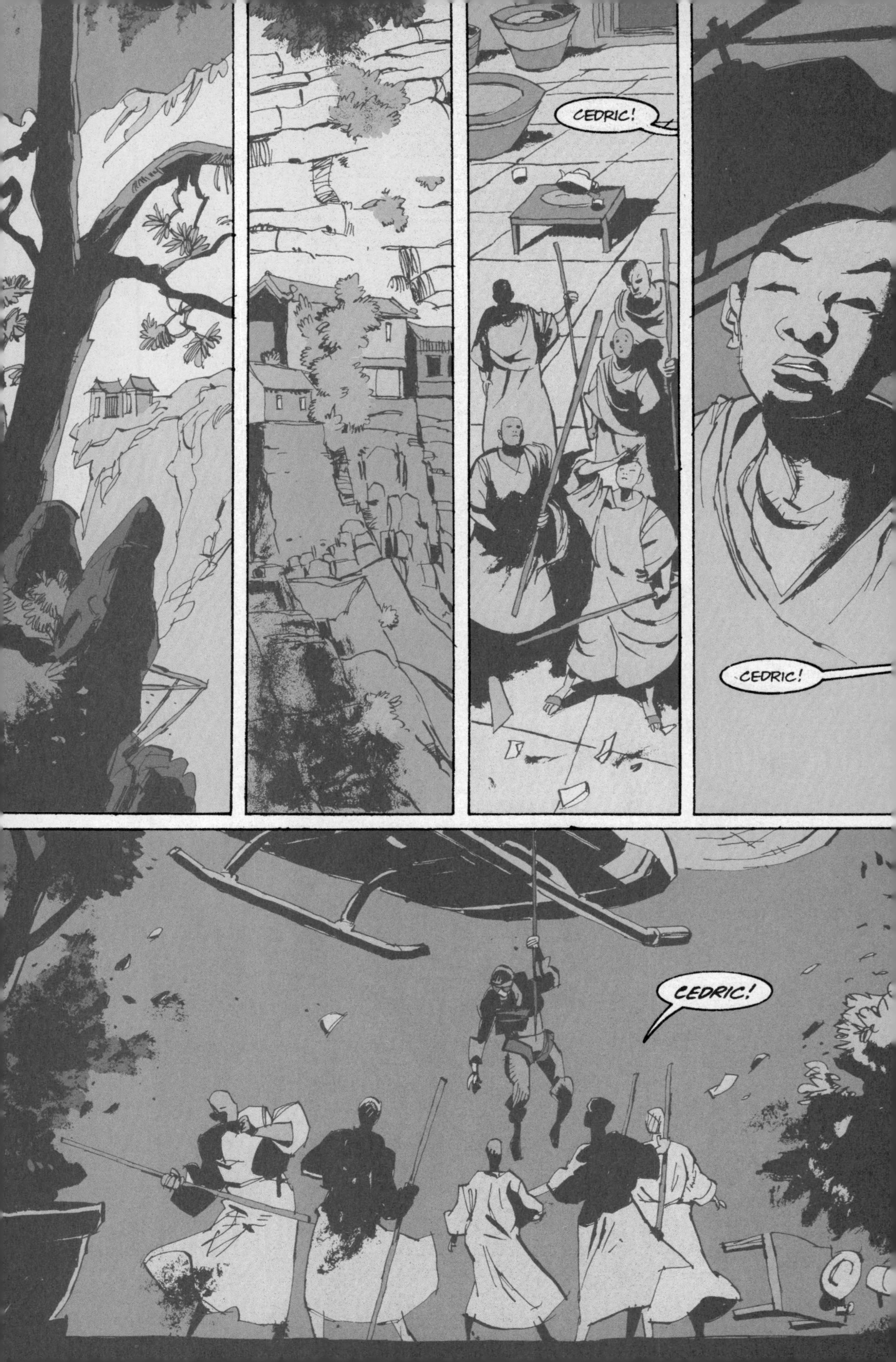
CEDRIC!
CEDRIC!
CEDRIC!

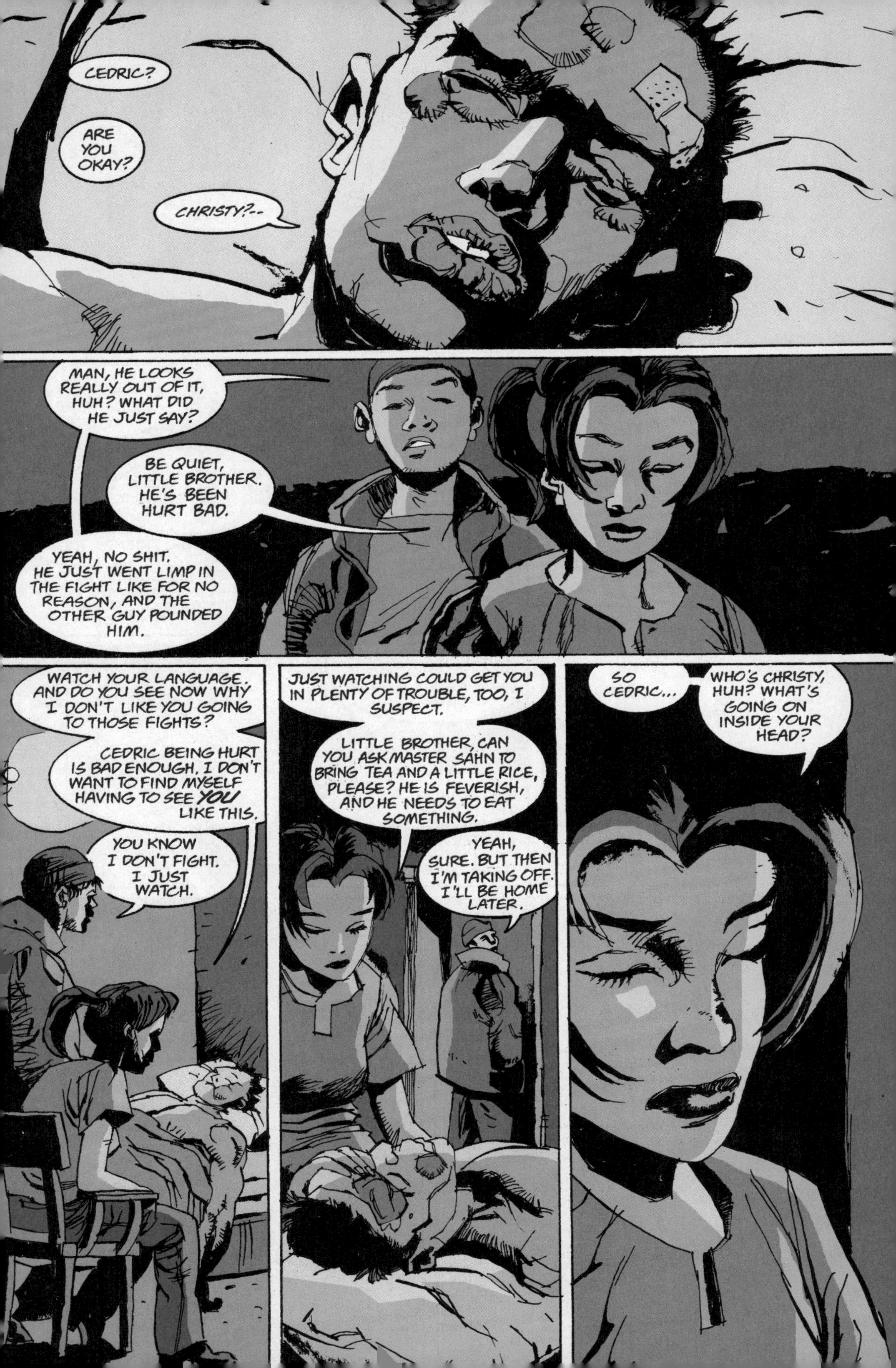
CEDRIC?
ARE YOU OKAY?
CHRISTY?--
MAN, HE LOOKS REALLY OUT OF IT, HUH? WHAT DID HE JUST SAY?
BE QUIET, LITTLE BROTHER. HE'S BEEN HURT BAD.
YEAH, NO SHIT. HE JUST WENT LIMP IN THE FIGHT LIKE FOR NO REASON, AND THE OTHER GUY POUNDED HIM.
WATCH YOUR LANGUAGE. AND DO YOU SEE NOW WHY I DON'T LIKE YOU GOING TO THOSE FIGHTS?
CEDRIC BEING HURT IS BAD ENOUGH. I DON'T WANT TO FIND MYSELF HAVING TO SEE YOU LIKE THIS.
YOU KNOW I DON'T FIGHT. I JUST WATCH.
JUST WATCHING COULD GET YOU IN PLENTY OF TROUBLE, TOO, I SUSPECT.
LITTLE BROTHER, CAN YOU ASK MASTER SAHN TO BRING TEA AND A LITTLE RICE, PLEASE? HE IS FEVERISH, AND HE NEEDS TO EAT SOMETHING.
YEAH, SURE. BUT THEN I'M TAKING OFF. I'LL BE HOME LATER.
SO CEDRIC...
WHO'S CHRISTY, HUH? WHAT'S GOING ON INSIDE YOUR HEAD?

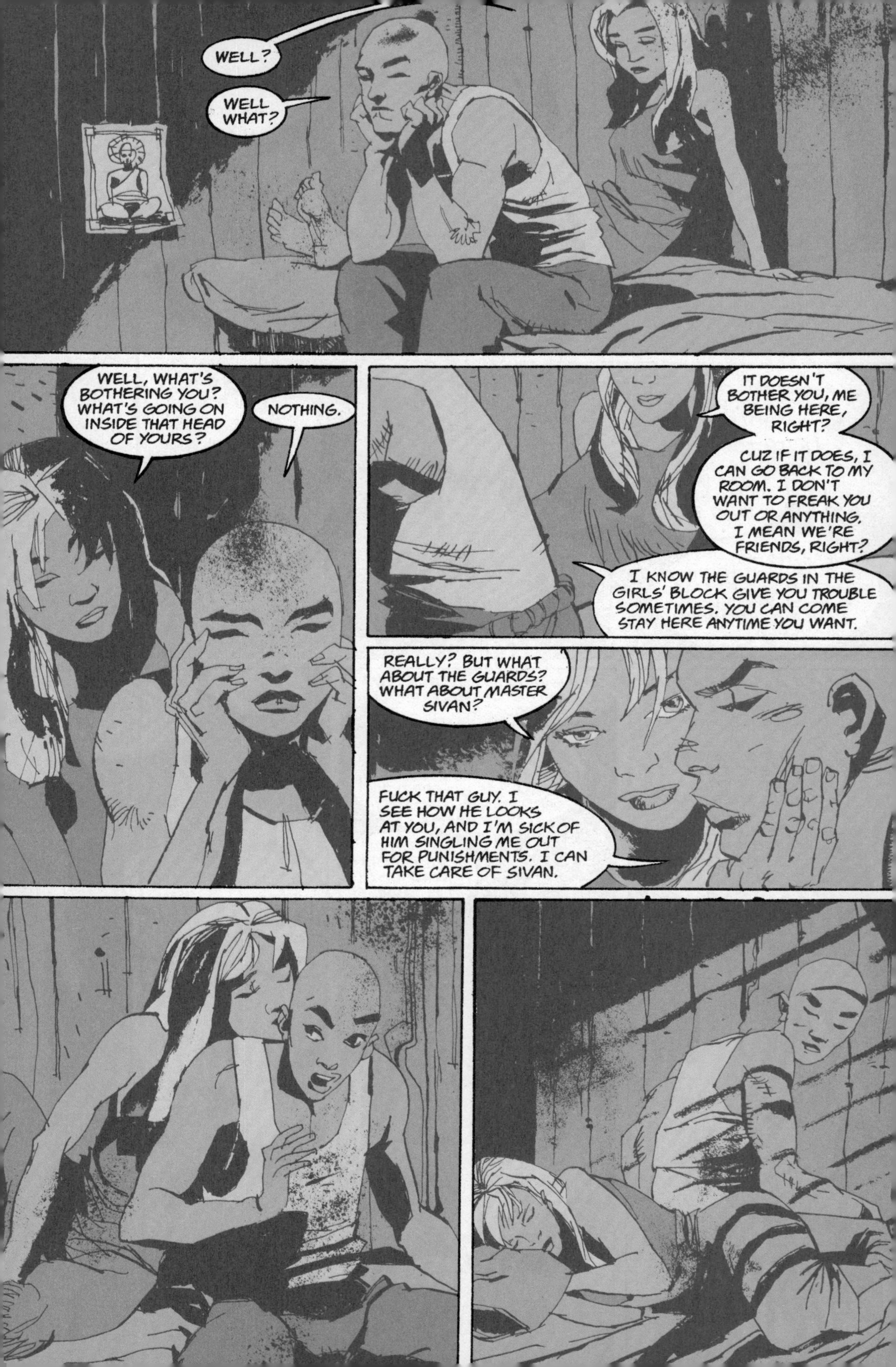
WELL?
WELL WHAT?
WELL, WHAT'S BOTHERING YOU? WHAT'S GOING ON INSIDE THAT HEAD OF YOURS?
NOTHING.
IT DOESN'T BOTHER YOU, ME BEING HERE, RIGHT?
CUZ IF IT DOES, I CAN GO BACK TO MY ROOM. I DON'T WANT TO FREAK YOU OUT OR ANYTHING. I MEAN WE'RE FRIENDS, RIGHT?
I KNOW THE GUARDS IN THE GIRLS' BLOCK GIVE YOU TROUBLE SOMETIMES. YOU CAN COME STAY HERE ANYTIME YOU WANT.
REALLY? BUT WHAT ABOUT THE GUARDS? WHAT ABOUT MASTER SIVAN?
FUCK THAT GUY. I SEE HOW HE LOOKS AT YOU, AND I'M SICK OF HIM SINGLING ME OUT FOR PUNISHMENTS. I CAN TAKE CARE OF SIVAN.

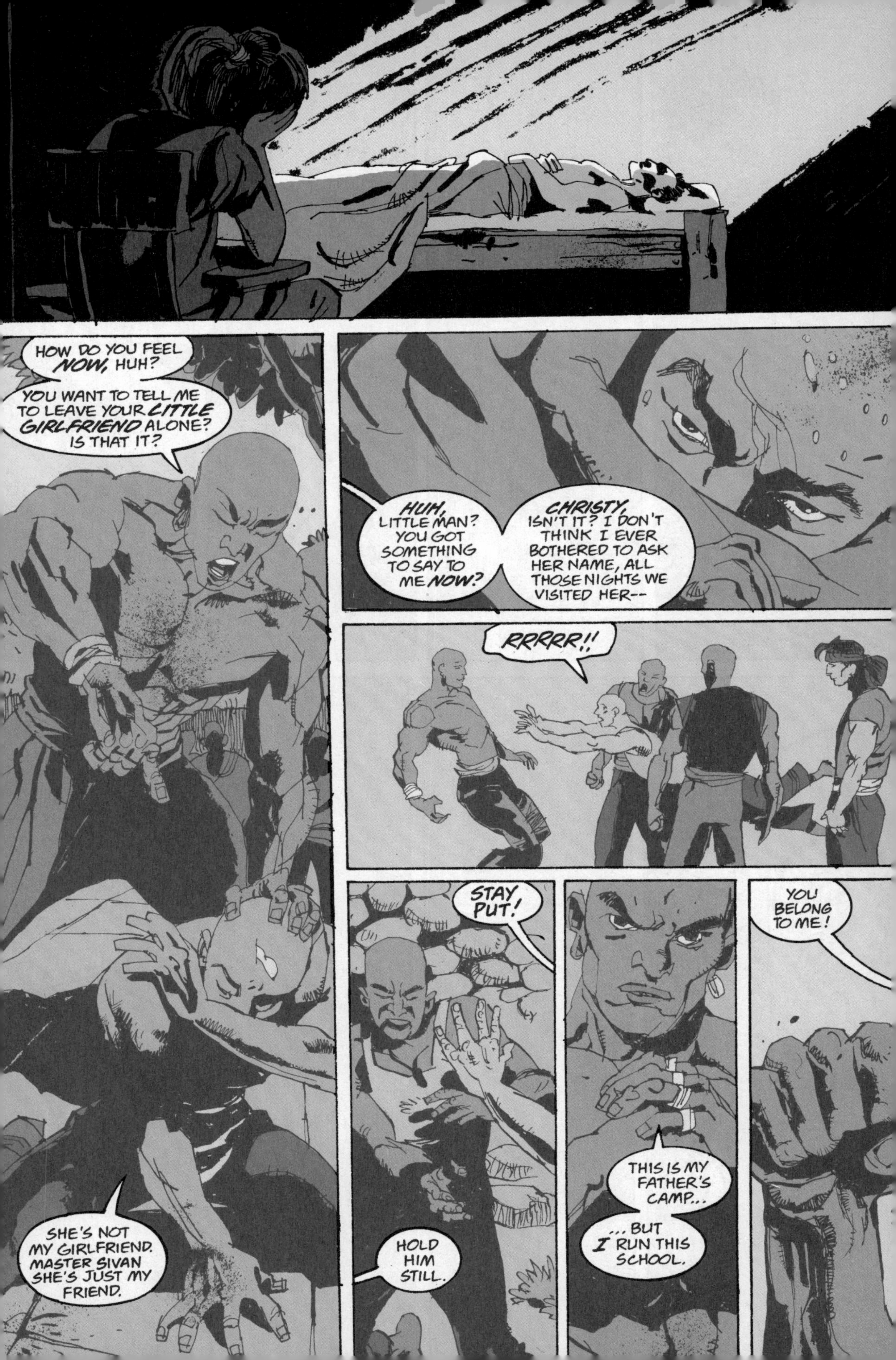

HOW DO YOU FEEL NOW, HUH?
YOU WANT TO TELL ME TO LEAVE YOUR LITTLE GIRLFRIEND ALONE? IS THAT IT?
SHE'S NOT MY GIRLFRIEND. MASTER SIVAN SHE'S JUST MY FRIEND.
HUH, LITTLE MAN? YOU GOT SOMETHING TO SAY TO ME NOW?
CHRISTY, ISN'T IT? I DON'T THINK I EVER BOTHERED TO ASK HER NAME, ALL THOSE NIGHTS WE VISITED HER--
RRRRR!!
STAY PUT!
HOLD HIM STILL.
THIS IS MY FATHER'S CAMP...
...BUT I RUN THIS SCHOOL.
YOU BELONG TO ME!

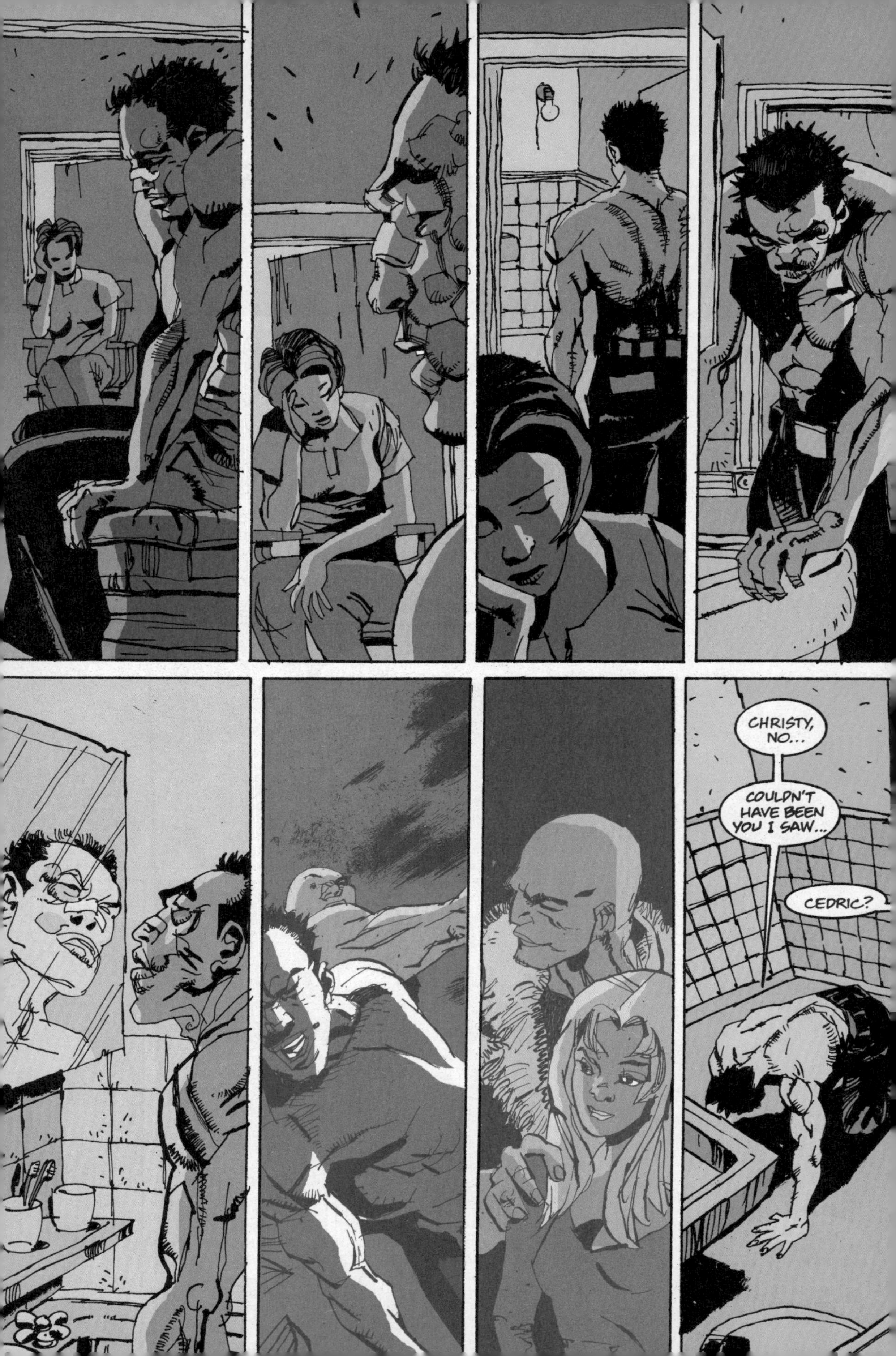
CHRISTY, NO...
COULDN'T HAVE BEEN YOU I SAW...
CEDRIC?

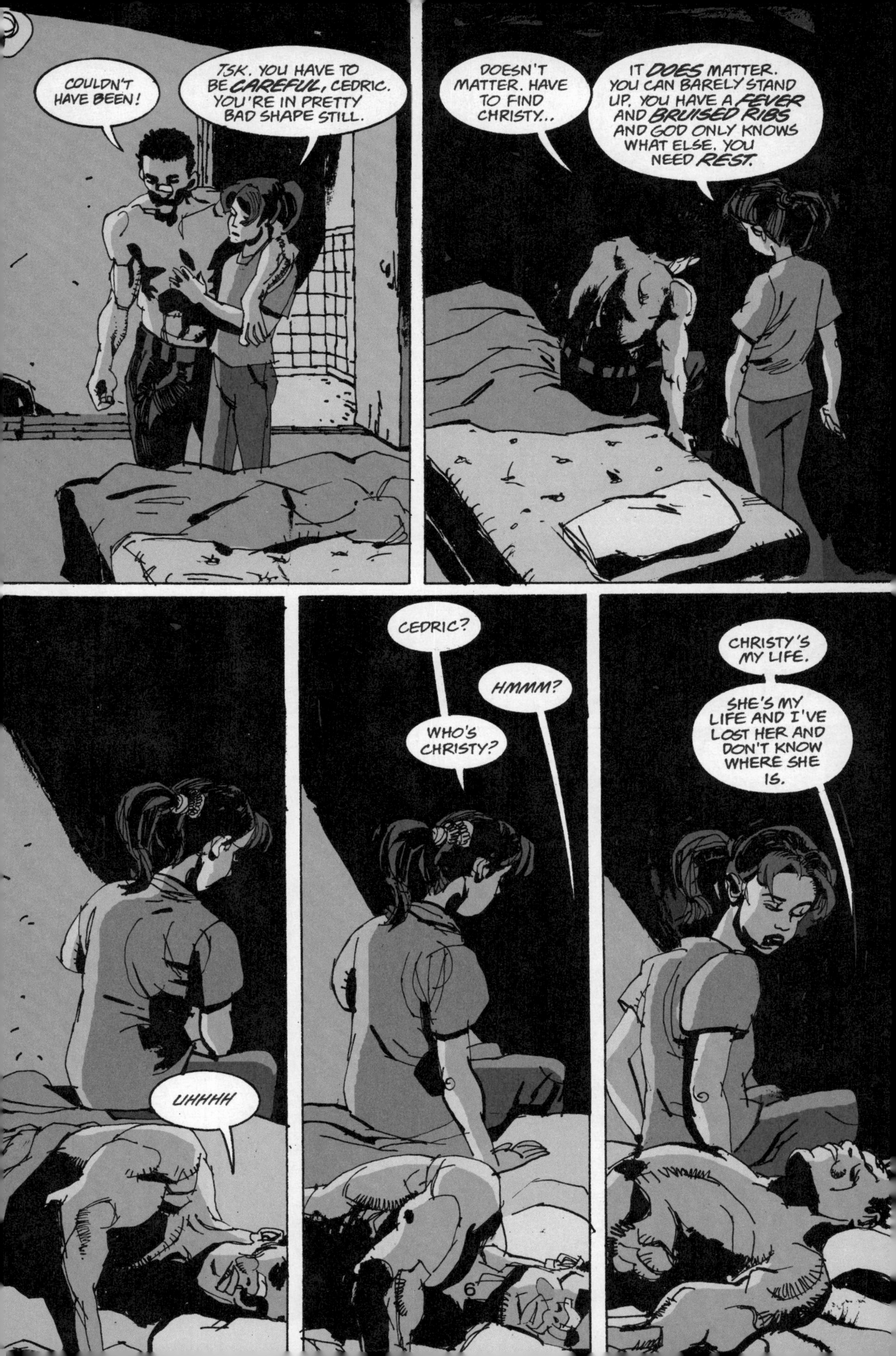
COULDN'T HAVE BEEN!
TSK. YOU HAVE TO BE CAREFUL, CEDRIC. YOU'RE IN PRETTY BAD SHAPE STILL.
DOESN'T MATTER. HAVE TO FIND CHRISTY...
IT DOES MATTER. YOU CAN BARELY STAND UP. YOU HAVE A FEVER AND BRUISED RIBS AND GOD ONLY KNOWS WHAT ELSE. YOU NEED REST.
UHHHH
CEDRIC?
HMMM?
WHO'S CHRISTY?
CHRISTY'S MY LIFE.
SHE'S MY LIFE AND I'VE LOST HER AND DON'T KNOW WHERE SHE IS.
6

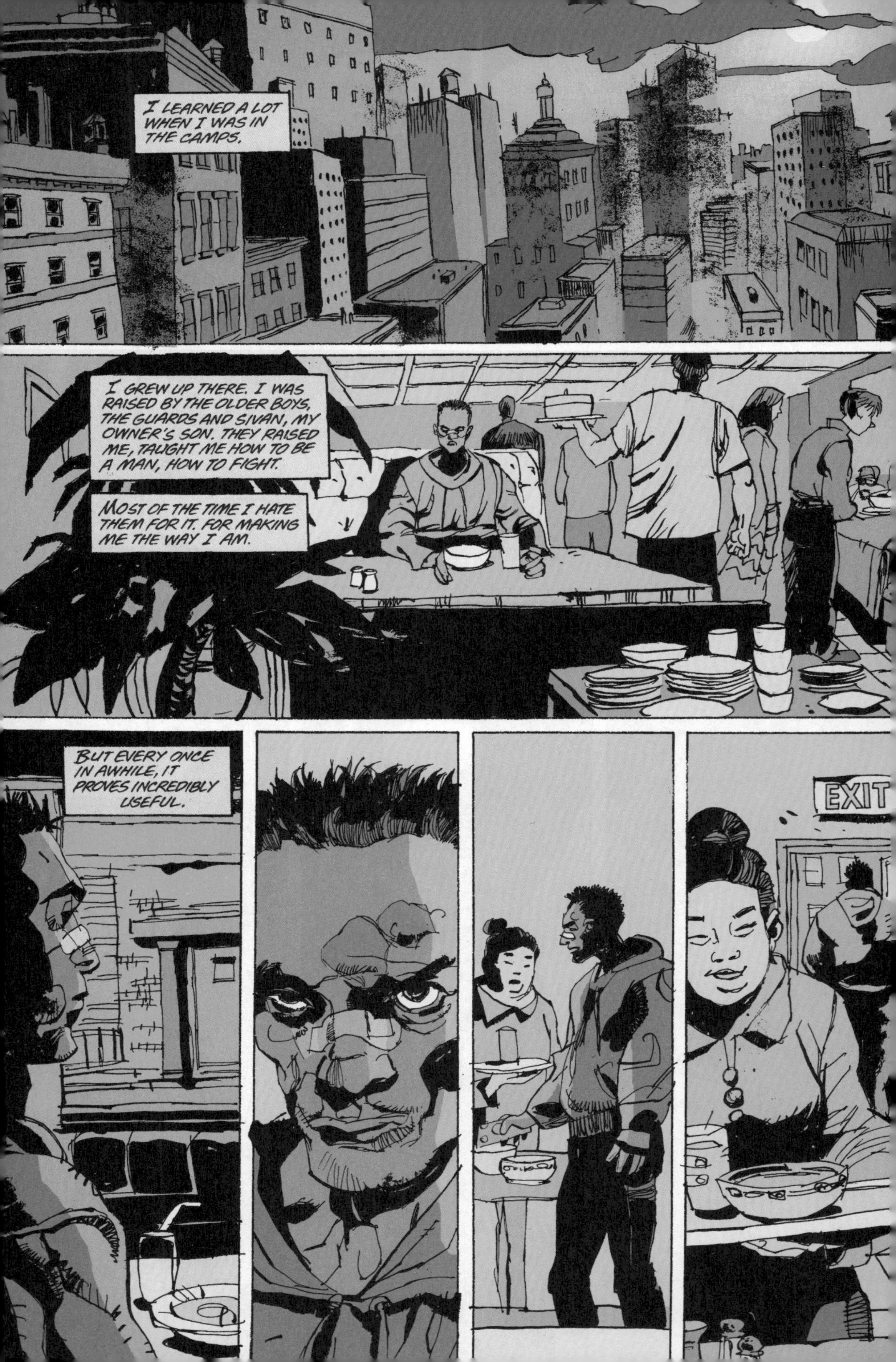
I LEARNED A LOT WHEN I WAS IN THE CAMPS.
I GREW UP THERE. I WAS RAISED BY THE OLDER BOYS, THE GUARDS AND SIVAN, MY OWNER'S SON. THEY RAISED ME, TAUGHT ME HOW TO BE A MAN, HOW TO FIGHT.
MOST OF THE TIME I HATE THEM FOR IT. FOR MAKING ME THE WAY I AM.
BUT EVERY ONCE IN AWHILE, IT PROVES INCREDIBLY USEFUL.
EXIT

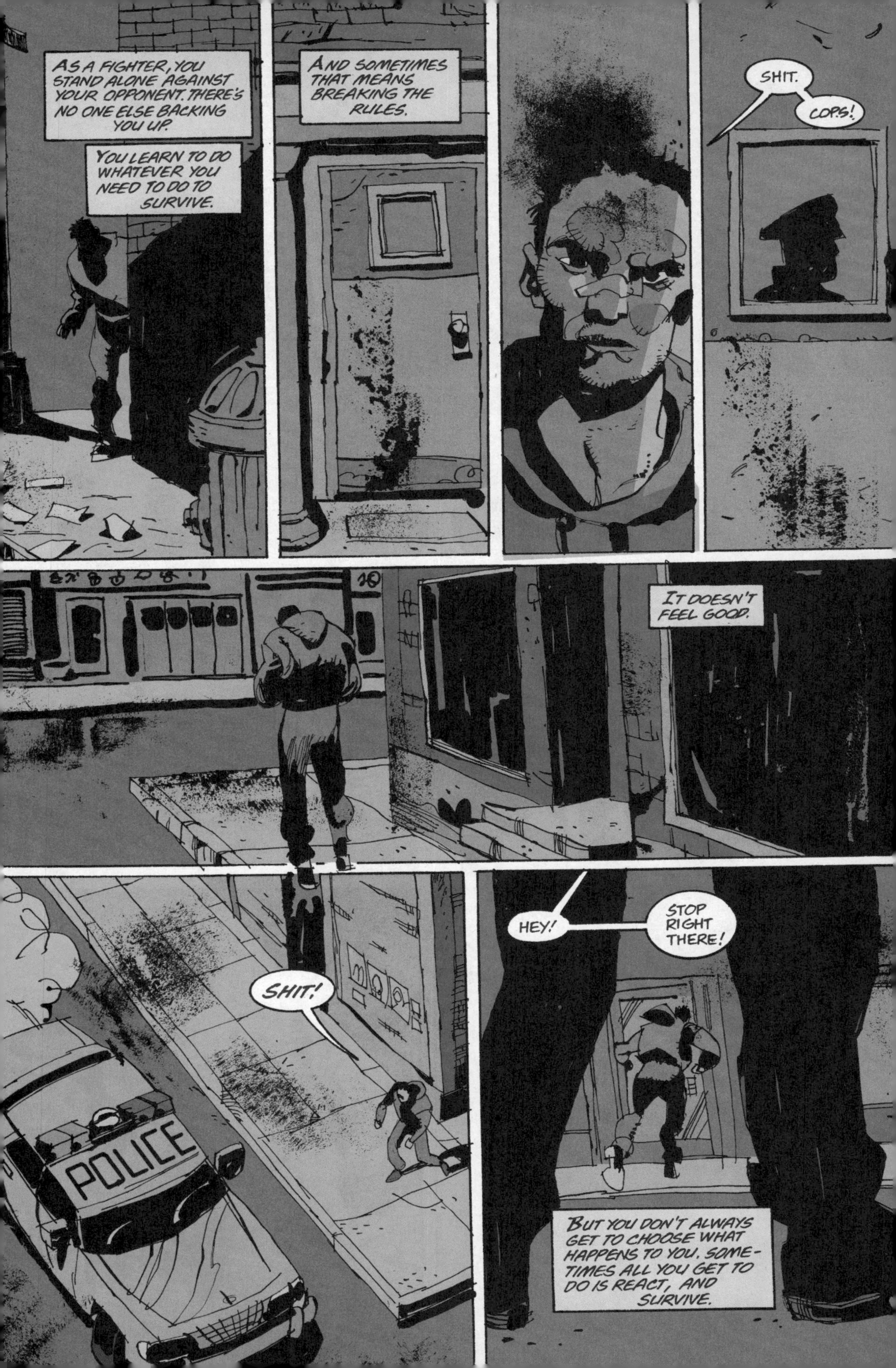

AS A FIGHTER, YOU STAND ALONE AGAINST YOUR OPPONENT. THERE'S NO ONE ELSE BACKING YOU UP.
YOU LEARN TO DO WHATEVER YOU NEED TO DO TO SURVIVE.
AND SOMETIMES THAT MEANS BREAKING THE RULES.
SHIT.
COPS!
IT DOESN'T FEEL GOOD.
SHIT!
HEY!
STOP RIGHT THERE!
BUT YOU DON'T ALWAYS GET TO CHOOSE WHAT HAPPENS TO YOU. SOME-TIMES ALL YOU GET TO DO IS REACT, AND SURVIVE.

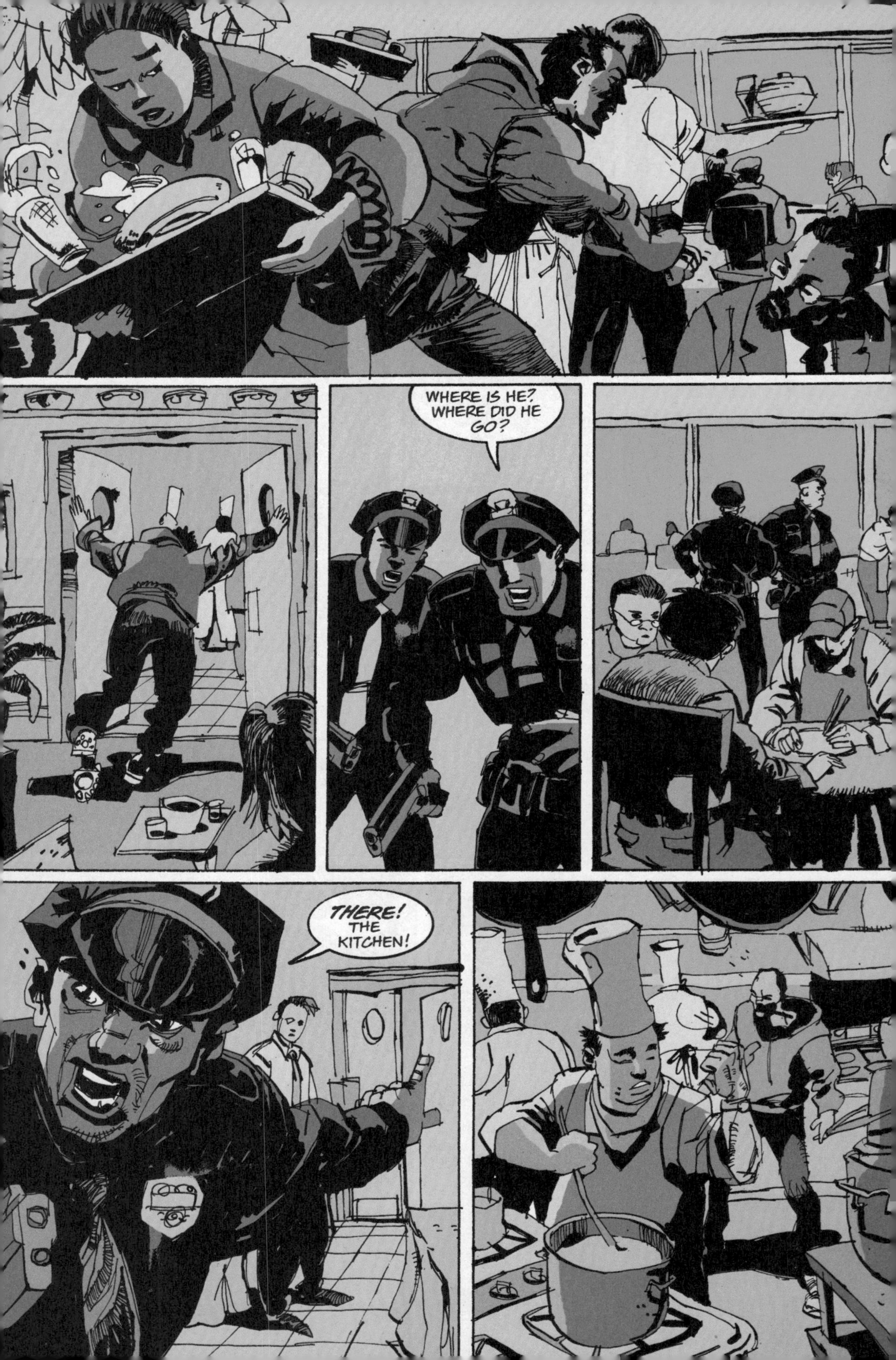
WHERE IS HE? WHERE DID HE GO?
THERE! THE KITCHEN!

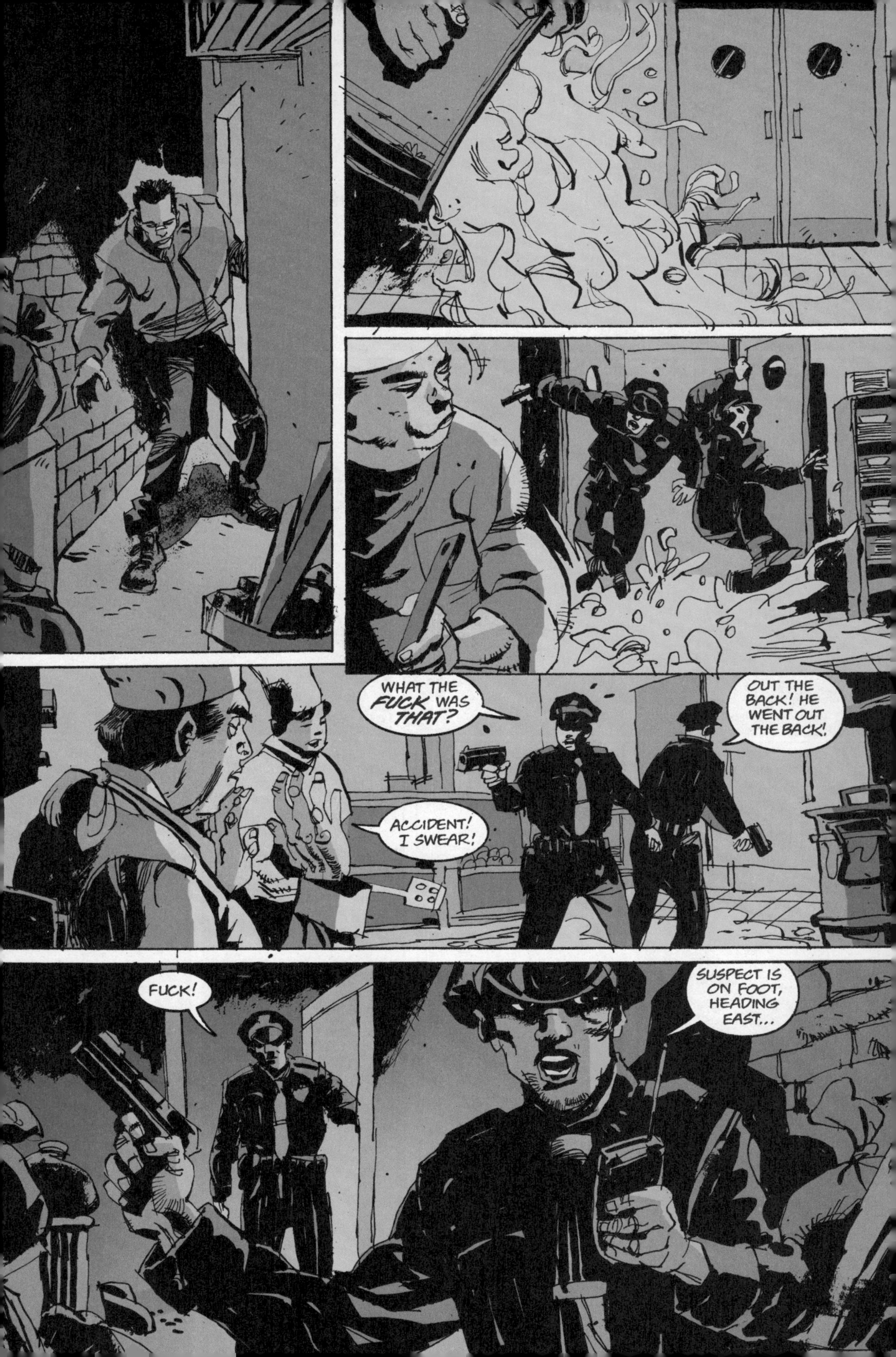
WHAT THE FUCK WAS THAT?
ACCIDENT! I SWEAR!
OUT THE BACK! HE WENT OUT THE BACK!
FUCK!
SUSPECT IS ON FOOT, HEADING EAST...

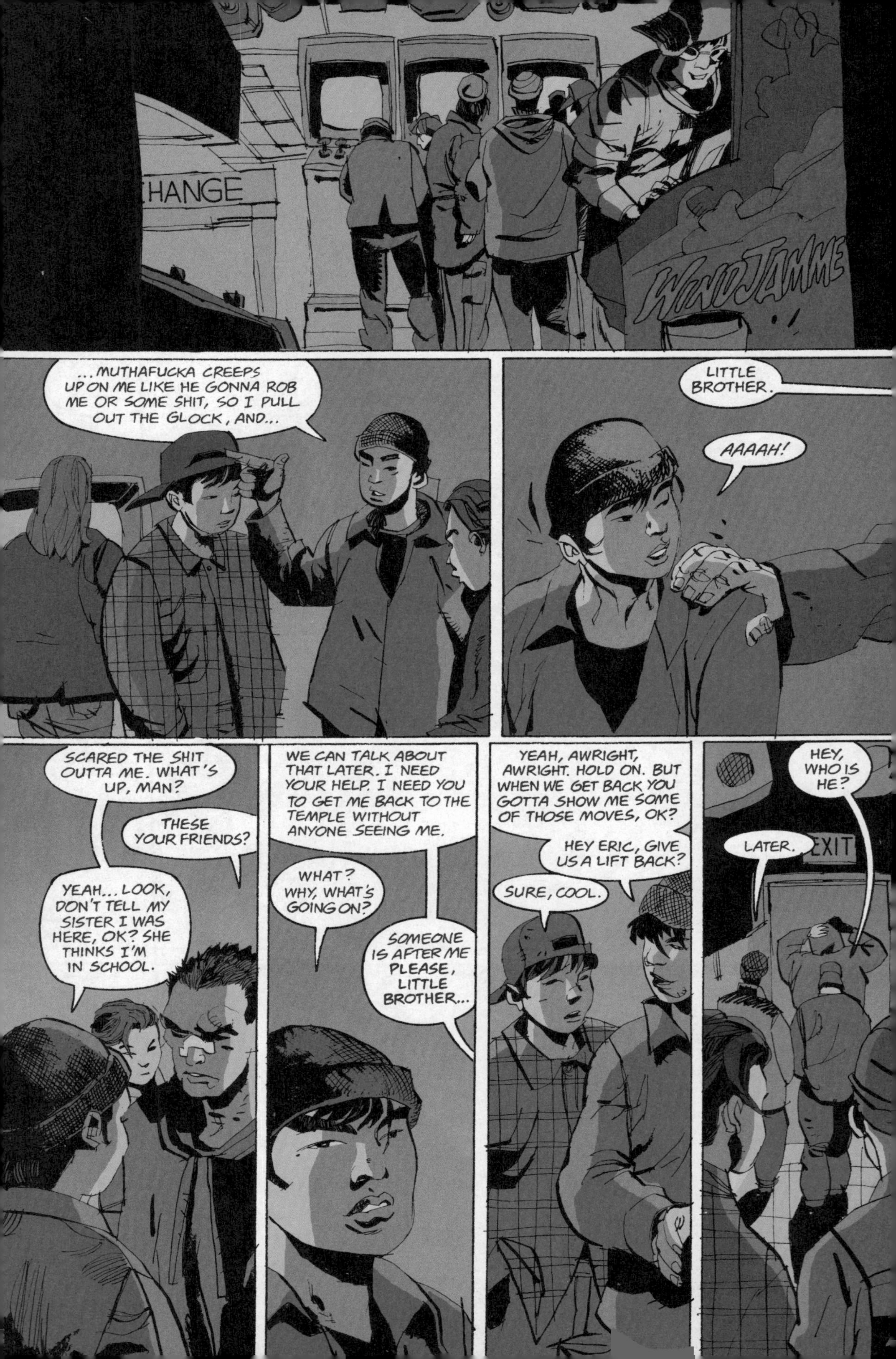

HANGE
WINDJAMME
...MUTHAFUCKA CREEPS UP ON ME LIKE HE GONNA ROB ME OR SOME SHIT, SO I PULL OUT THE GLOCK, AND...
LITTLE BROTHER.
AAAAH!
SCARED THE SHIT OUTTA ME. WHAT'S UP, MAN?
THESE YOUR FRIENDS?
YEAH... LOOK, DON'T TELL MY SISTER I WAS HERE, OK? SHE THINKS I'M IN SCHOOL.
WE CAN TALK ABOUT THAT LATER. I NEED YOUR HELP. I NEED YOU TO GET ME BACK TO THE TEMPLE WITHOUT ANYONE SEEING ME.
WHAT? WHY, WHAT'S GOING ON?
SOMEONE IS AFTER ME PLEASE, LITTLE BROTHER...
YEAH, AWRIGHT, AWRIGHT. HOLD ON. BUT WHEN WE GET BACK YOU GOTTA SHOW ME SOME OF THOSE MOVES, OK?
HEY ERIC, GIVE US A LIFT BACK?
SURE, COOL.
HEY, WHO IS HE?
LATER.
EXIT

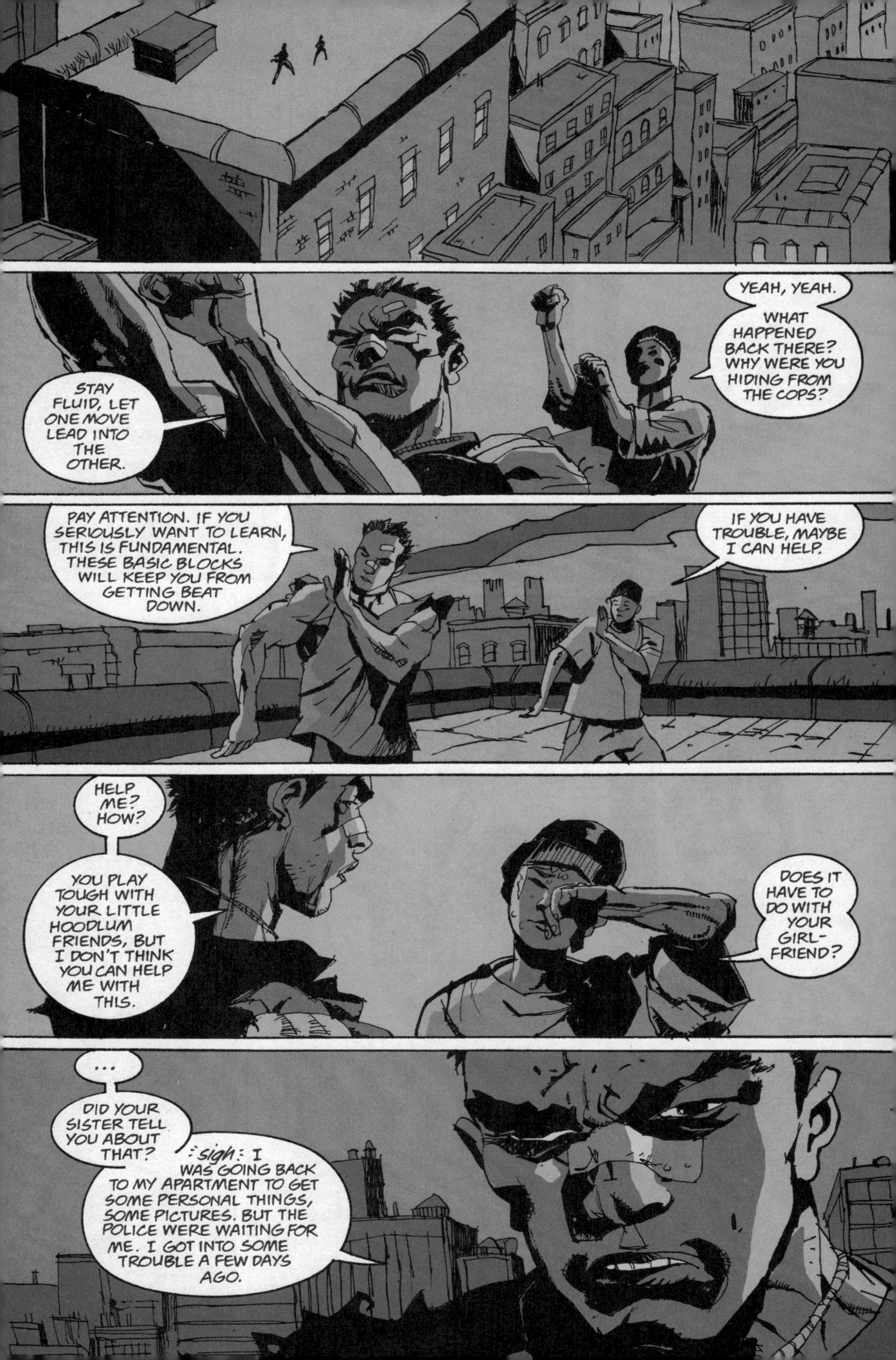
STAY FLUID, LET ONE MOVE LEAD INTO THE OTHER.
YEAH, YEAH.
WHAT HAPPENED BACK THERE? WHY WERE YOU HIDING FROM THE COPS?
PAY ATTENTION. IF YOU SERIOUSLY WANT TO LEARN, THIS IS FUNDAMENTAL. THESE BASIC BLOCKS WILL KEEP YOU FROM GETTING BEAT DOWN.
IF YOU HAVE TROUBLE, MAYBE I CAN HELP.
HELP ME? HOW?
YOU PLAY TOUGH WITH YOUR LITTLE HOODLUM FRIENDS, BUT I DON'T THINK YOU CAN HELP ME WITH THIS.
DOES IT HAVE TO DO WITH YOUR GIRL-FRIEND?
...
DID YOUR SISTER TELL YOU ABOUT THAT?
:sigh: I WAS GOING BACK TO MY APARTMENT TO GET SOME PERSONAL THINGS, SOME PICTURES. BUT THE POLICE WERE WAITING FOR ME. I GOT INTO SOME TROUBLE A FEW DAYS AGO.

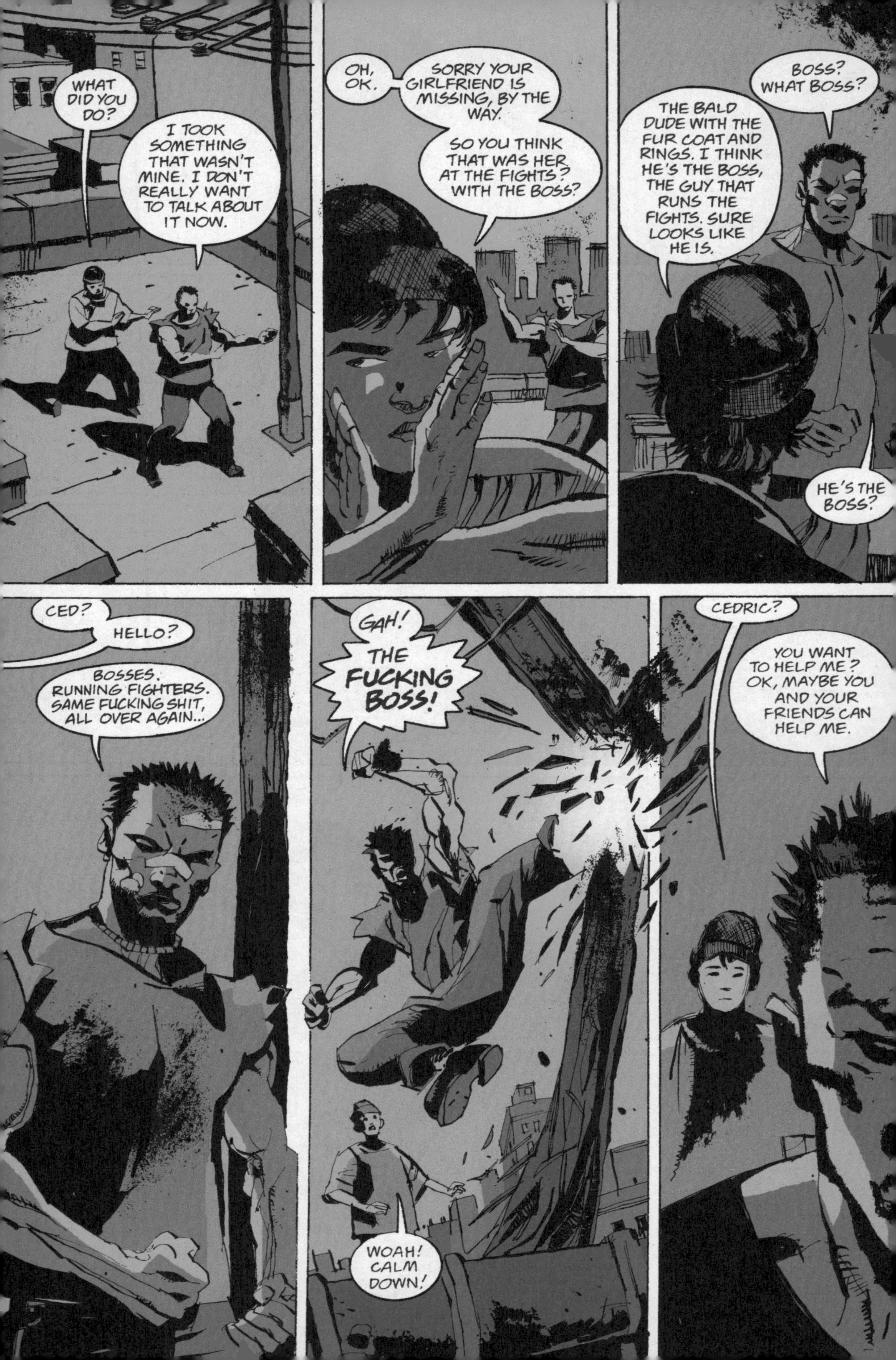
WHAT DID YOU DO?
I TOOK SOMETHING THAT WASN'T MINE. I DON'T REALLY WANT TO TALK ABOUT IT NOW.
OH, OK.
SORRY YOUR GIRLFRIEND IS MISSING, BY THE WAY.
SO YOU THINK THAT WAS HER AT THE FIGHTS? WITH THE BOSS?
BOSS? WHAT BOSS?
THE BALD DUDE WITH THE FUR COAT AND RINGS. I THINK HE'S THE BOSS, THE GUY THAT RUNS THE FIGHTS. SURE LOOKS LIKE HE IS.
HE'S THE BOSS?
CED?
HELLO?
BOSSES. RUNNING FIGHTERS. SAME FUCKING SHIT, ALL OVER AGAIN...
GAH!
THE FUCKING BOSS!
WOAH! CALM DOWN!
CEDRIC?
YOU WANT TO HELP ME? OK, MAYBE YOU AND YOUR FRIENDS CAN HELP ME.

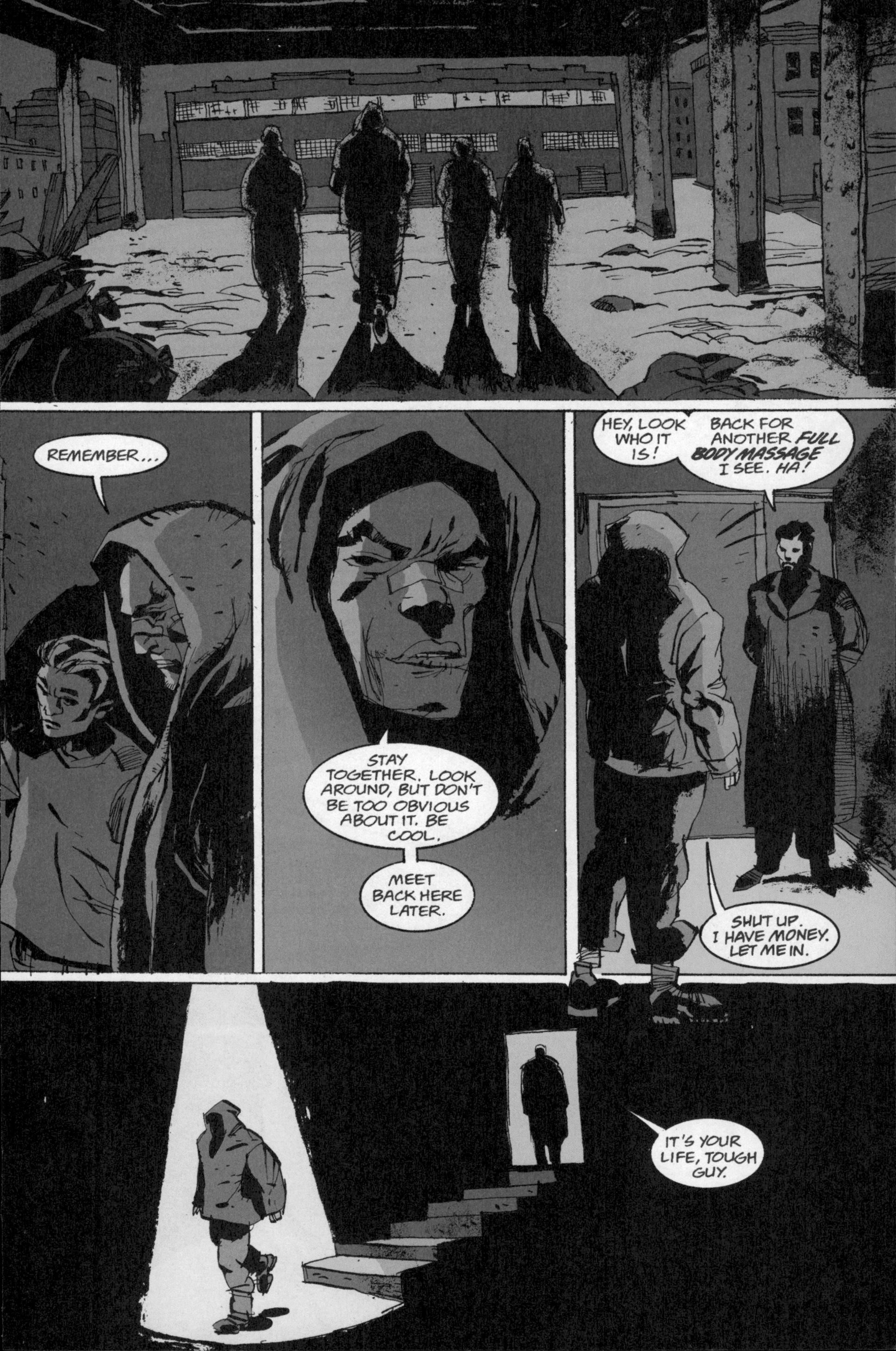
REMEMBER...
STAY TOGETHER. LOOK AROUND, BUT DON'T BE TOO OBVIOUS ABOUT IT. BE COOL.
MEET BACK HERE LATER.
HEY, LOOK WHO IT IS!
BACK FOR ANOTHER FULL BODY MASSAGE I SEE. HA!
SHUT UP. I HAVE MONEY. LET ME IN.
IT'S YOUR LIFE, TOUGH GUY.

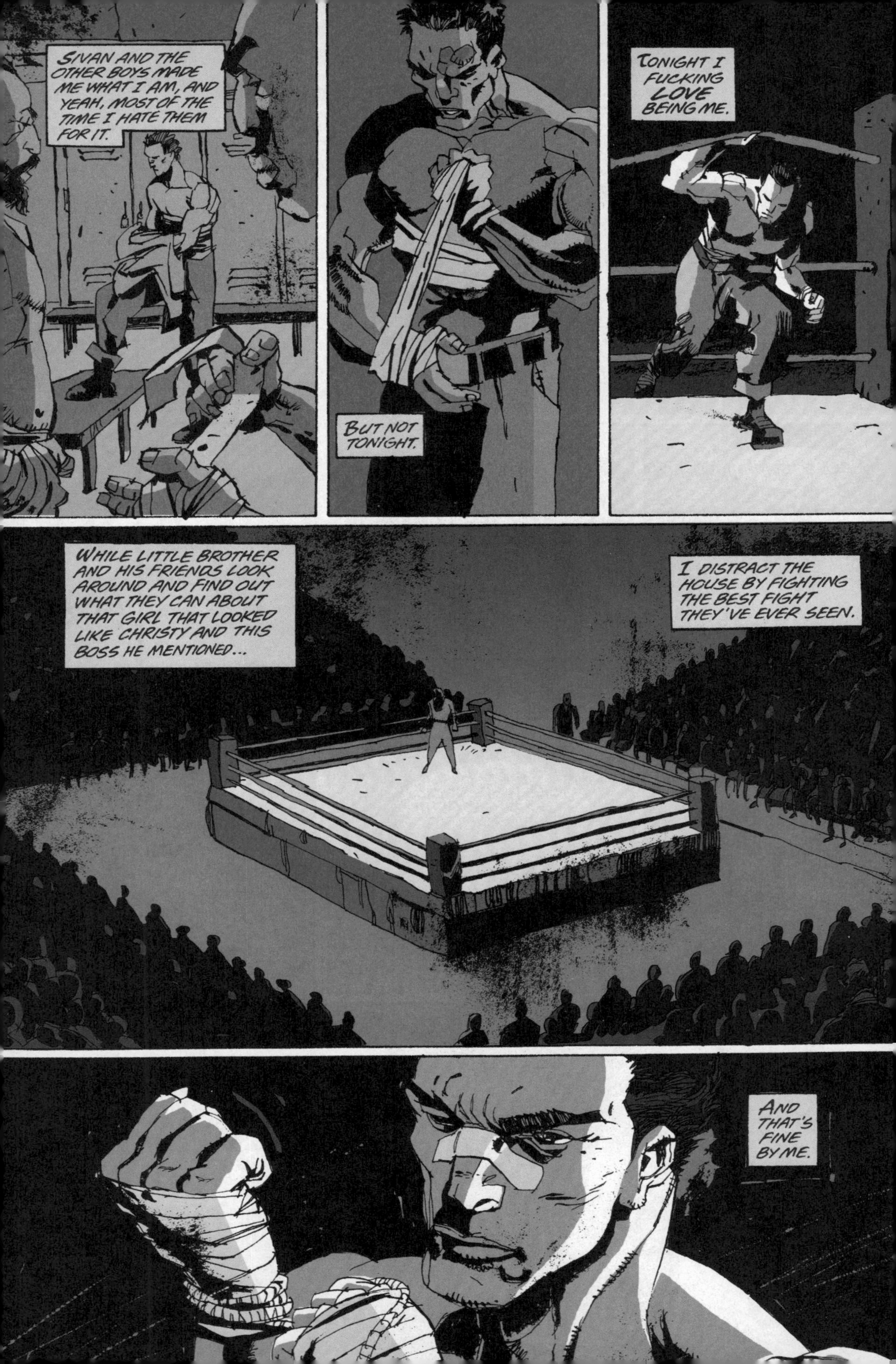
SIVAN AND THE OTHER BOYS MADE ME WHAT I AM, AND YEAH, MOST OF THE TIME I HATE THEM FOR IT.
BUT NOT TONIGHT.
TONIGHT I FUCKING LOVE BEING ME.
WHILE LITTLE BROTHER AND HIS FRIENDS LOOK AROUND AND FIND OUT WHAT THEY CAN ABOUT THAT GIRL THAT LOOKED LIKE CHRISTY AND THIS BOSS HE MENTIONED...
I DISTRACT THE HOUSE BY FIGHTING THE BEST FIGHT THEY'VE EVER SEEN.
AND THAT'S FINE BY ME.

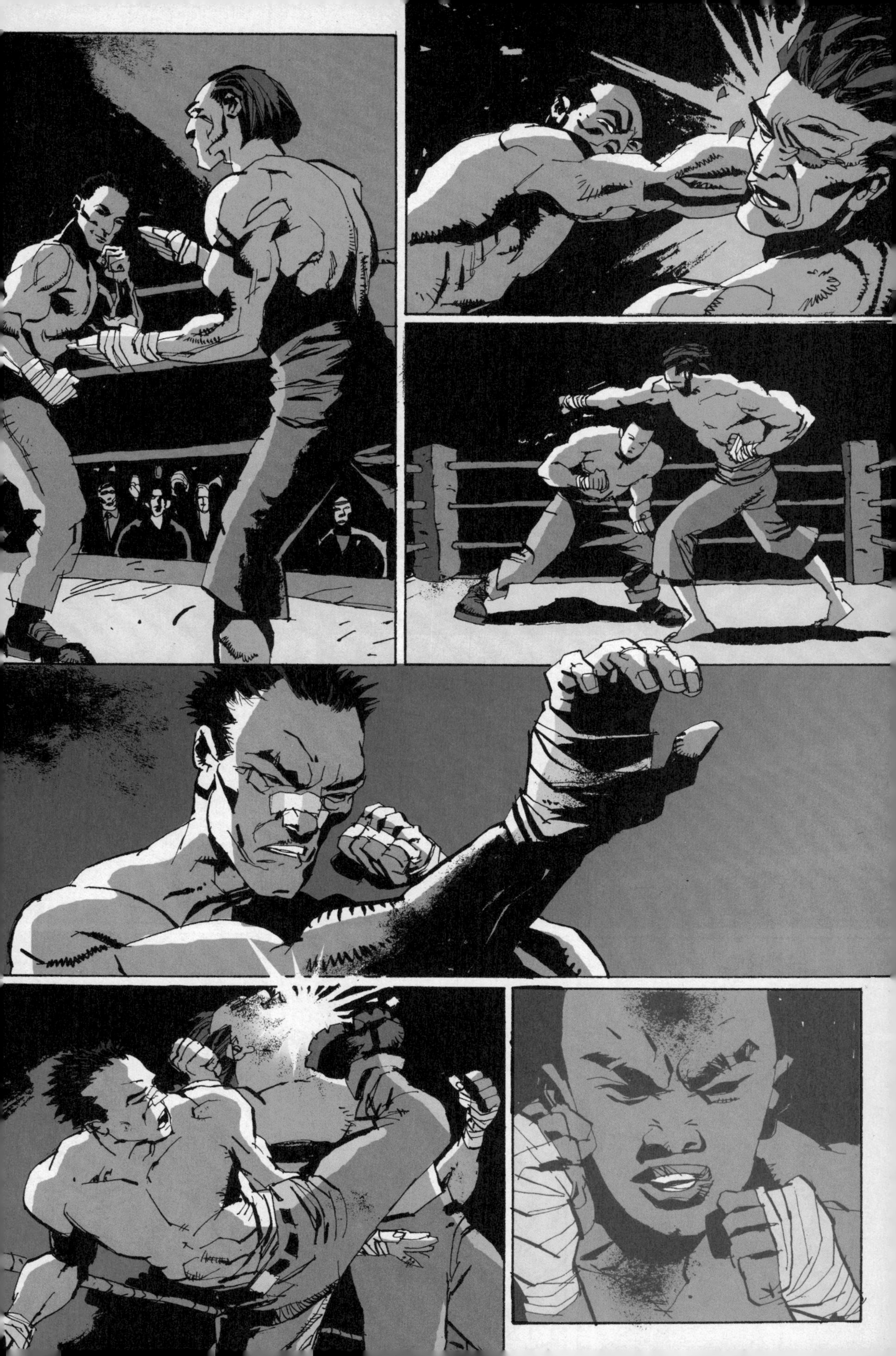

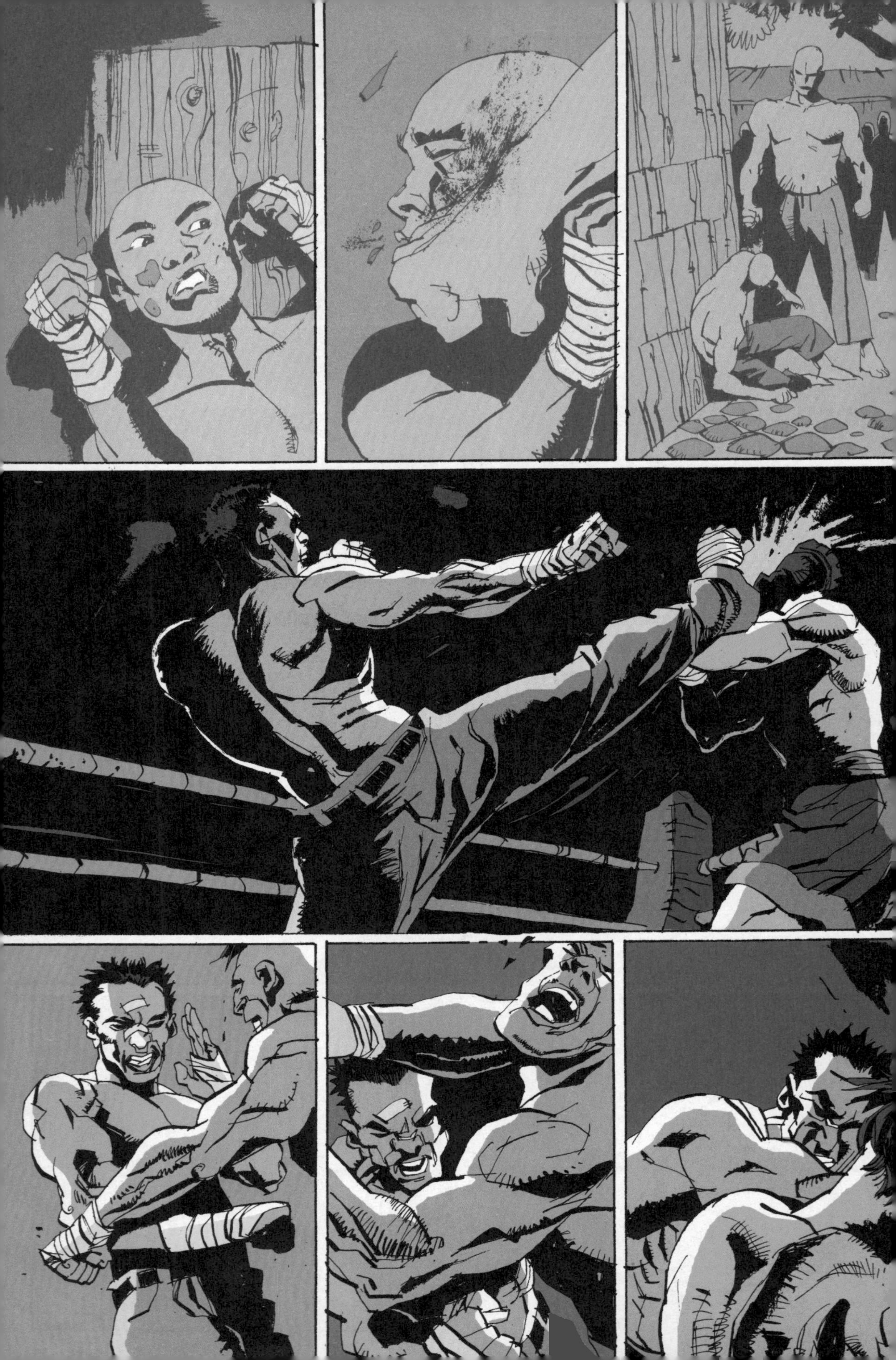

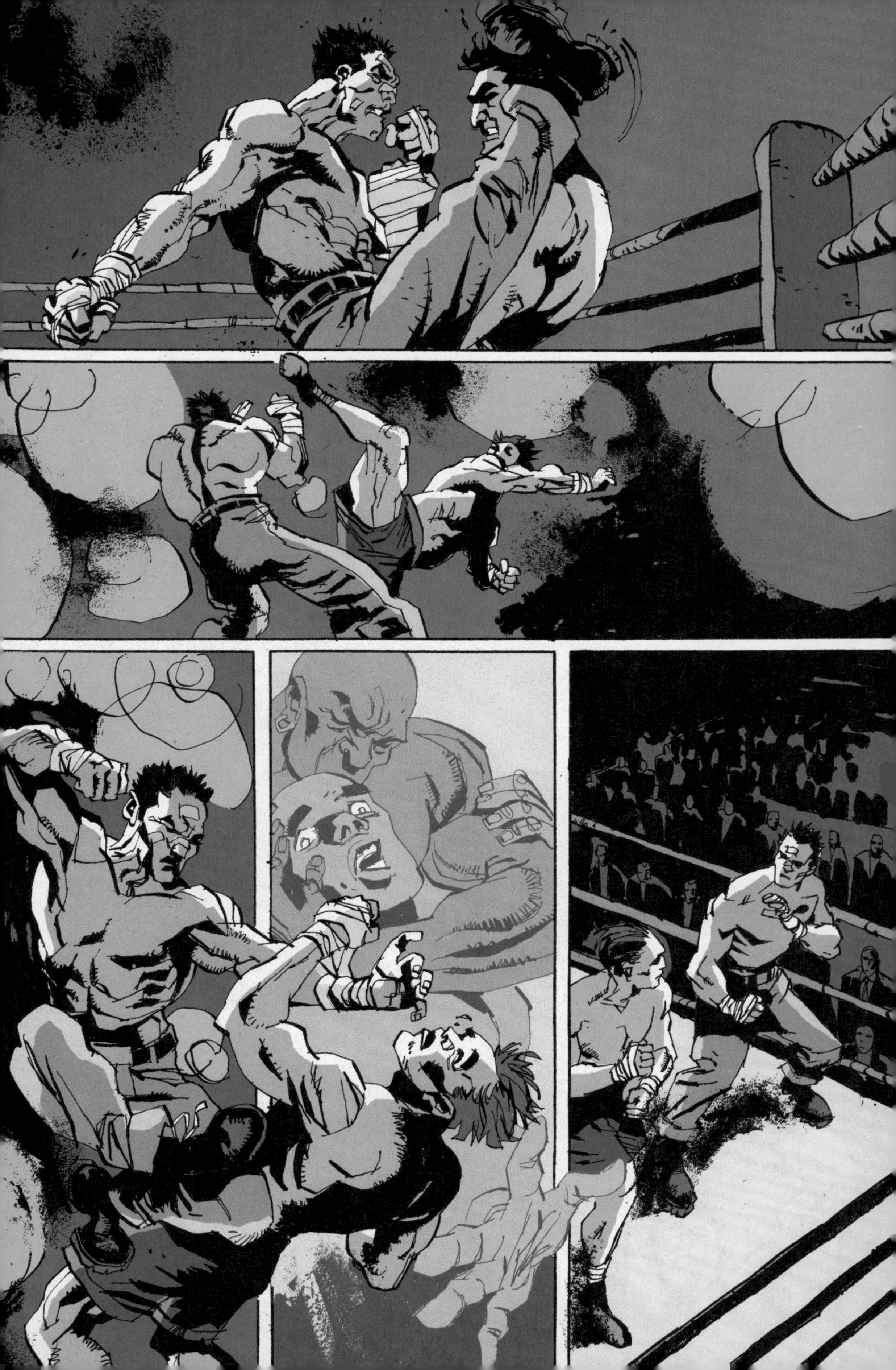

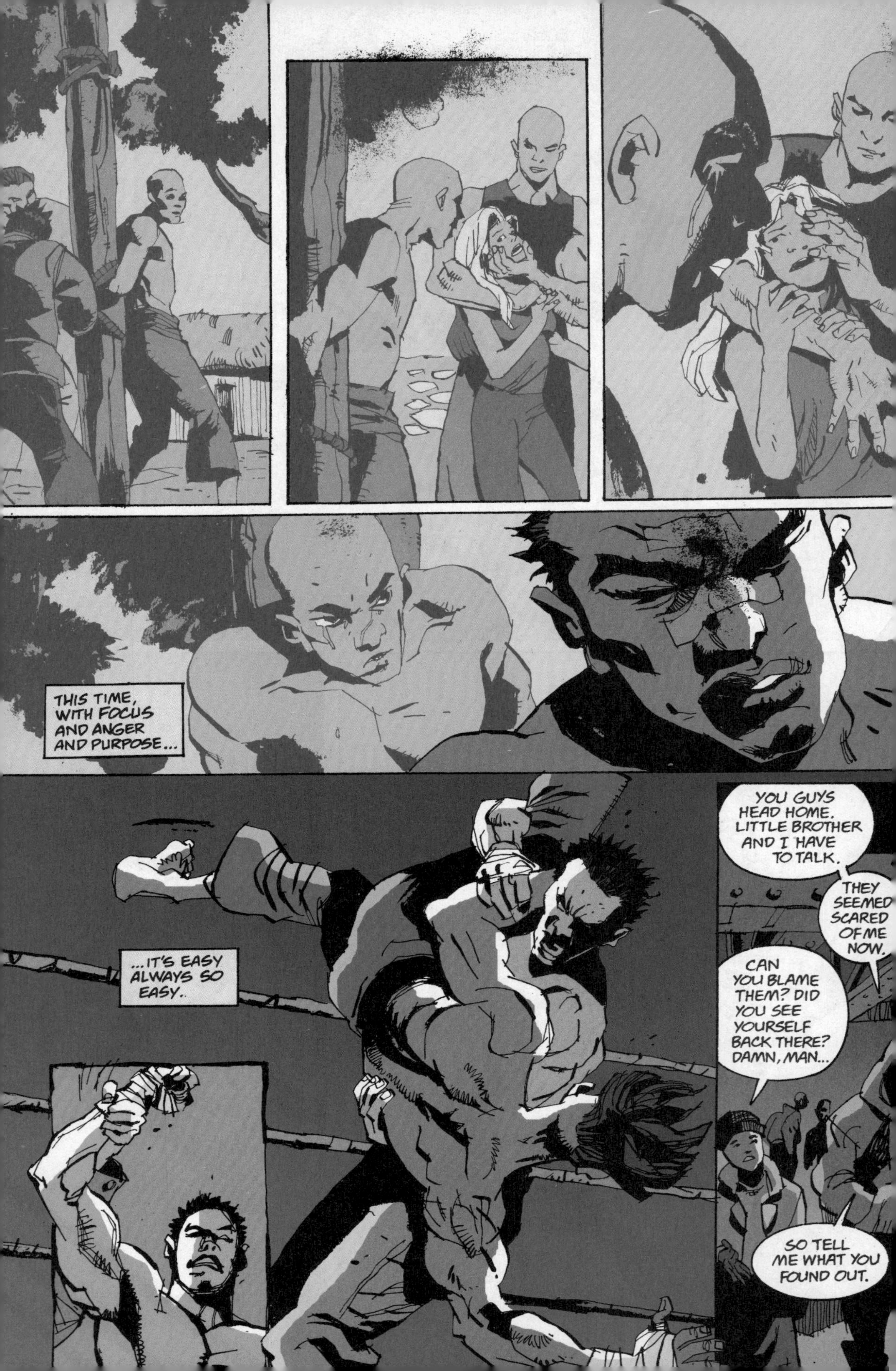
THIS TIME, WITH FOCUS AND ANGER AND PURPOSE...
...IT'S EASY ALWAYS SO EASY..
YOU GUYS HEAD HOME. LITTLE BROTHER AND I HAVE TO TALK.
THEY SEEMED SCARED OF ME NOW.
CAN YOU BLAME THEM? DID YOU SEE YOURSELF BACK THERE? DAMN, MAN...
SO TELL ME WHAT YOU FOUND OUT.

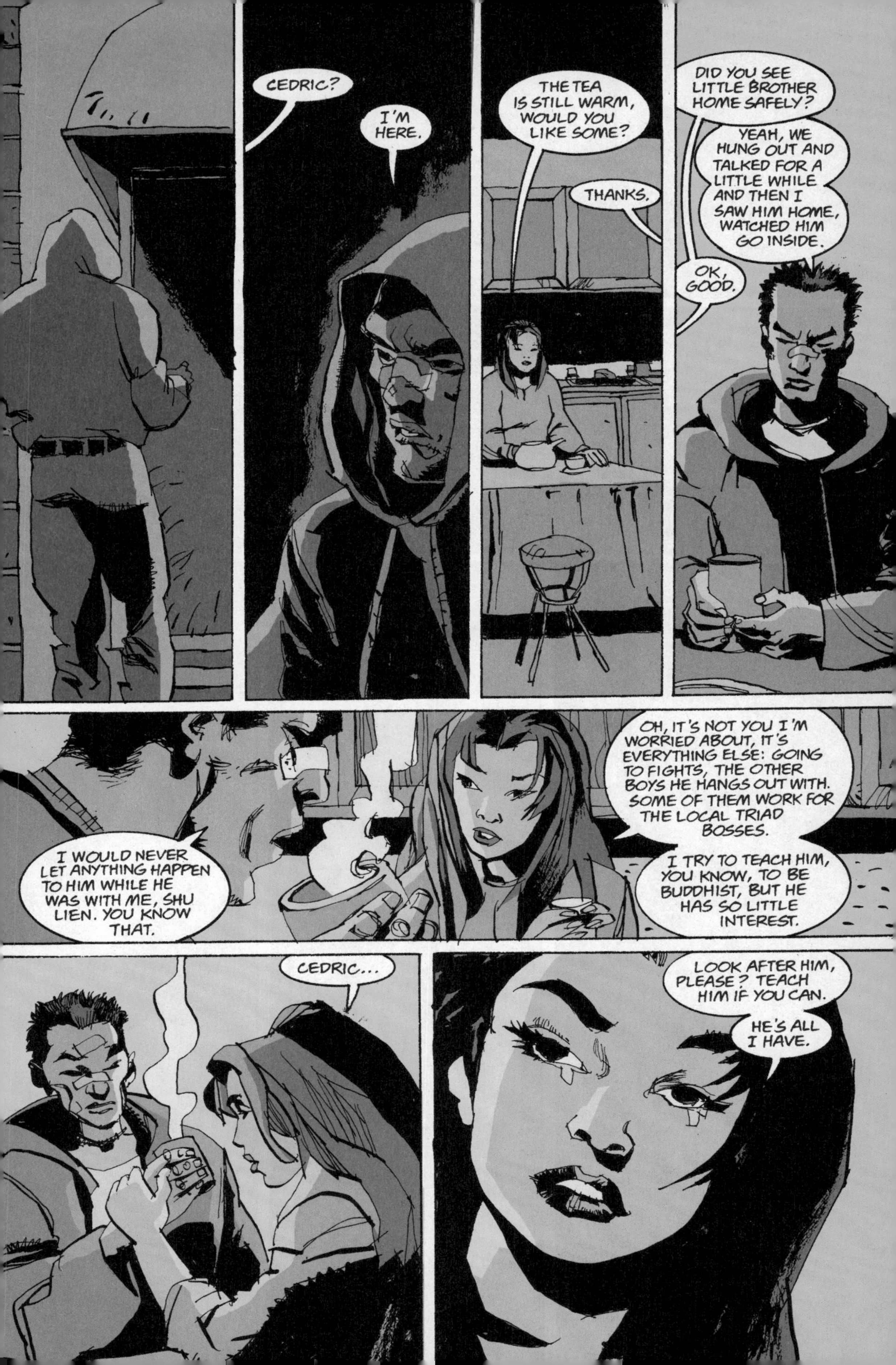
CEDRIC?
I'M HERE.
THE TEA IS STILL WARM, WOULD YOU LIKE SOME?
THANKS.
DID YOU SEE LITTLE BROTHER HOME SAFELY?
YEAH, WE HUNG OUT AND TALKED FOR A LITTLE WHILE AND THEN I SAW HIM HOME, WATCHED HIM GO INSIDE.
OK, GOOD.
I WOULD NEVER LET ANYTHING HAPPEN TO HIM WHILE HE WAS WITH ME, SHU LIEN. YOU KNOW THAT.
OH, IT'S NOT YOU I'M WORRIED ABOUT, IT'S EVERYTHING ELSE: GOING TO FIGHTS, THE OTHER BOYS HE HANGS OUT WITH. SOME OF THEM WORK FOR THE LOCAL TRIAD BOSSES.
I TRY TO TEACH HIM, YOU KNOW, TO BE BUDDHIST, BUT HE HAS SO LITTLE INTEREST.
CEDRIC...
LOOK AFTER HIM, PLEASE? TEACH HIM IF YOU CAN.
HE'S ALL I HAVE.

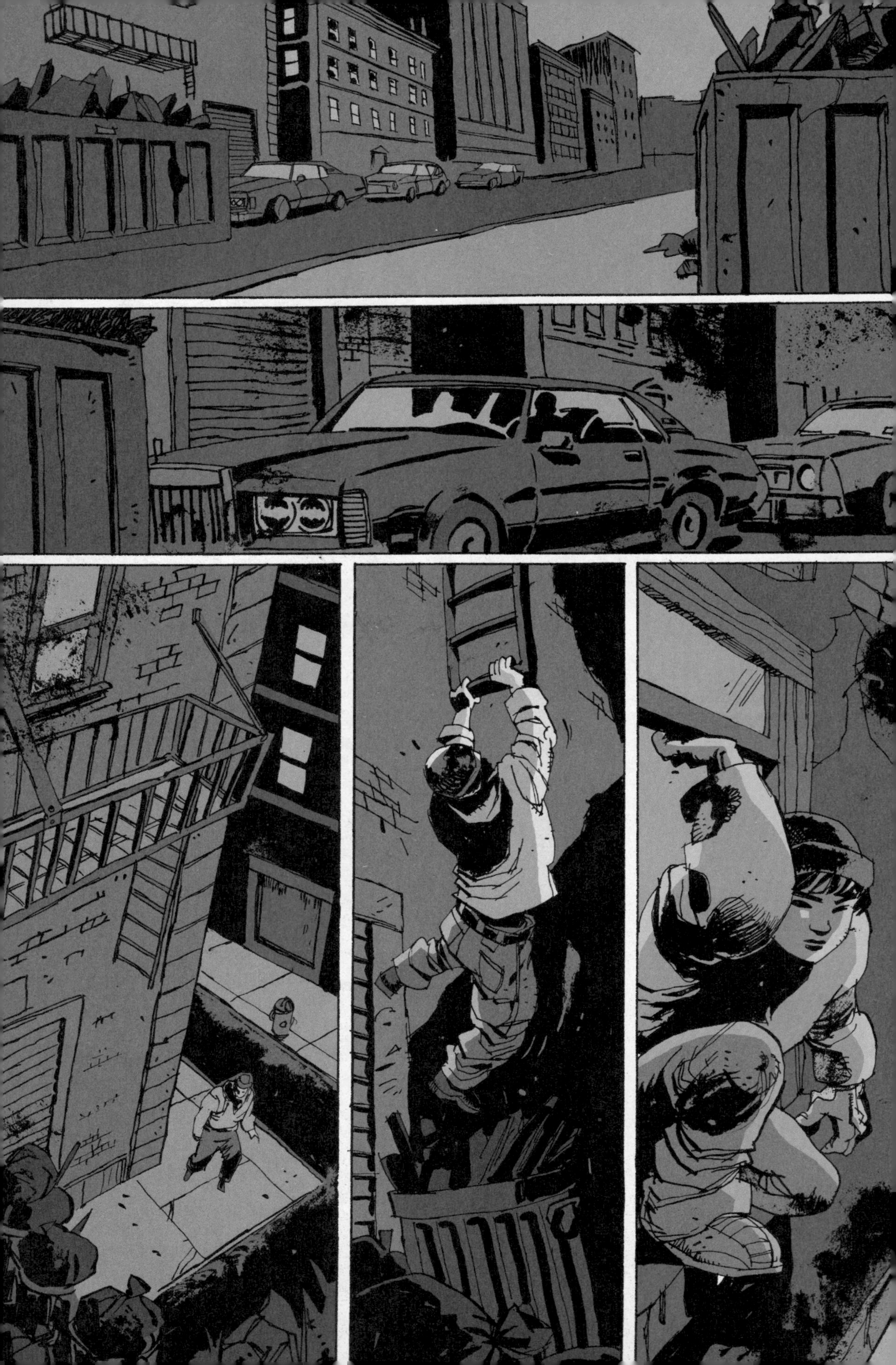

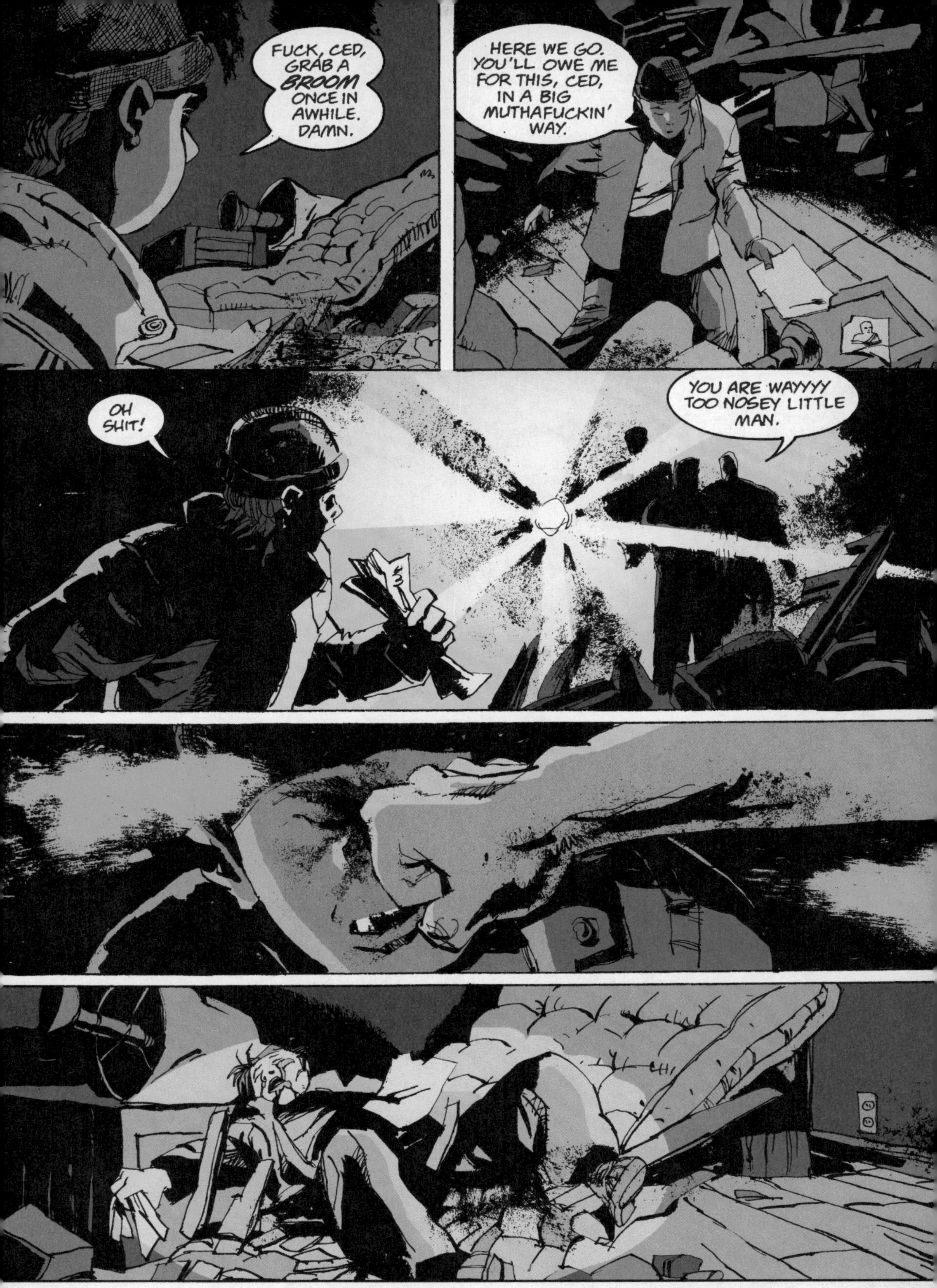
FUCK, CED, GRAB A BROOM ONCE IN AWHILE. DAMN.
HERE WE GO. YOU'LL OWE ME FOR THIS, CED, IN A BIG MUTHAFUCKIN' WAY.
OH SHIT!
YOU ARE WAYYYY TOO NOSEY LITTLE MAN.

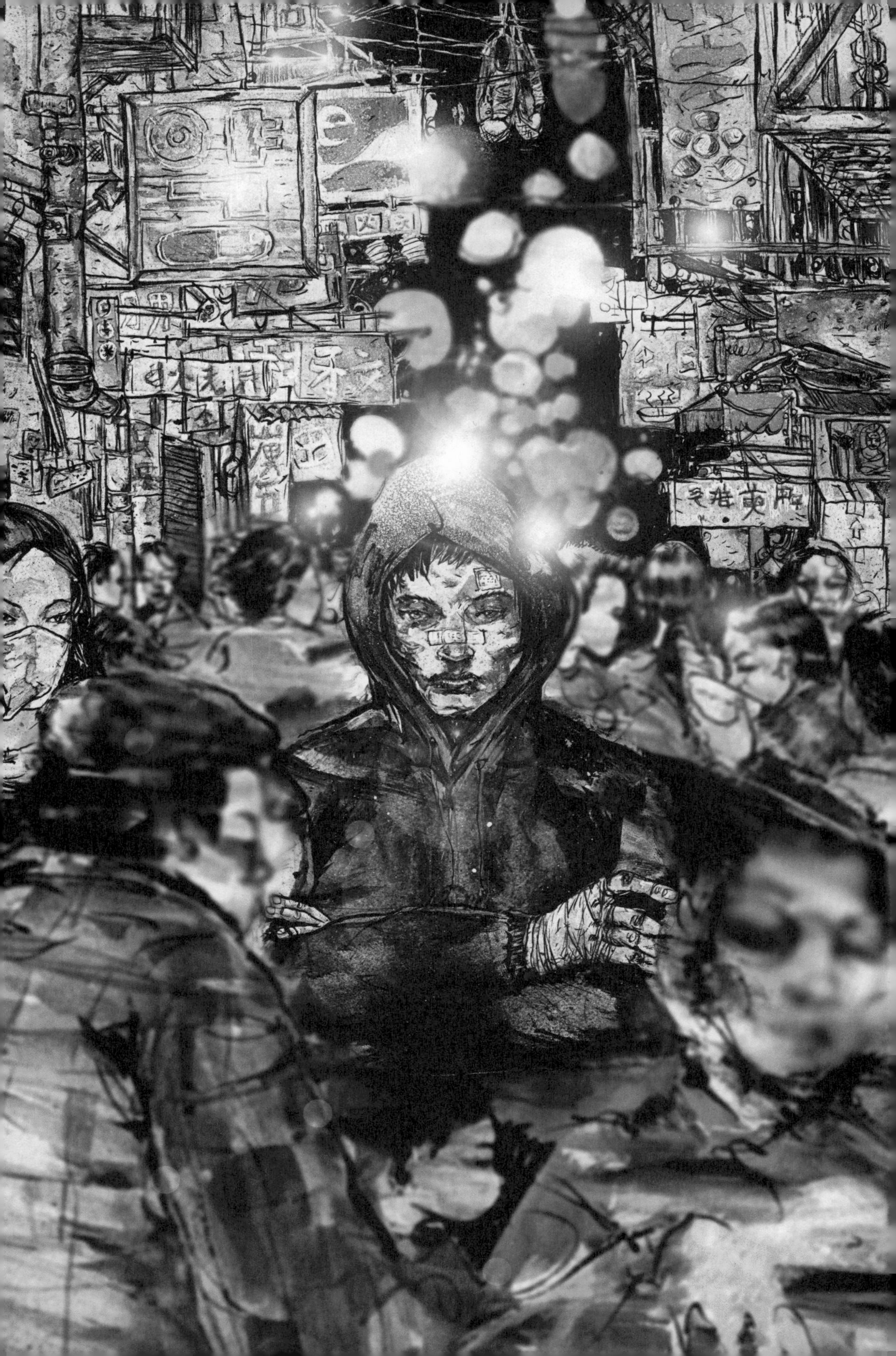

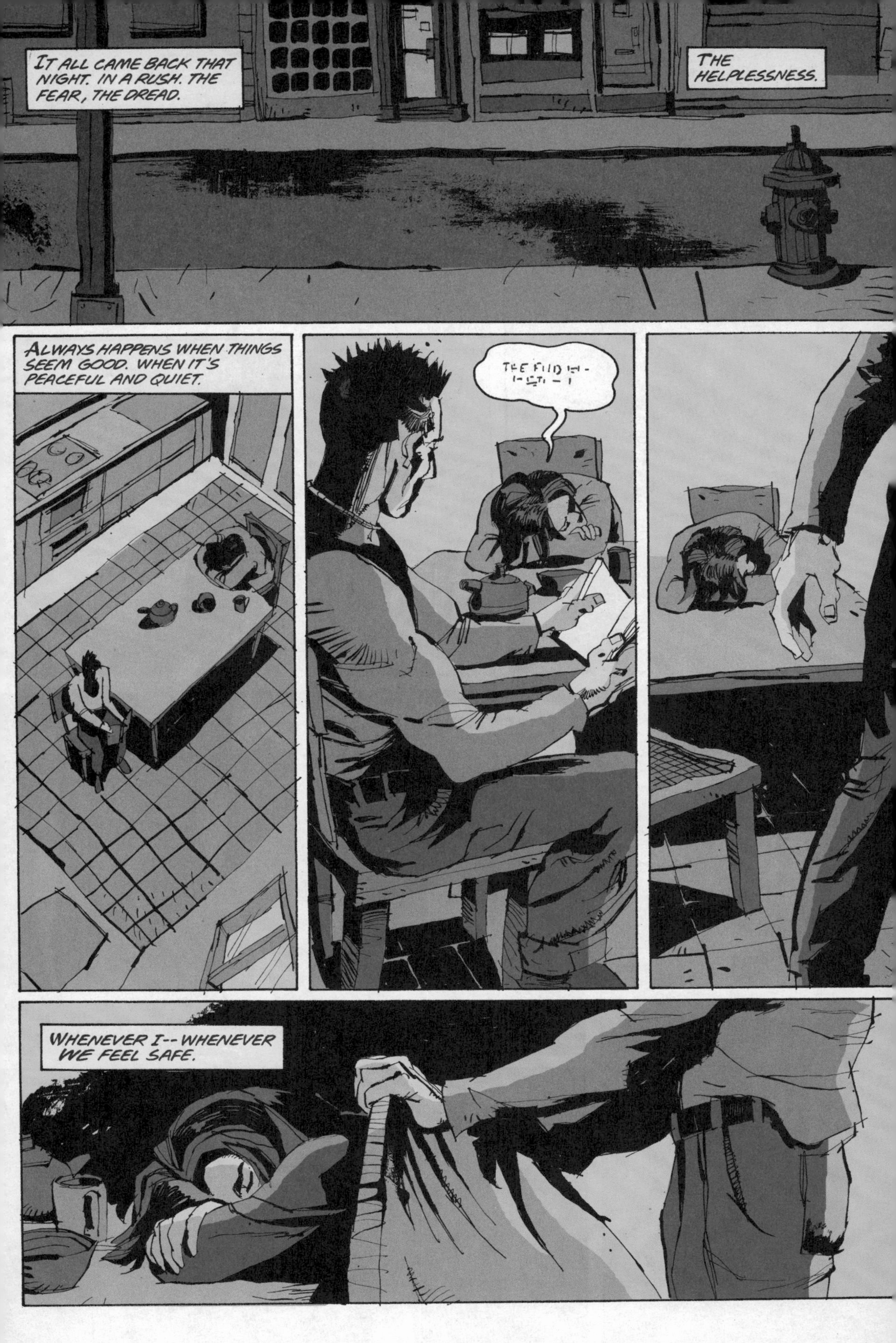
IT ALL CAME BACK THAT NIGHT. IN A RUSH. THE FEAR, THE DREAD.
THE HELPLESSNESS.
ALWAYS HAPPENS WHEN THINGS SEEM GOOD. WHEN IT'S PEACEFUL AND QUIET.
WHENEVER I--WHENEVER WE FEEL SAFE.

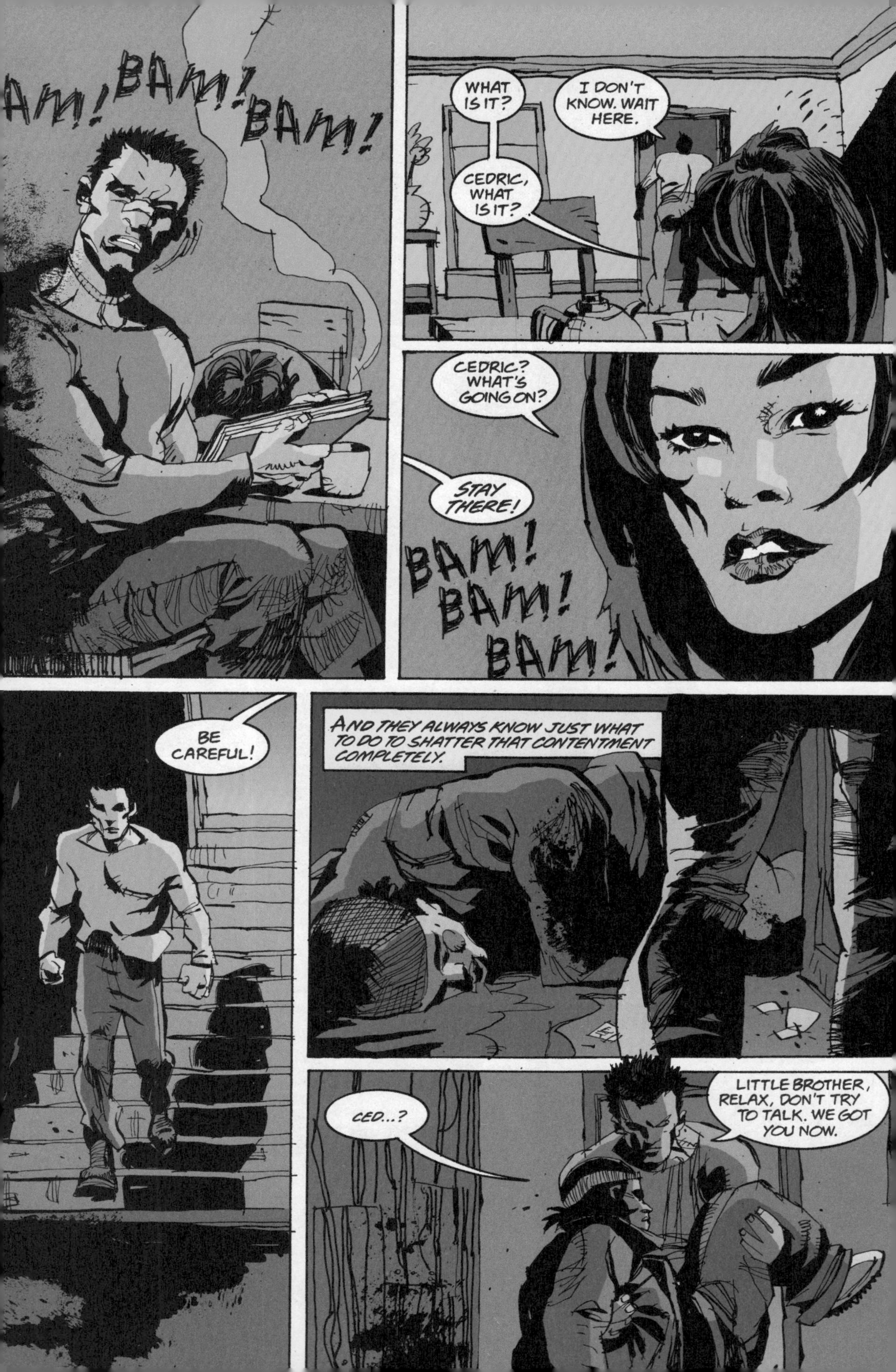
AM! BAM! BAM!
WHAT IS IT?
CEDRIC, WHAT IS IT?
I DON'T KNOW. WAIT HERE.
CEDRIC? WHAT'S GOING ON?
STAY THERE!
BAM! BAM! BAM!
BE CAREFUL!
AND THEY ALWAYS KNOW JUST WHAT TO DO TO SHATTER THAT CONTENTMENT COMPLETELY.
CED...?
LITTLE BROTHER, RELAX, DON'T TRY TO TALK. WE GOT YOU NOW.

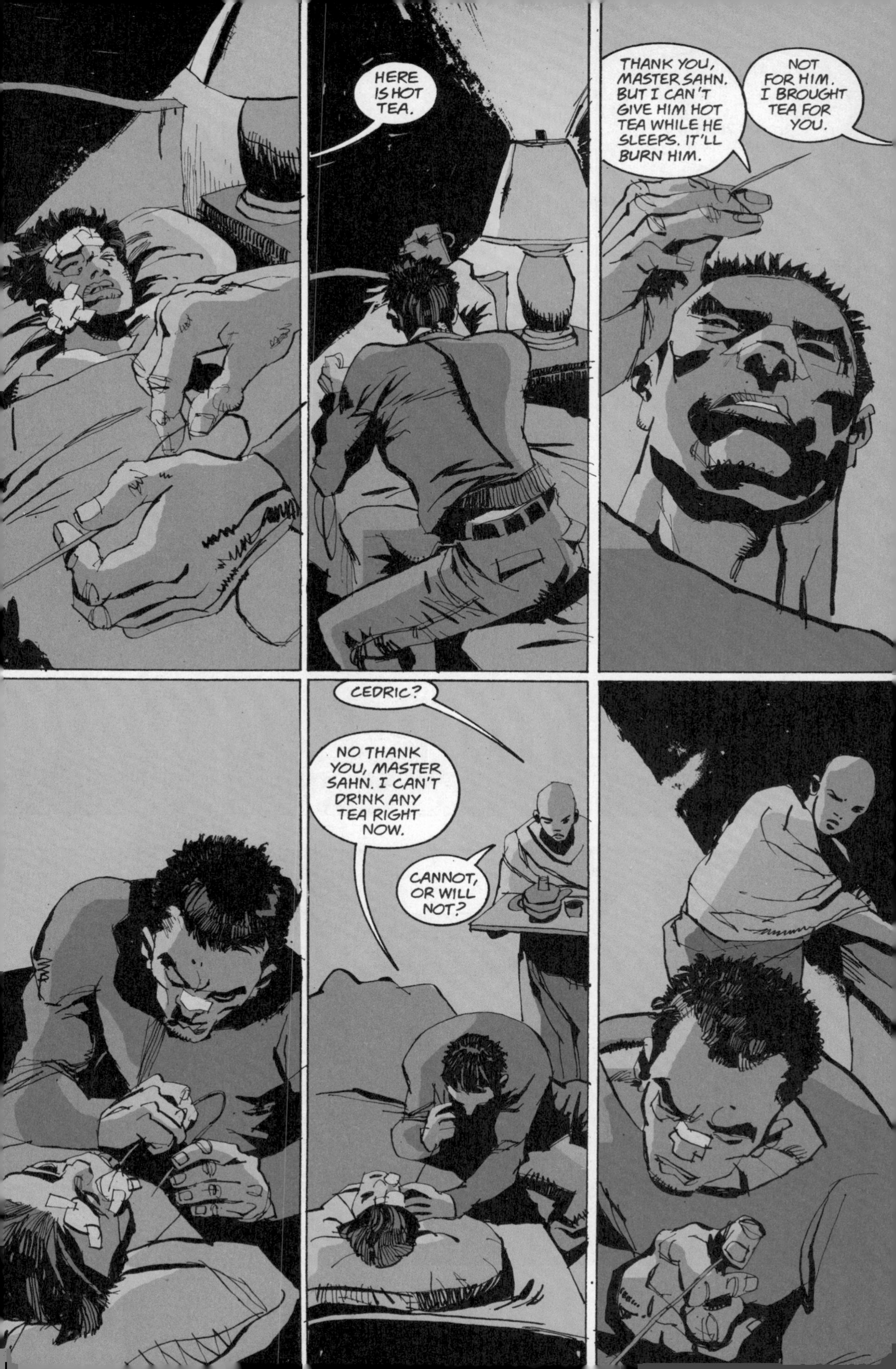
HERE IS HOT TEA.
THANK YOU, MASTER SAHN. BUT I CAN'T GIVE HIM HOT TEA WHILE HE SLEEPS. IT'LL BURN HIM.
NOT FOR HIM. I BROUGHT TEA FOR YOU.
CEDRIC?
NO THANK YOU, MASTER SAHN. I CAN'T DRINK ANY TEA RIGHT NOW.
CANNOT, OR WILL NOT?

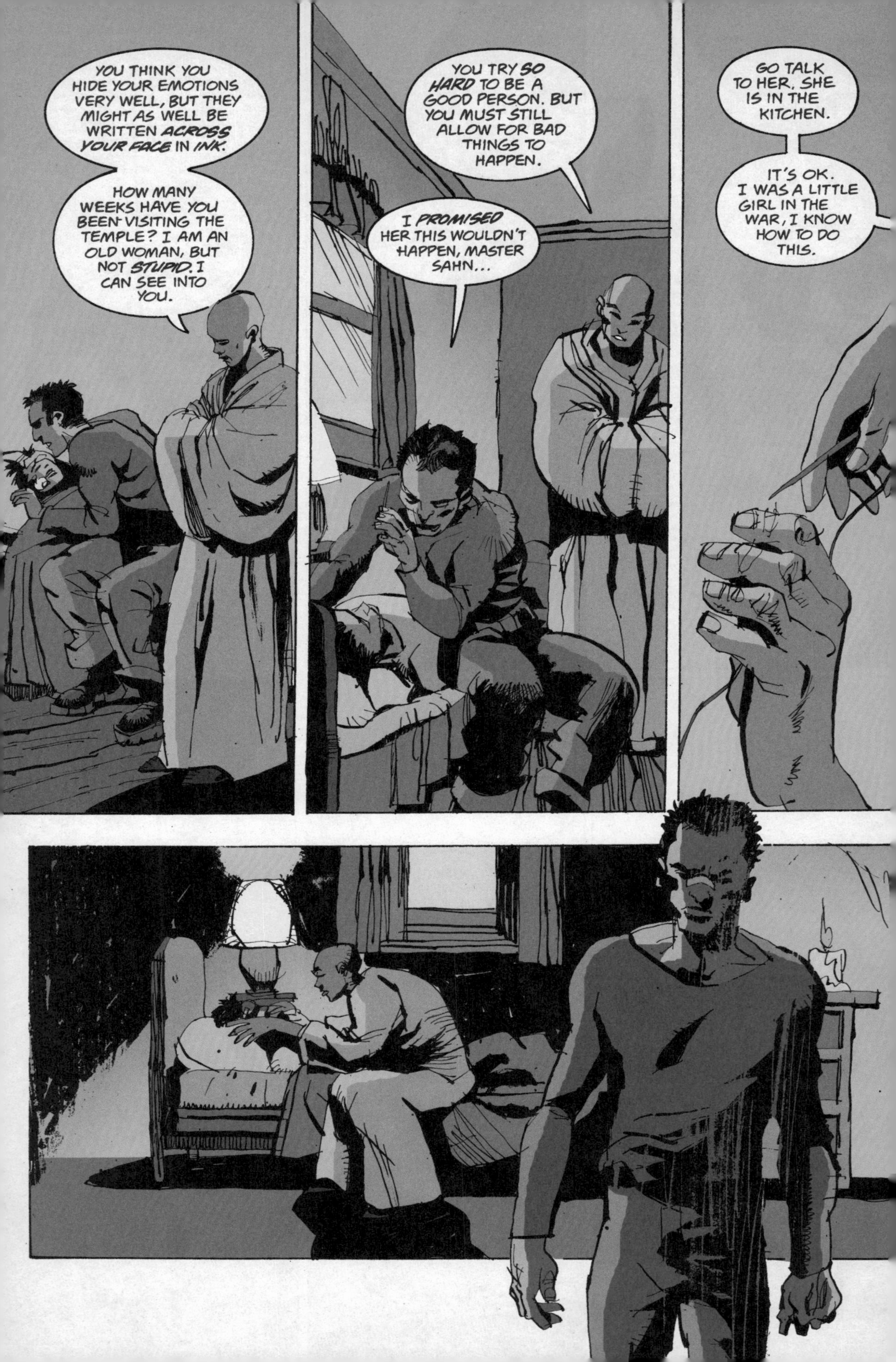
YOU THINK YOU HIDE YOUR EMOTIONS VERY WELL, BUT THEY MIGHT AS WELL BE WRITTEN ACROSS YOUR FACE IN INK.
HOW MANY WEEKS HAVE YOU BEEN VISITING THE TEMPLE? I AM AN OLD WOMAN, BUT NOT STUPID. I CAN SEE INTO YOU.
YOU TRY SO HARD TO BE A GOOD PERSON. BUT YOU MUST STILL ALLOW FOR BAD THINGS TO HAPPEN.
I PROMISED HER THIS WOULDN'T HAPPEN, MASTER SAHN...
GO TALK TO HER. SHE IS IN THE KITCHEN.
IT'S OK. I WAS A LITTLE GIRL IN THE WAR, I KNOW HOW TO DO THIS.

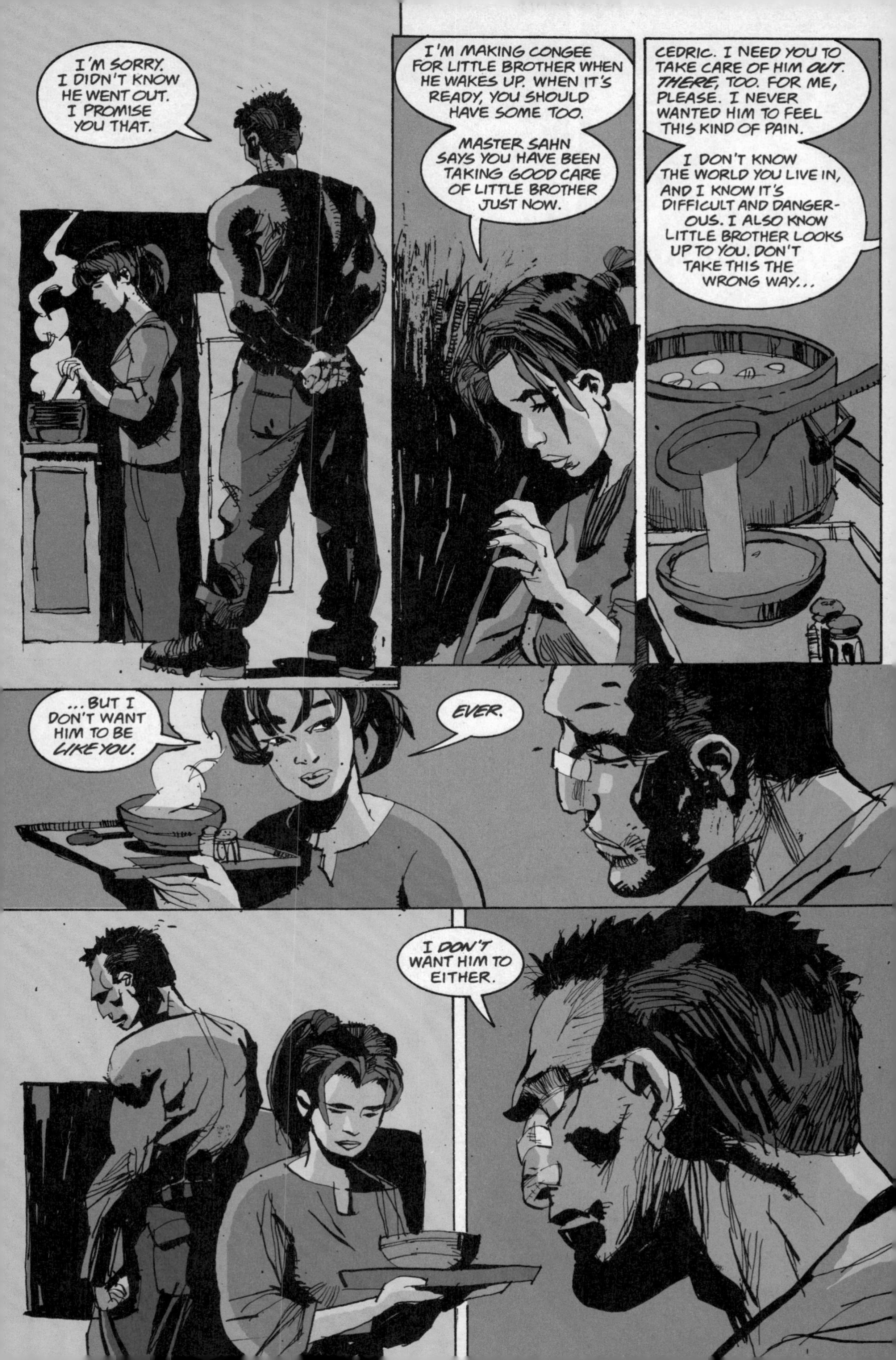
I'M SORRY. I DIDN'T KNOW HE WENT OUT. I PROMISE YOU THAT.
I'M MAKING CONGEE FOR LITTLE BROTHER WHEN HE WAKES UP. WHEN IT'S READY, YOU SHOULD HAVE SOME TOO.
MASTER SAHN SAYS YOU HAVE BEEN TAKING GOOD CARE OF LITTLE BROTHER JUST NOW.
CEDRIC. I NEED YOU TO TAKE CARE OF HIM OUT THERE, TOO. FOR ME, PLEASE. I NEVER WANTED HIM TO FEEL THIS KIND OF PAIN.
I DON'T KNOW THE WORLD YOU LIVE IN, AND I KNOW IT'S DIFFICULT AND DANGEROUS. I ALSO KNOW LITTLE BROTHER LOOKS UP TO YOU. DON'T TAKE THIS THE WRONG WAY...
...BUT I DON'T WANT HIM TO BE LIKE YOU.
EVER.
I DON'T WANT HIM TO EITHER.

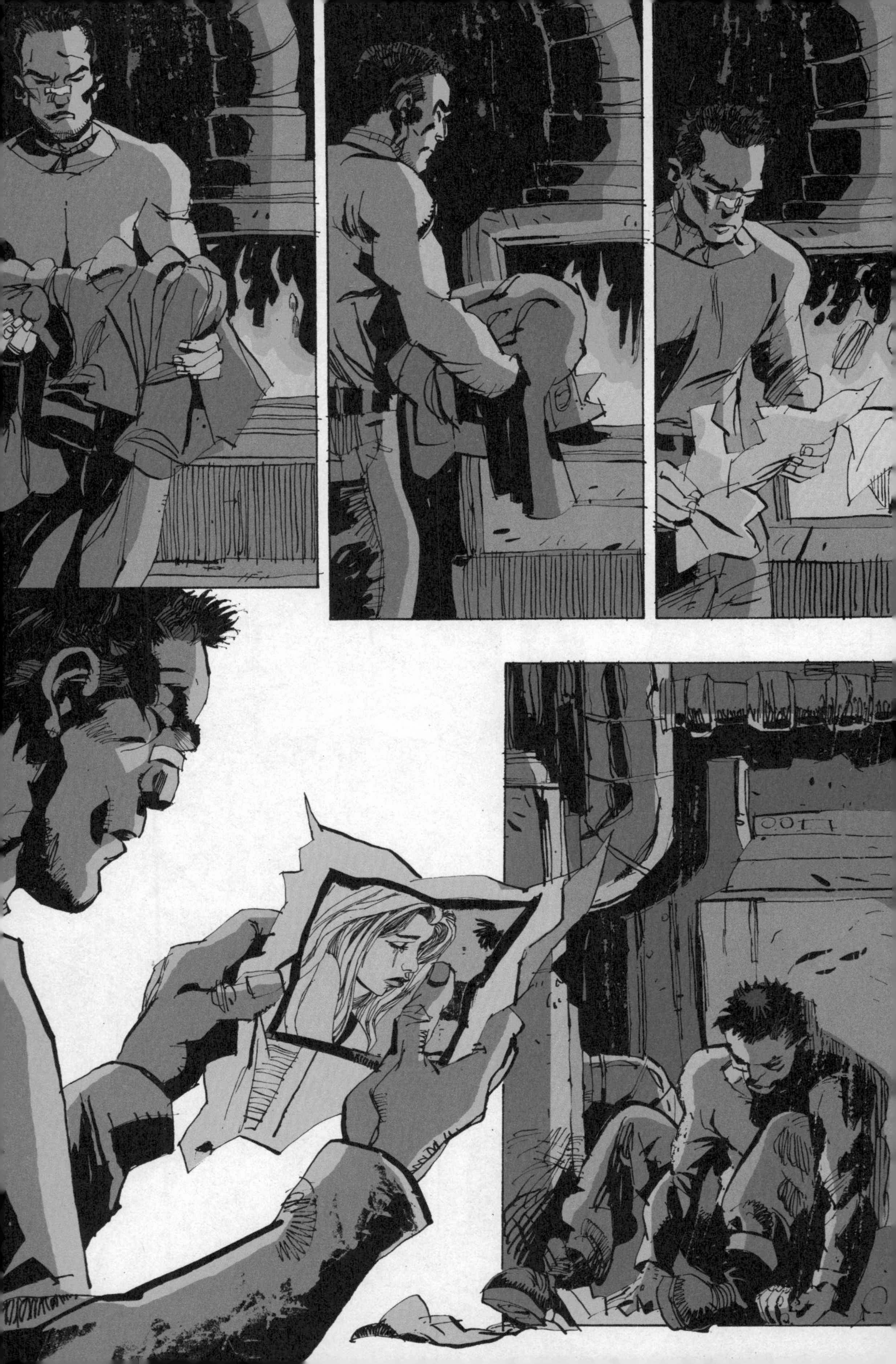

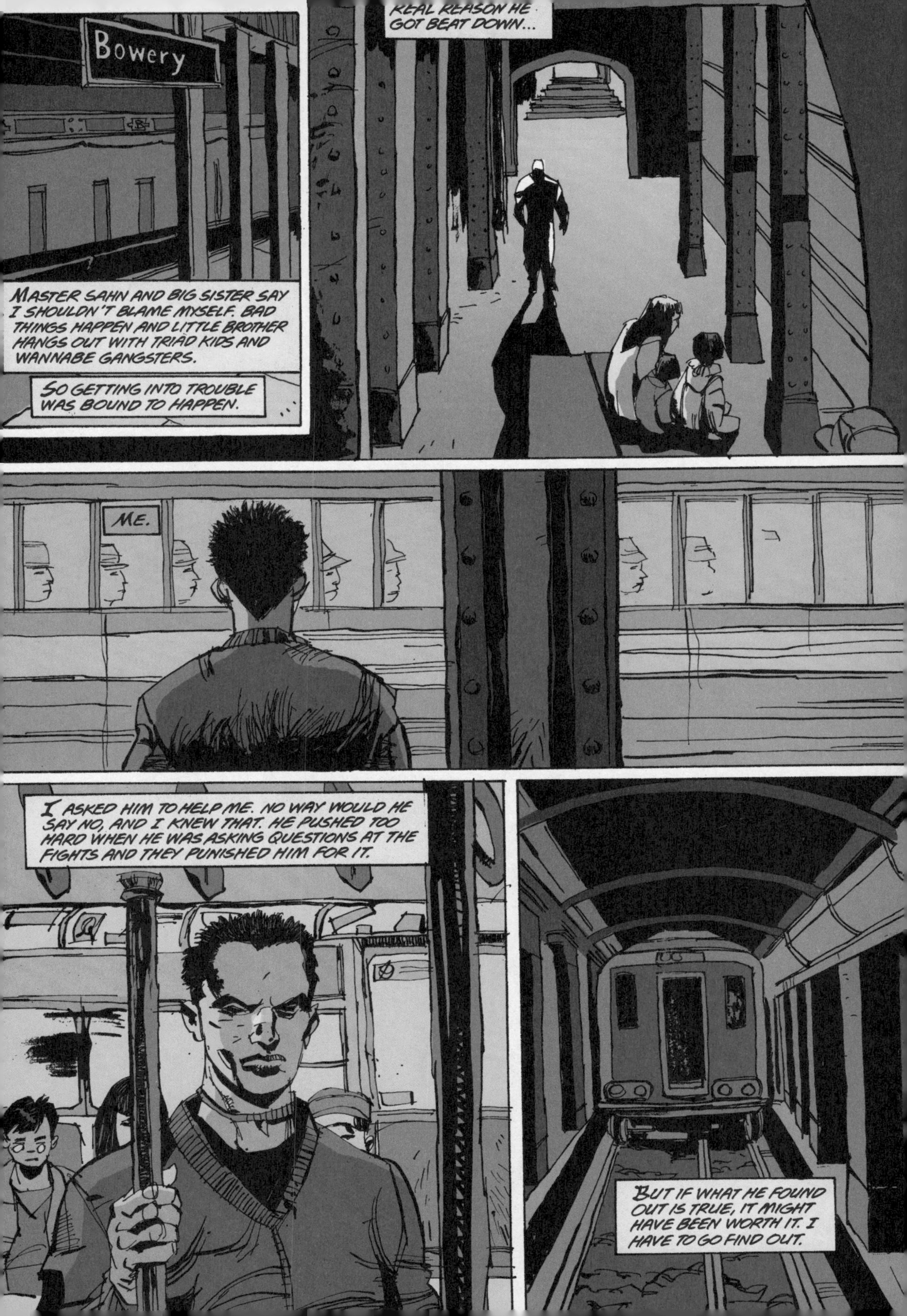
Bowery
REAL REASON HE GOT BEAT DOWN...
MASTER SAHN AND BIG SISTER SAY I SHOULDN'T BLAME MYSELF. BAD THINGS HAPPEN AND LITTLE BROTHER HANGS OUT WITH TRIAD KIDS AND WANNABE GANGSTERS.
SO GETTING INTO TROUBLE WAS BOUND TO HAPPEN.
ME.
I ASKED HIM TO HELP ME. NO WAY WOULD HE SAY NO, AND I KNEW THAT. HE PUSHED TOO HARD WHEN HE WAS ASKING QUESTIONS AT THE FIGHTS AND THEY PUNISHED HIM FOR IT.
BUT IF WHAT HE FOUND OUT IS TRUE, IT MIGHT HAVE BEEN WORTH IT. I HAVE TO GO FIND OUT.

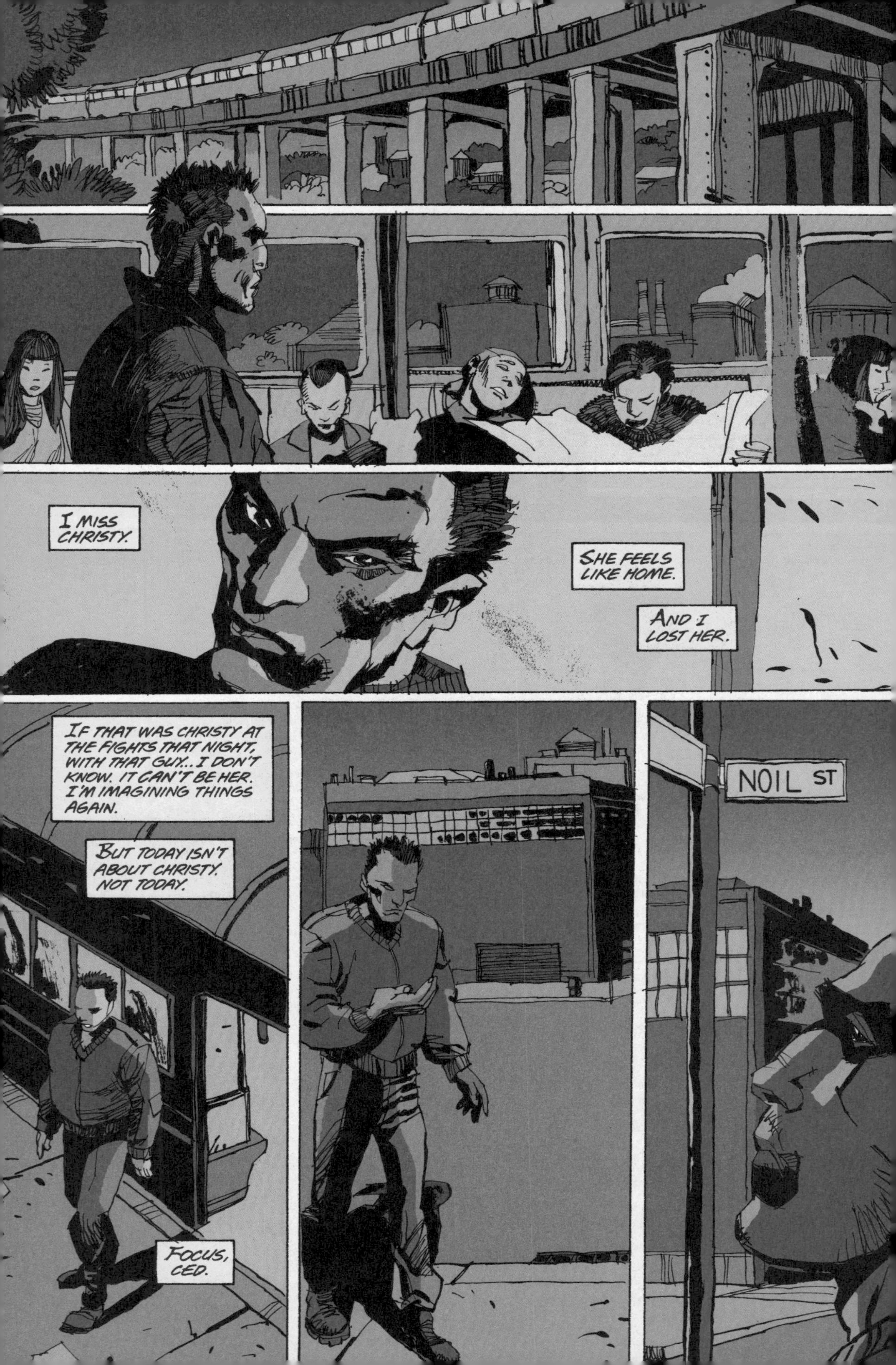
I MISS CHRISTY.
SHE FEELS LIKE HOME.
AND I LOST HER.
IF THAT WAS CHRISTY AT THE FIGHTS THAT NIGHT, WITH THAT GUY... I DON'T KNOW. IT CAN'T BE HER. I'M IMAGINING THINGS AGAIN.
BUT TODAY ISN'T ABOUT CHRISTY. NOT TODAY.
FOCUS, CED.
NOIL ST

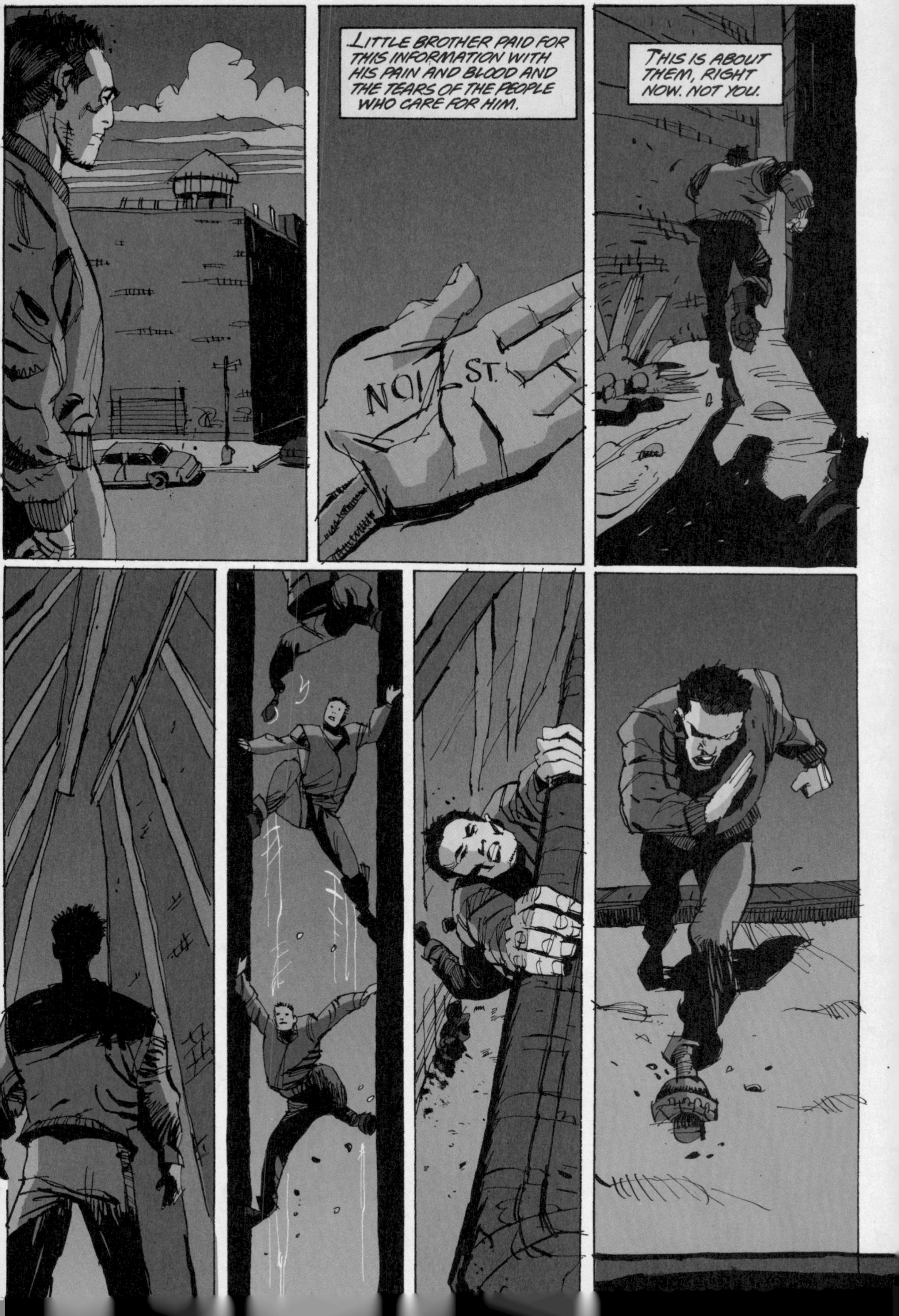
LITTLE BROTHER PAID FOR THIS INFORMATION WITH HIS PAIN AND BLOOD AND THE TEARS OF THE PEOPLE WHO CARE FOR HIM.
NO1 ST.
THIS IS ABOUT THEM, RIGHT NOW. NOT YOU.

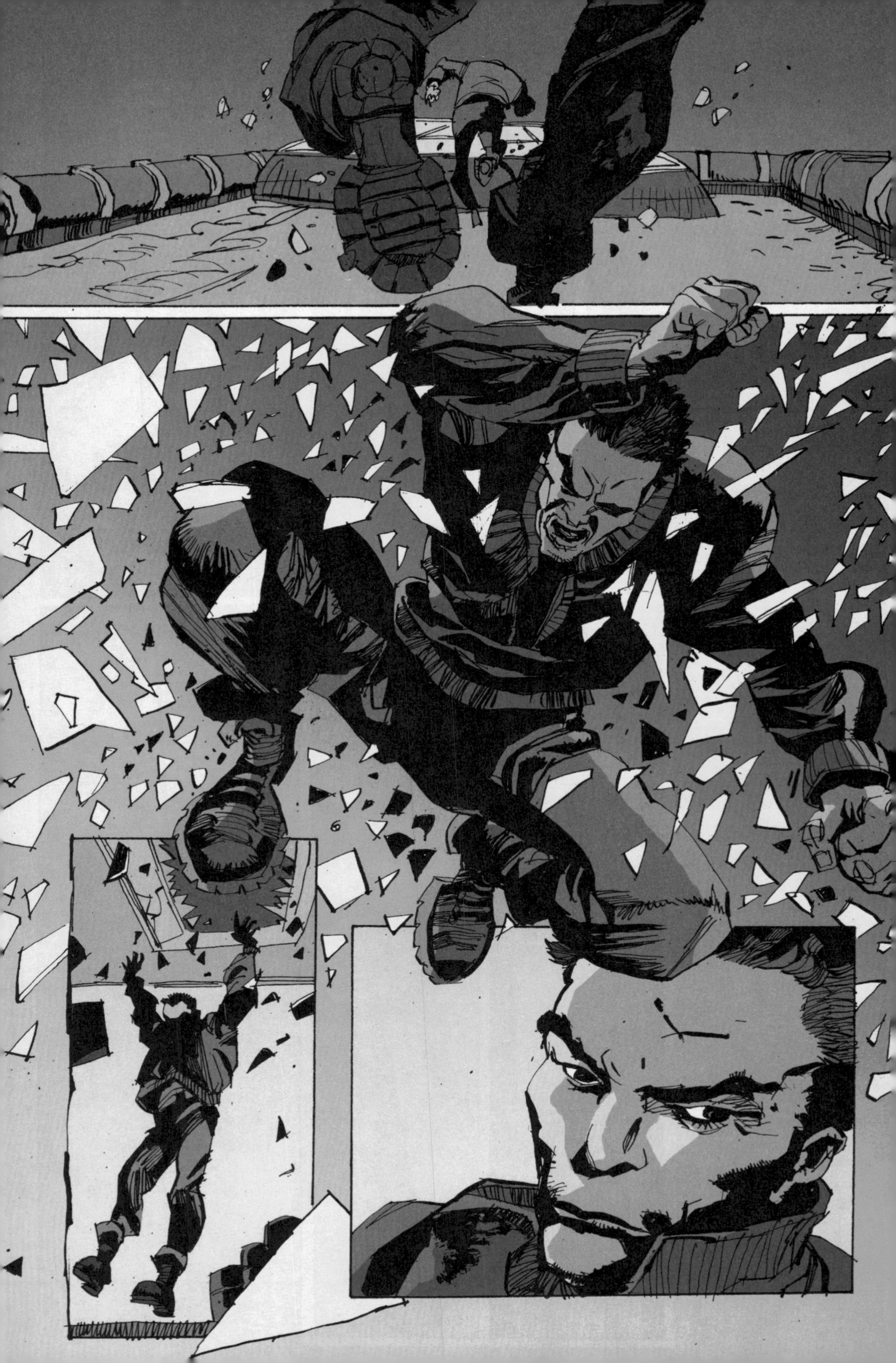

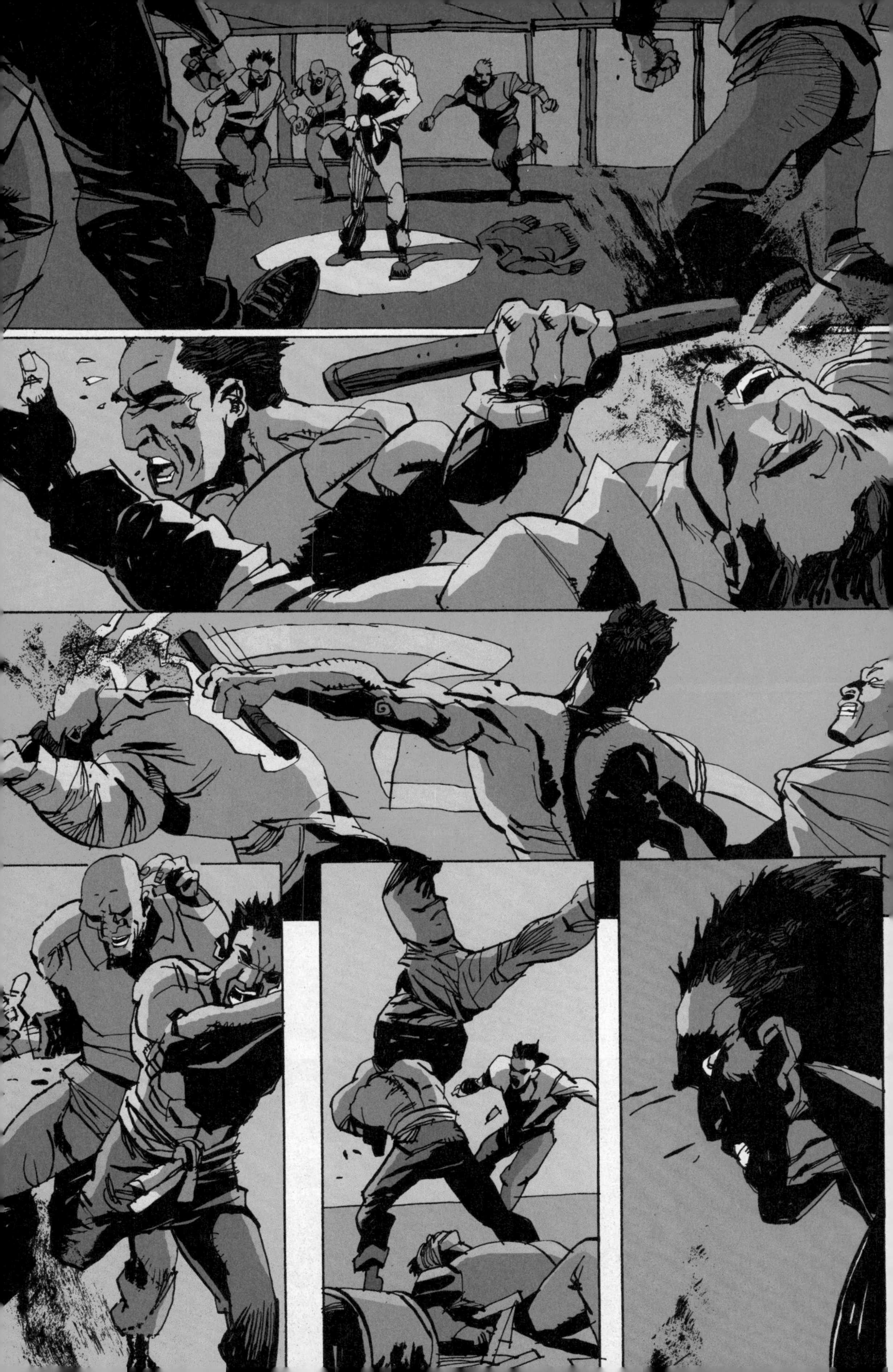

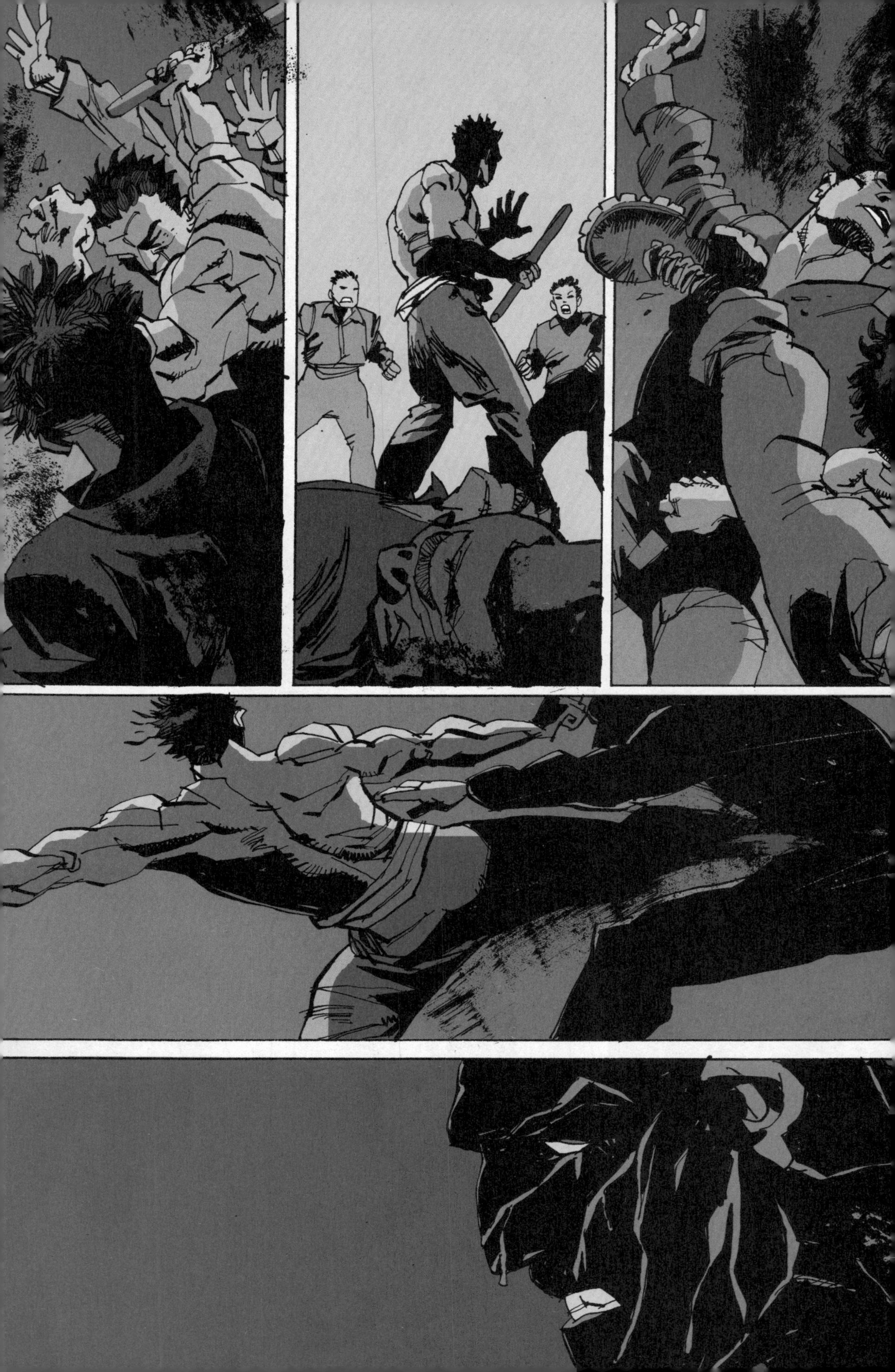

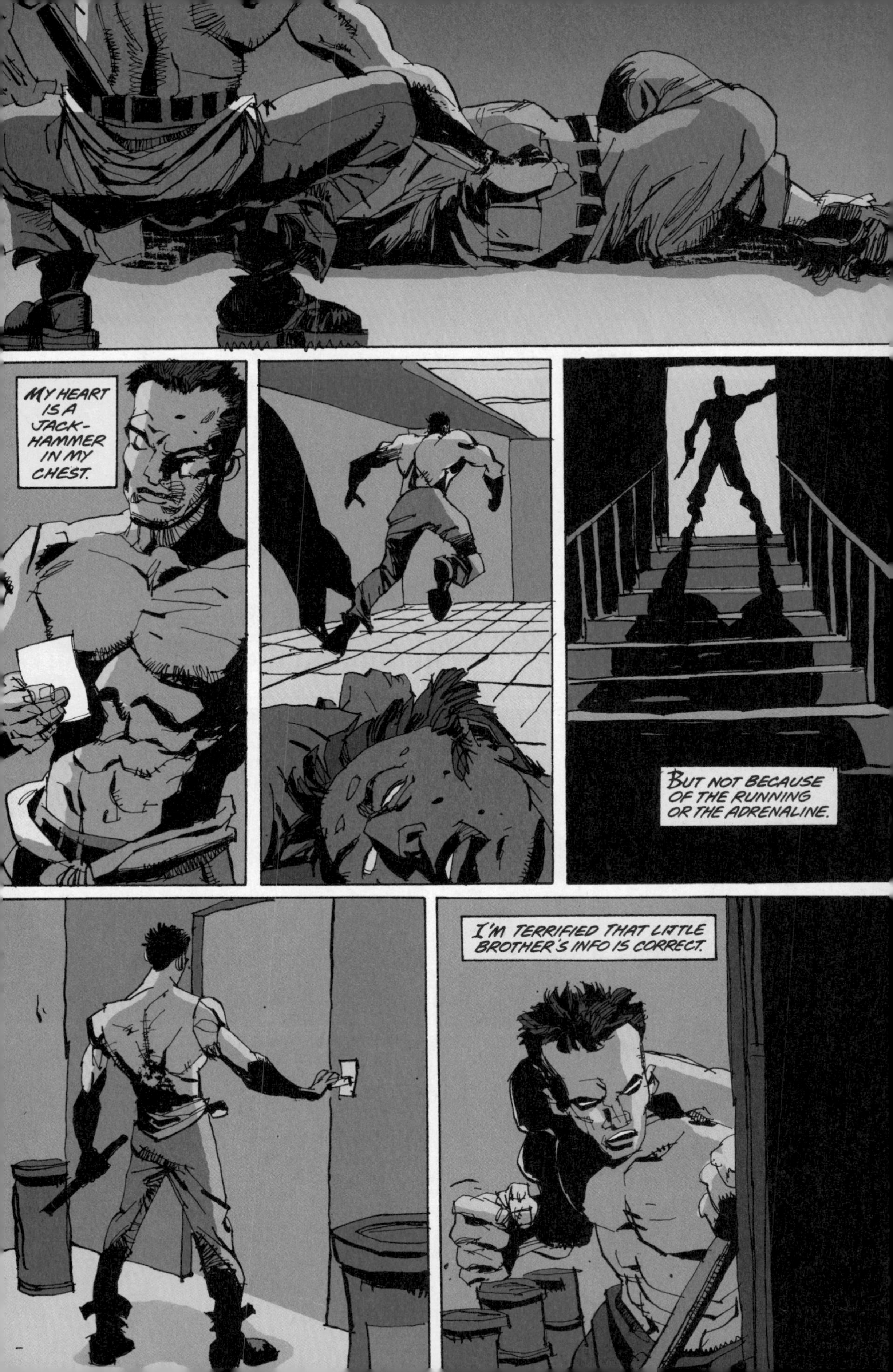
MY HEART IS A JACK-HAMMER IN MY CHEST.
BUT NOT BECAUSE OF THE RUNNING OR THE ADRENALINE.
I'M TERRIFIED THAT LITTLE BROTHER'S INFO IS CORRECT.

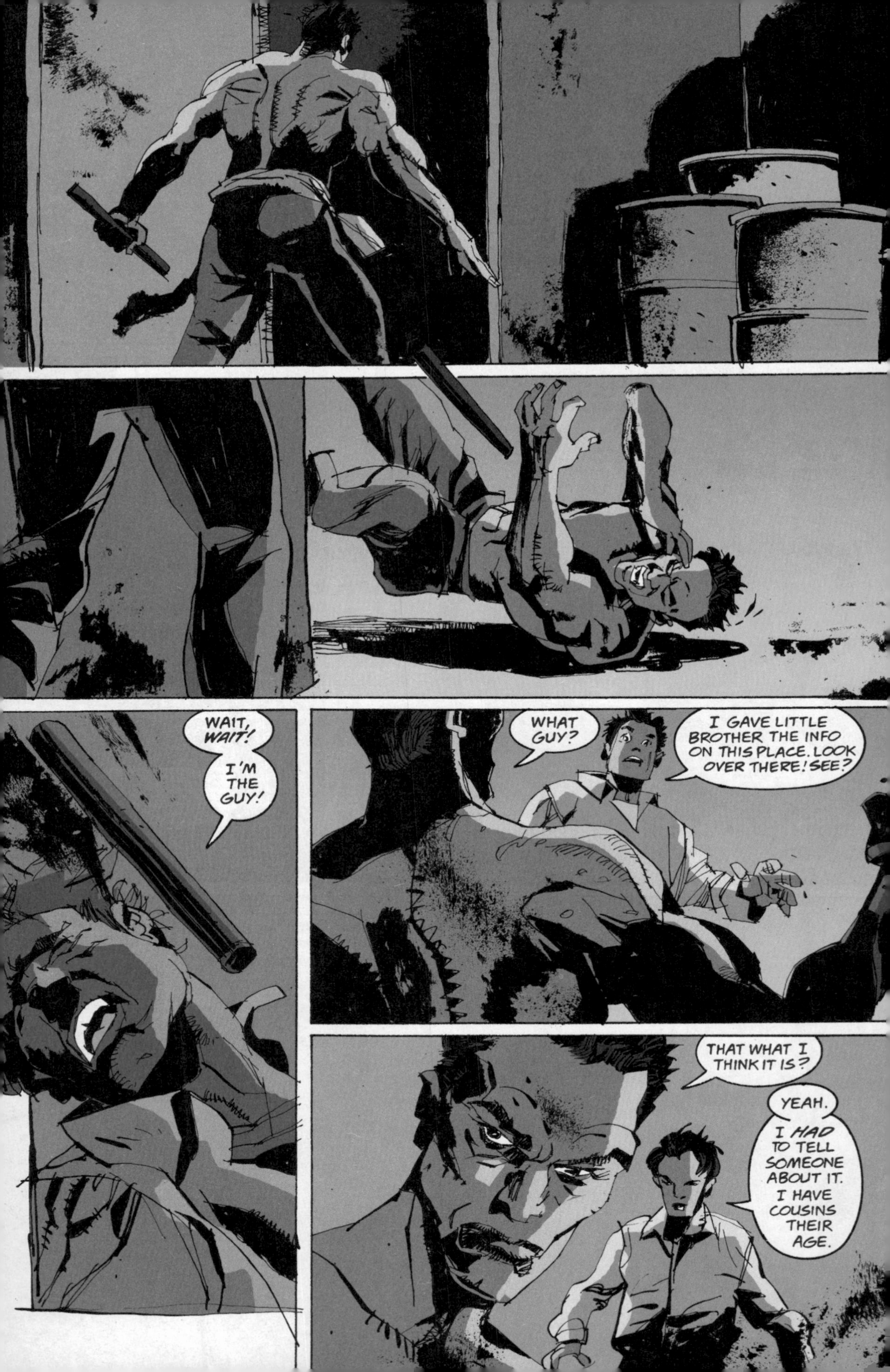
WAIT, *WAIT!*
I'M THE GUY!
WHAT GUY?
I GAVE LITTLE BROTHER THE INFO ON THIS PLACE. LOOK OVER THERE! SEE?
THAT WHAT I THINK IT IS?
YEAH.
I *HAD* TO TELL SOMEONE ABOUT IT. I HAVE COUSINS THEIR AGE.

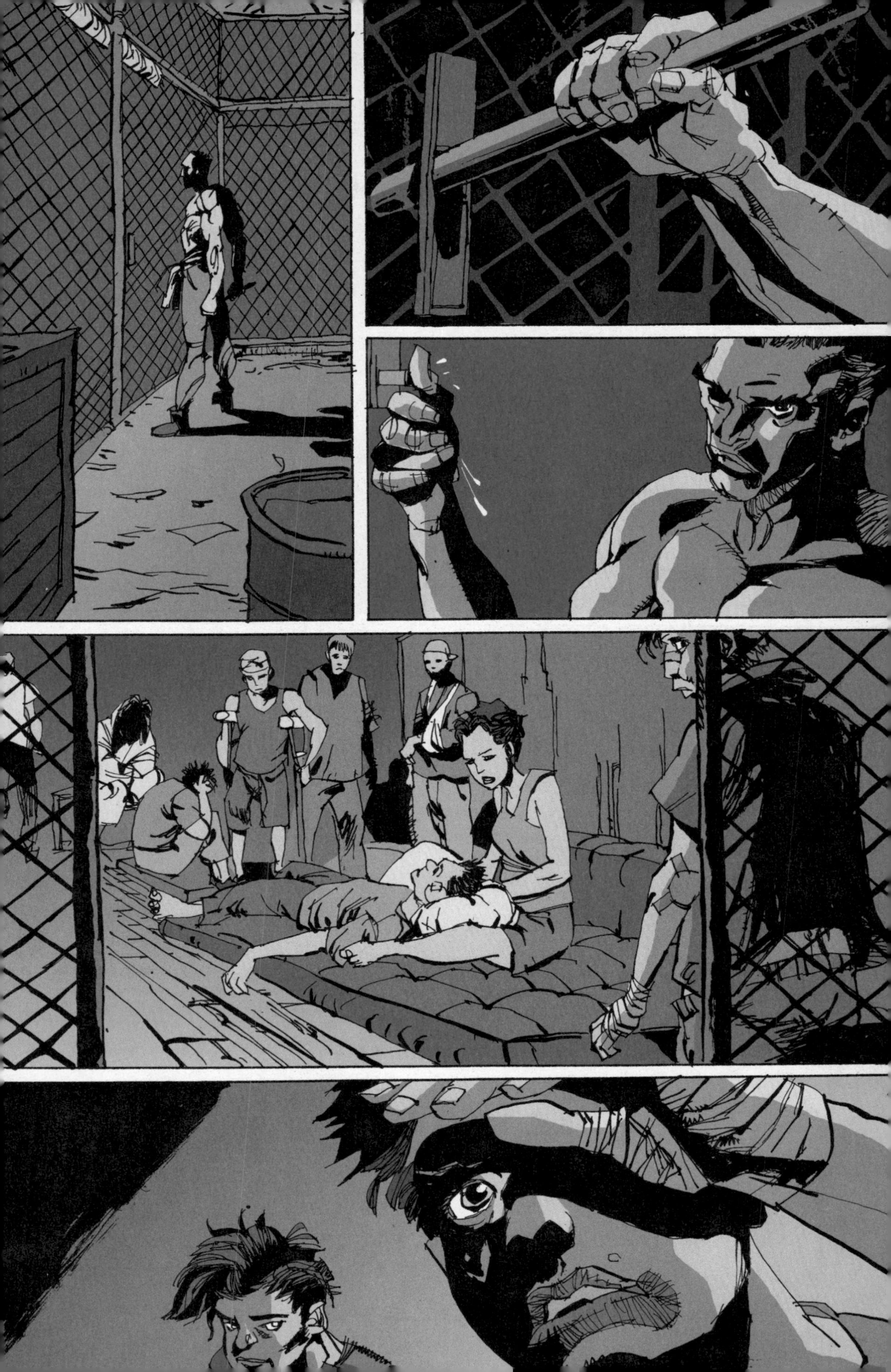

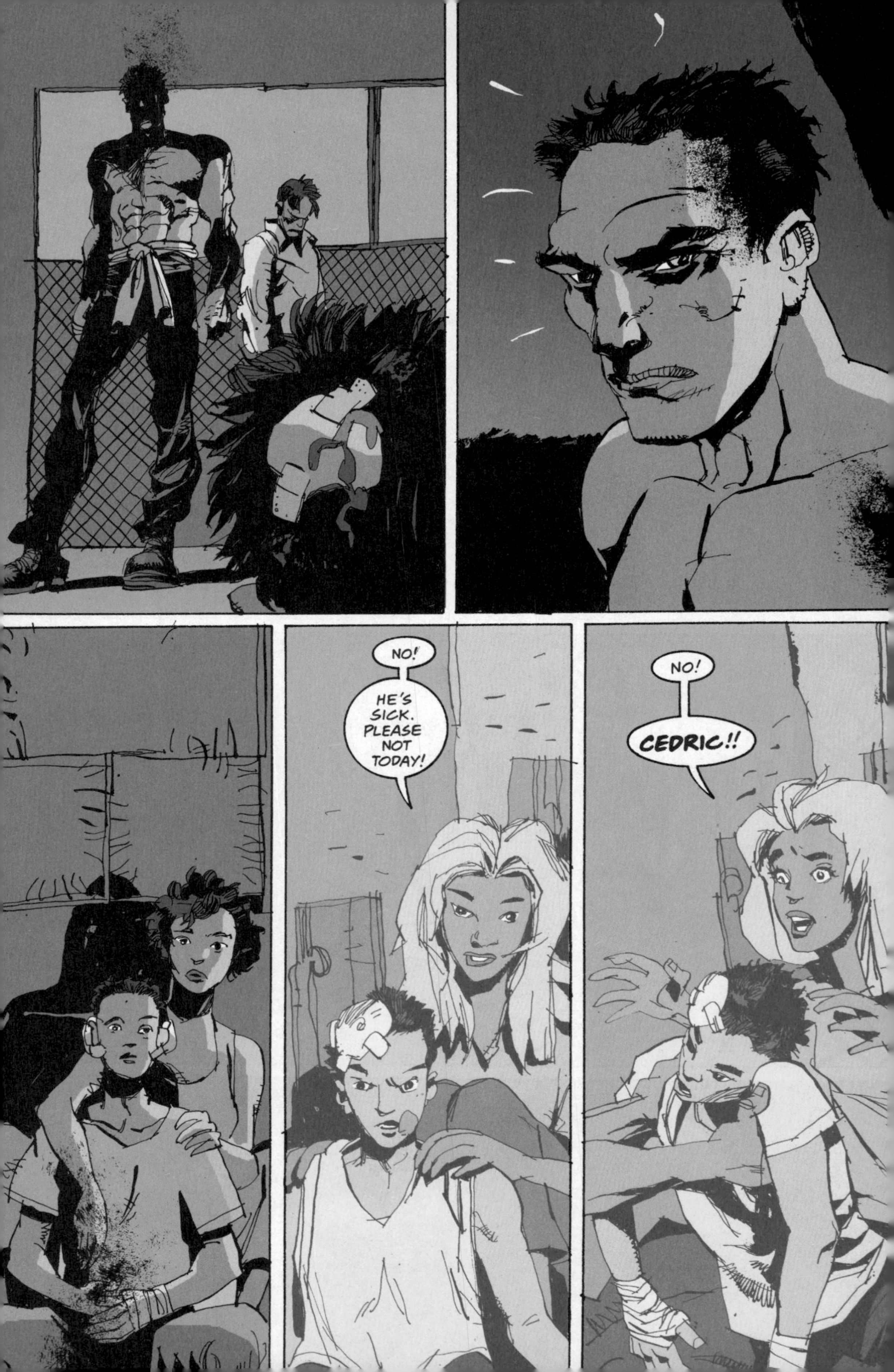
NO!
HE'S SICK. PLEASE NOT TODAY!
NO!
CEDRIC!!

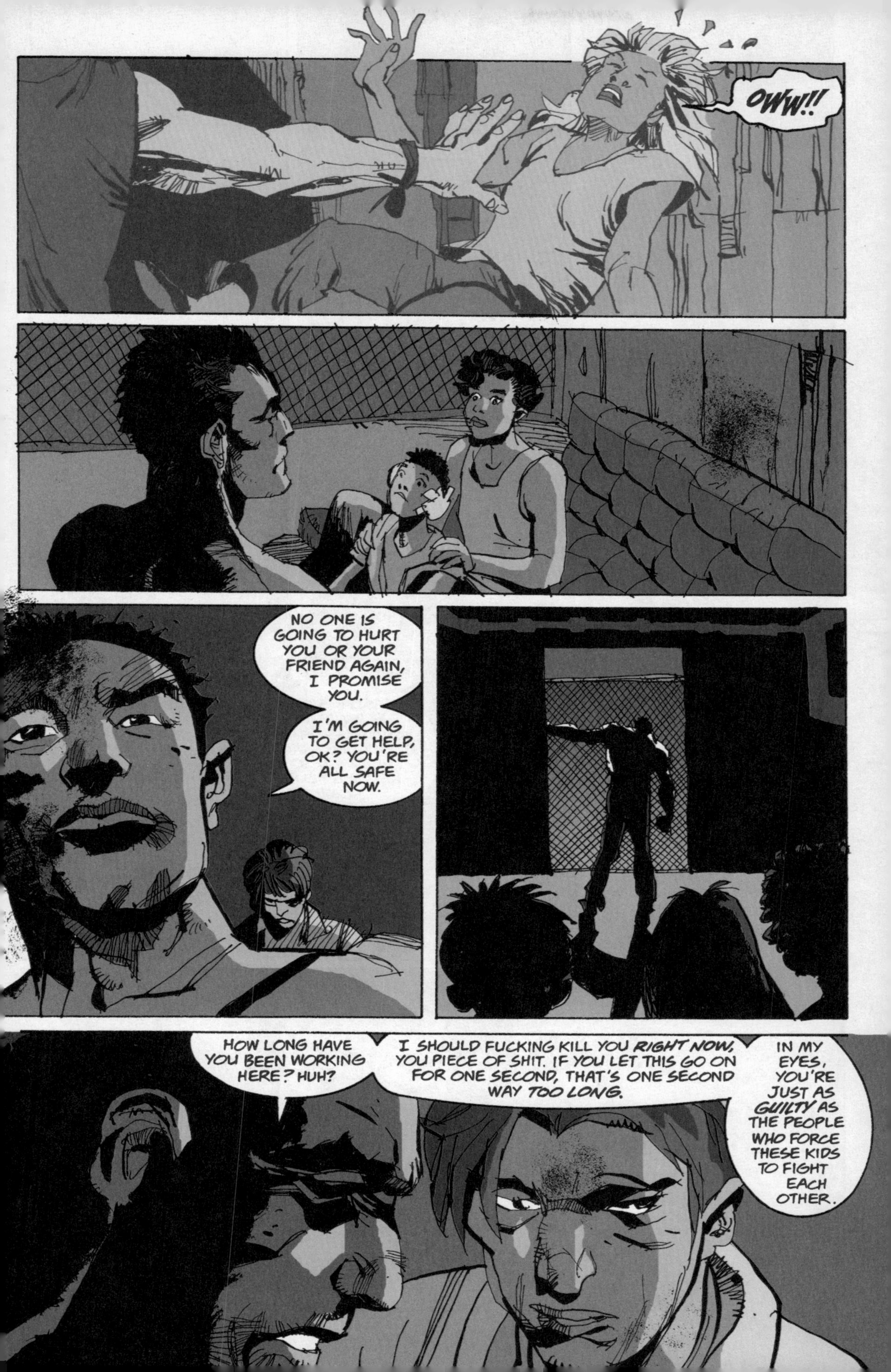
OWW!!
NO ONE IS GOING TO HURT YOU OR YOUR FRIEND AGAIN, I PROMISE YOU.
I'M GOING TO GET HELP, OK? YOU'RE ALL SAFE NOW.
HOW LONG HAVE YOU BEEN WORKING HERE? HUH?
I SHOULD FUCKING KILL YOU RIGHT NOW, YOU PIECE OF SHIT. IF YOU LET THIS GO ON FOR ONE SECOND, THAT'S ONE SECOND WAY TOO LONG.
IN MY EYES, YOU'RE JUST AS GUILTY AS THE PEOPLE WHO FORCE THESE KIDS TO FIGHT EACH OTHER.

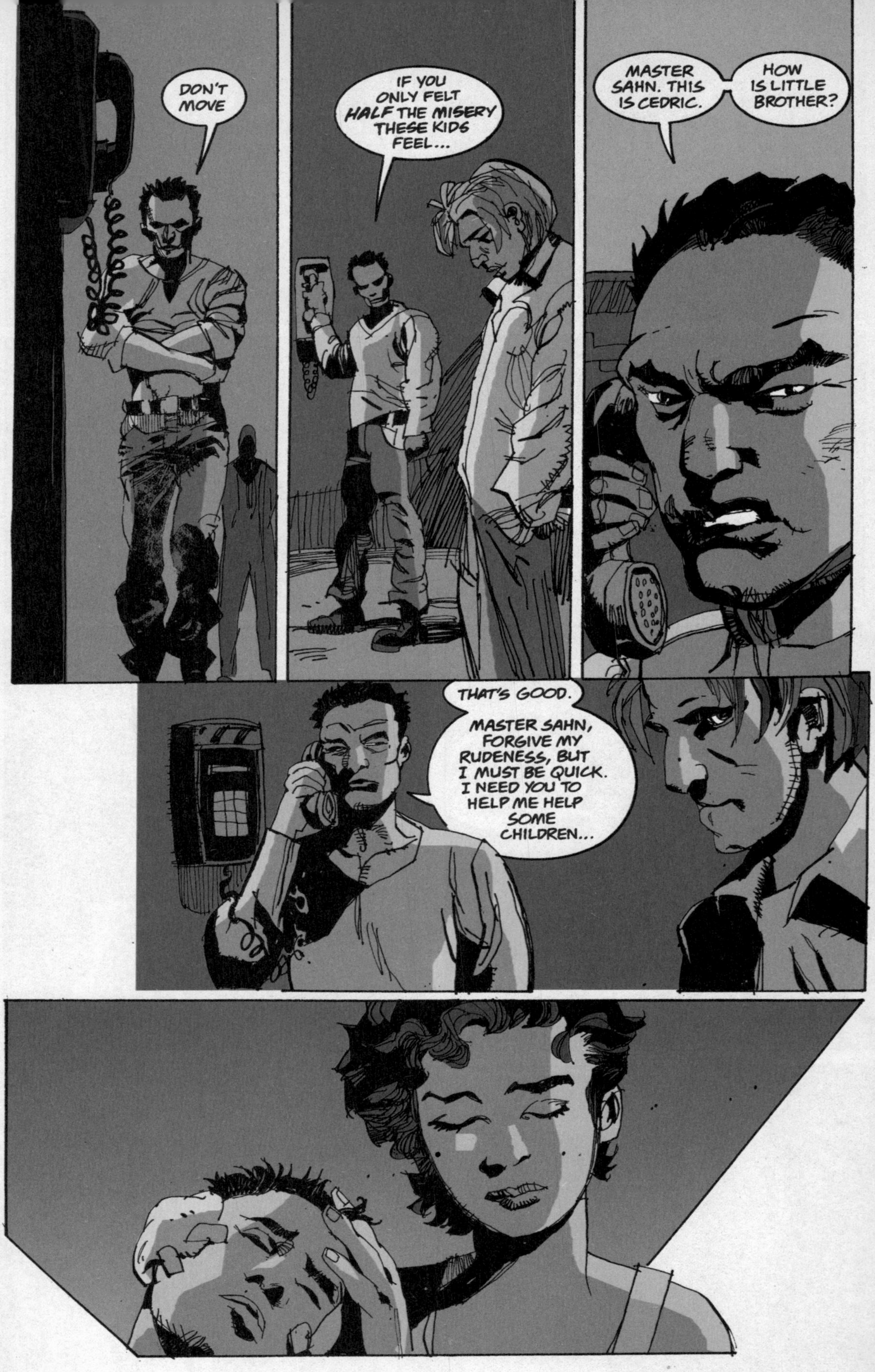
DON'T MOVE
IF YOU ONLY FELT HALF THE MISERY THESE KIDS FEEL...
MASTER SAHN. THIS IS CEDRIC.
HOW IS LITTLE BROTHER?
THAT'S GOOD.
MASTER SAHN, FORGIVE MY RUDENESS, BUT I MUST BE QUICK. I NEED YOU TO HELP ME HELP SOME CHILDREN...

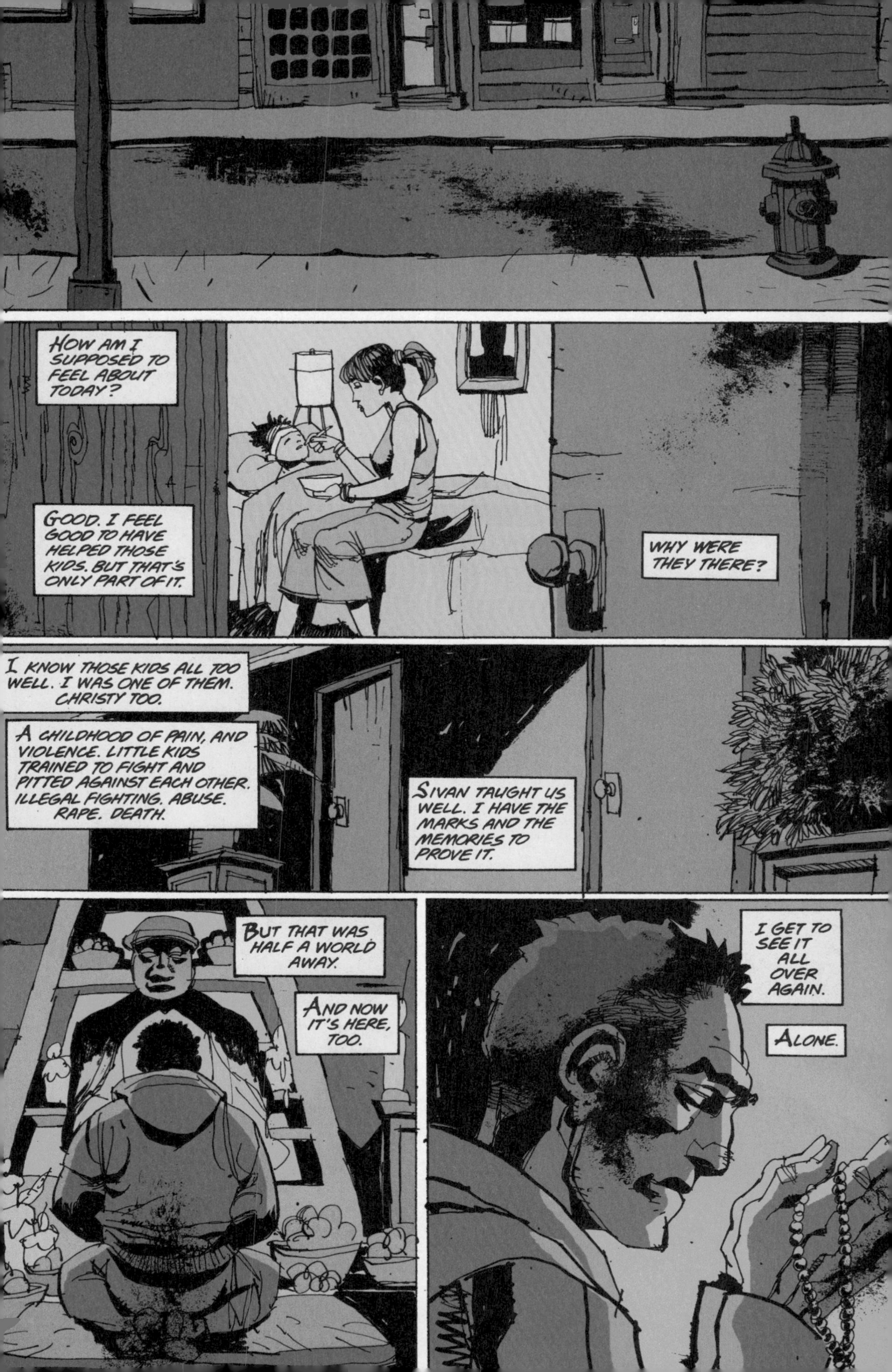
HOW AM I SUPPOSED TO FEEL ABOUT TODAY?
GOOD. I FEEL GOOD TO HAVE HELPED THOSE KIDS. BUT THAT'S ONLY PART OF IT.
WHY WERE THEY THERE?
I KNOW THOSE KIDS ALL TOO WELL. I WAS ONE OF THEM. CHRISTY TOO.
A CHILDHOOD OF PAIN, AND VIOLENCE. LITTLE KIDS TRAINED TO FIGHT AND PITTED AGAINST EACH OTHER. ILLEGAL FIGHTING. ABUSE. RAPE. DEATH.
SIVAN TAUGHT US WELL. I HAVE THE MARKS AND THE MEMORIES TO PROVE IT.
BUT THAT WAS HALF A WORLD AWAY.
AND NOW IT'S HERE, TOO.
I GET TO SEE IT ALL OVER AGAIN.
ALONE.

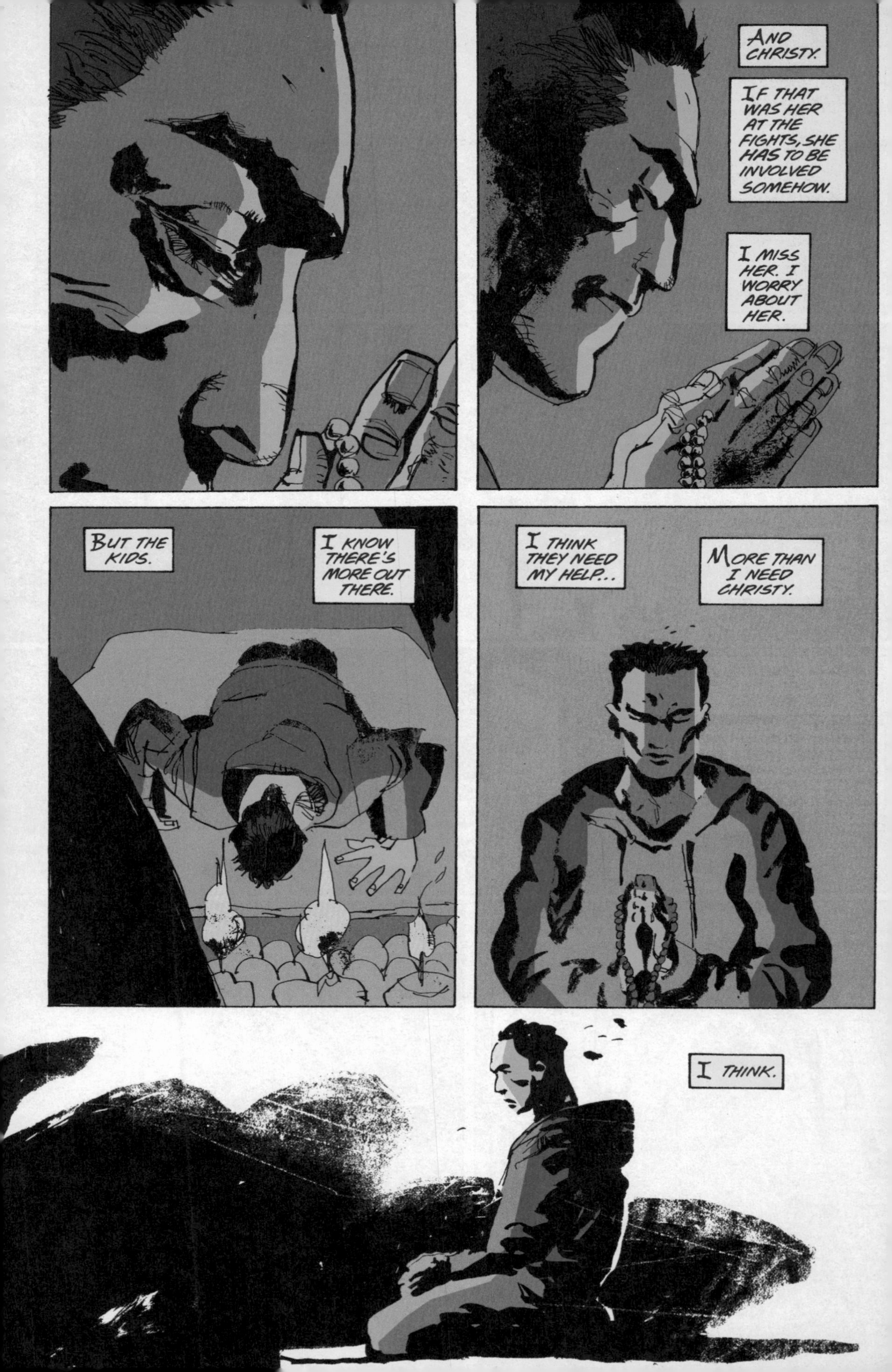
AND CHRISTY.
IF THAT WAS HER AT THE FIGHTS, SHE HAS TO BE INVOLVED SOMEHOW.
I MISS HER. I WORRY ABOUT HER.
BUT THE KIDS.
I KNOW THERE'S MORE OUT THERE.
I THINK THEY NEED MY HELP...
MORE THAN I NEED CHRISTY.
I THINK.

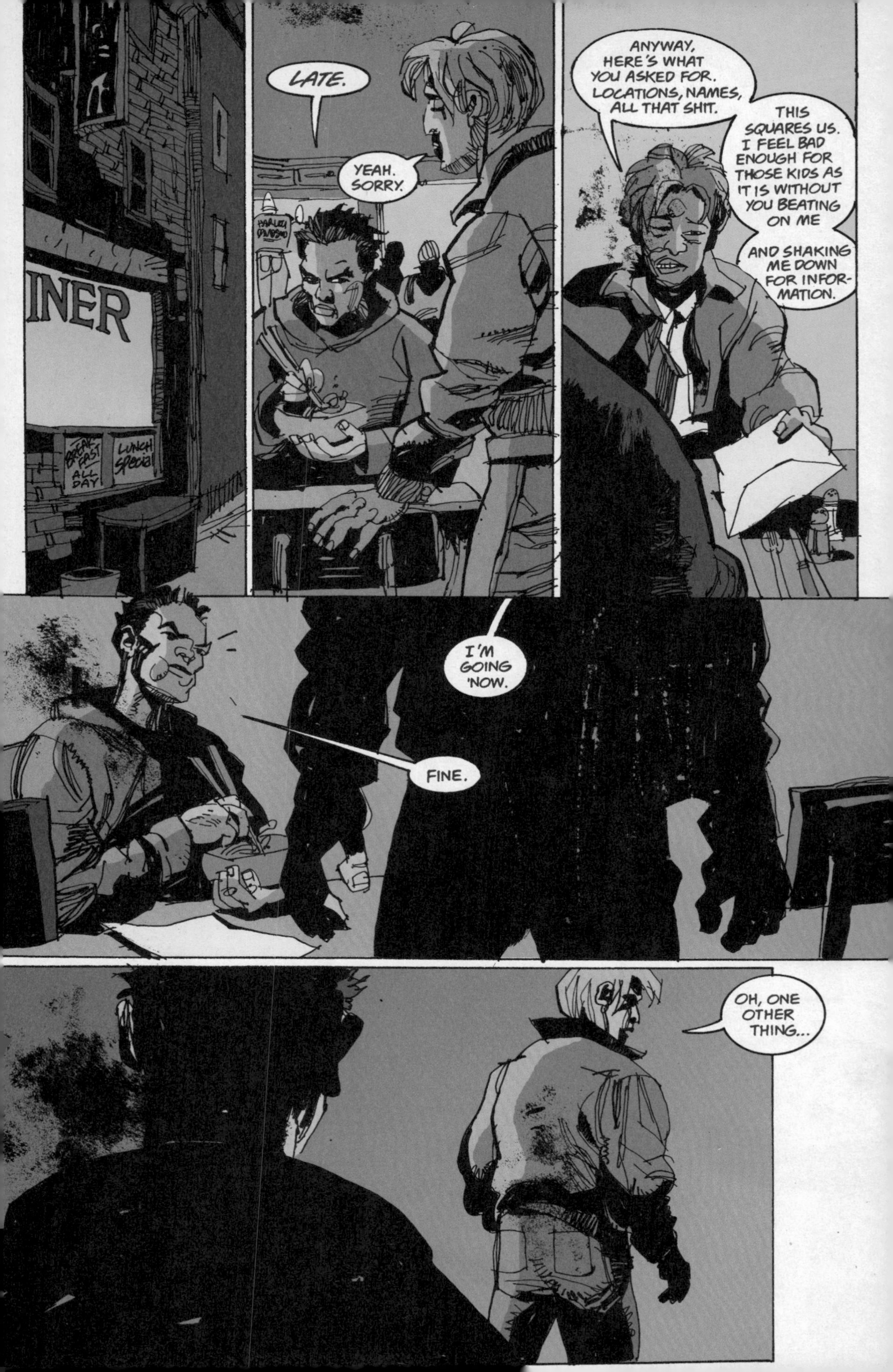
INER
BREAKFAST ALL DAY
LUNCH SPECIAL
LATE.
YEAH. SORRY.
ANYWAY, HERE'S WHAT YOU ASKED FOR. LOCATIONS, NAMES, ALL THAT SHIT.
THIS SQUARES US. I FEEL BAD ENOUGH FOR THOSE KIDS AS IT IS WITHOUT YOU BEATING ON ME
AND SHAKING ME DOWN FOR INFORMATION.
I'M GOING 'NOW.
FINE.
OH, ONE OTHER THING...

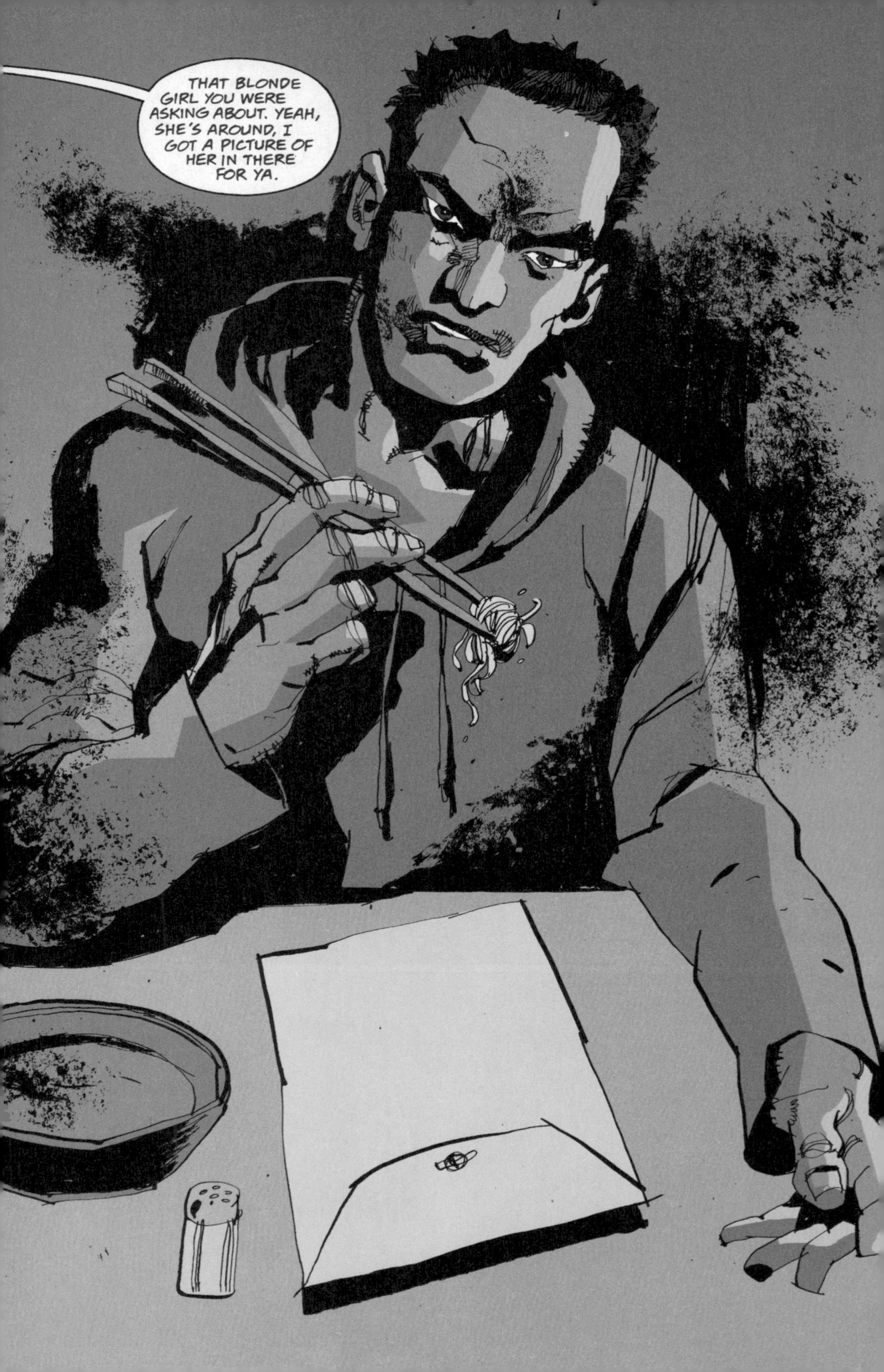
THAT BLONDE GIRL YOU WERE ASKING ABOUT. YEAH, SHE'S AROUND, I GOT A PICTURE OF HER IN THERE FOR YA.

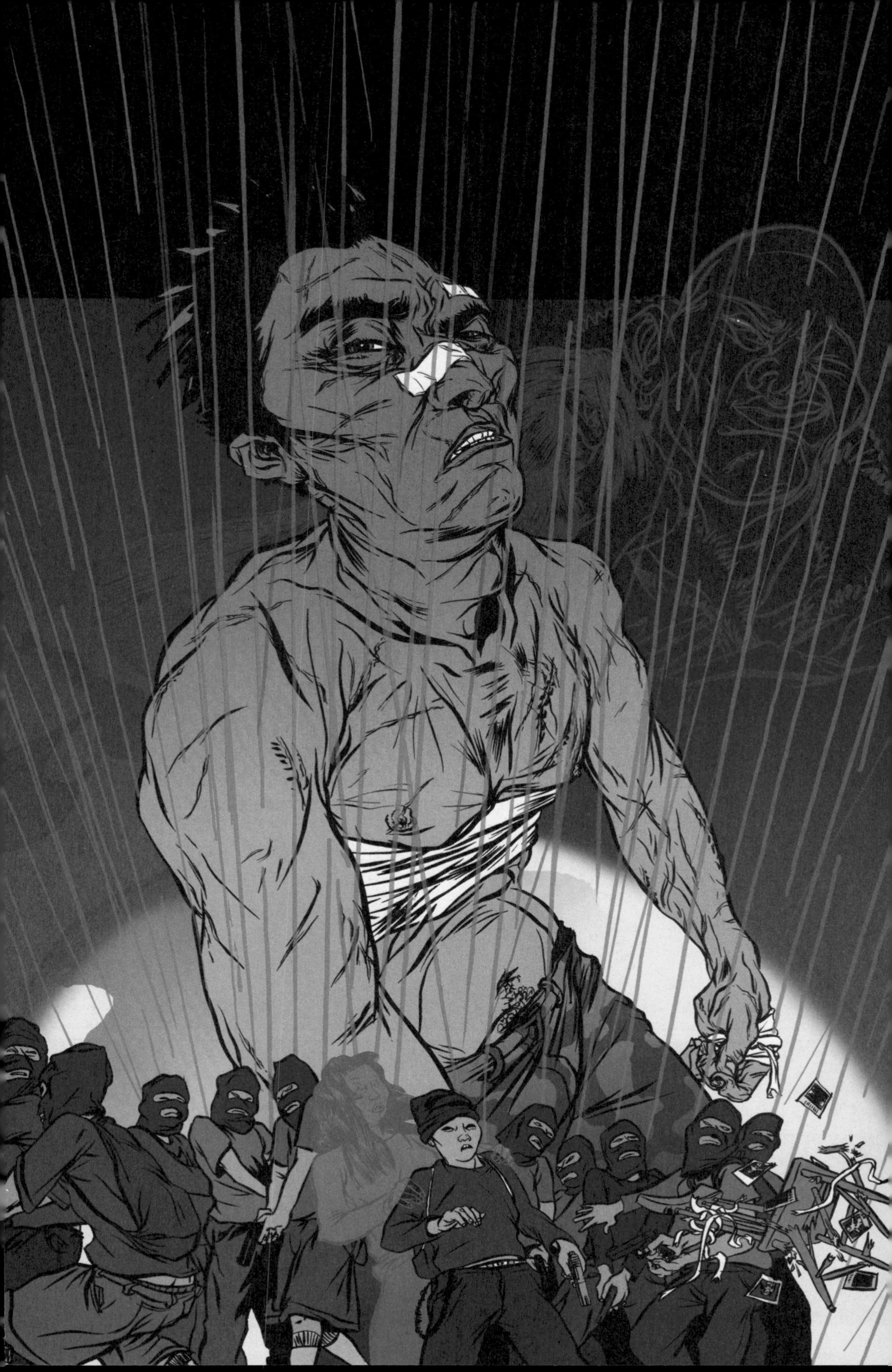

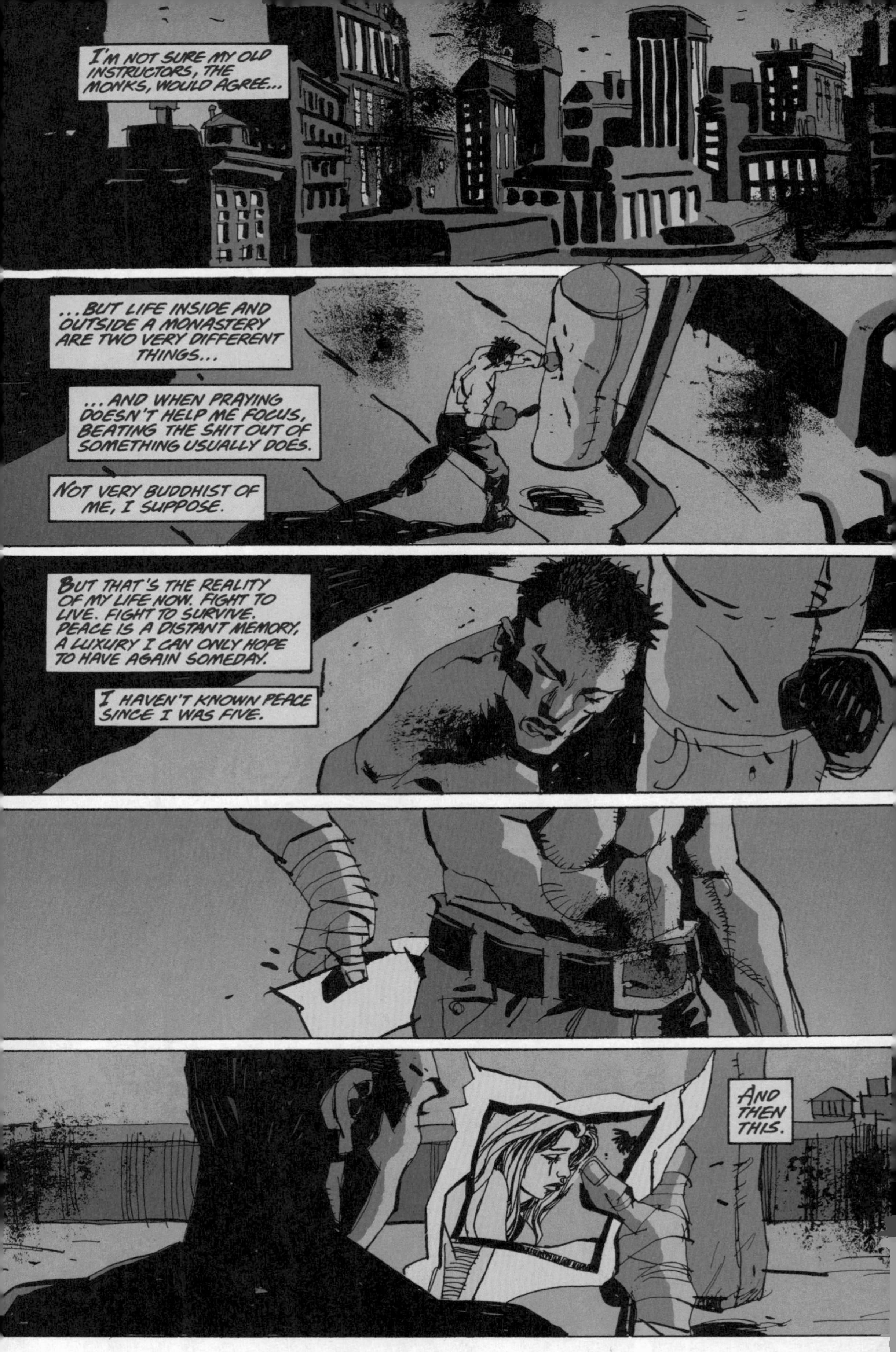
I'M NOT SURE MY OLD INSTRUCTORS, THE MONKS, WOULD AGREE...
...BUT LIFE INSIDE AND OUTSIDE A MONASTERY ARE TWO VERY DIFFERENT THINGS...
...AND WHEN PRAYING DOESN'T HELP ME FOCUS, BEATING THE SHIT OUT OF SOMETHING USUALLY DOES.
NOT VERY BUDDHIST OF ME, I SUPPOSE.
BUT THAT'S THE REALITY OF MY LIFE NOW. FIGHT TO LIVE. FIGHT TO SURVIVE. PEACE IS A DISTANT MEMORY, A LUXURY I CAN ONLY HOPE TO HAVE AGAIN SOMEDAY.
I HAVEN'T KNOWN PEACE SINCE I WAS FIVE.
AND THEN THIS.

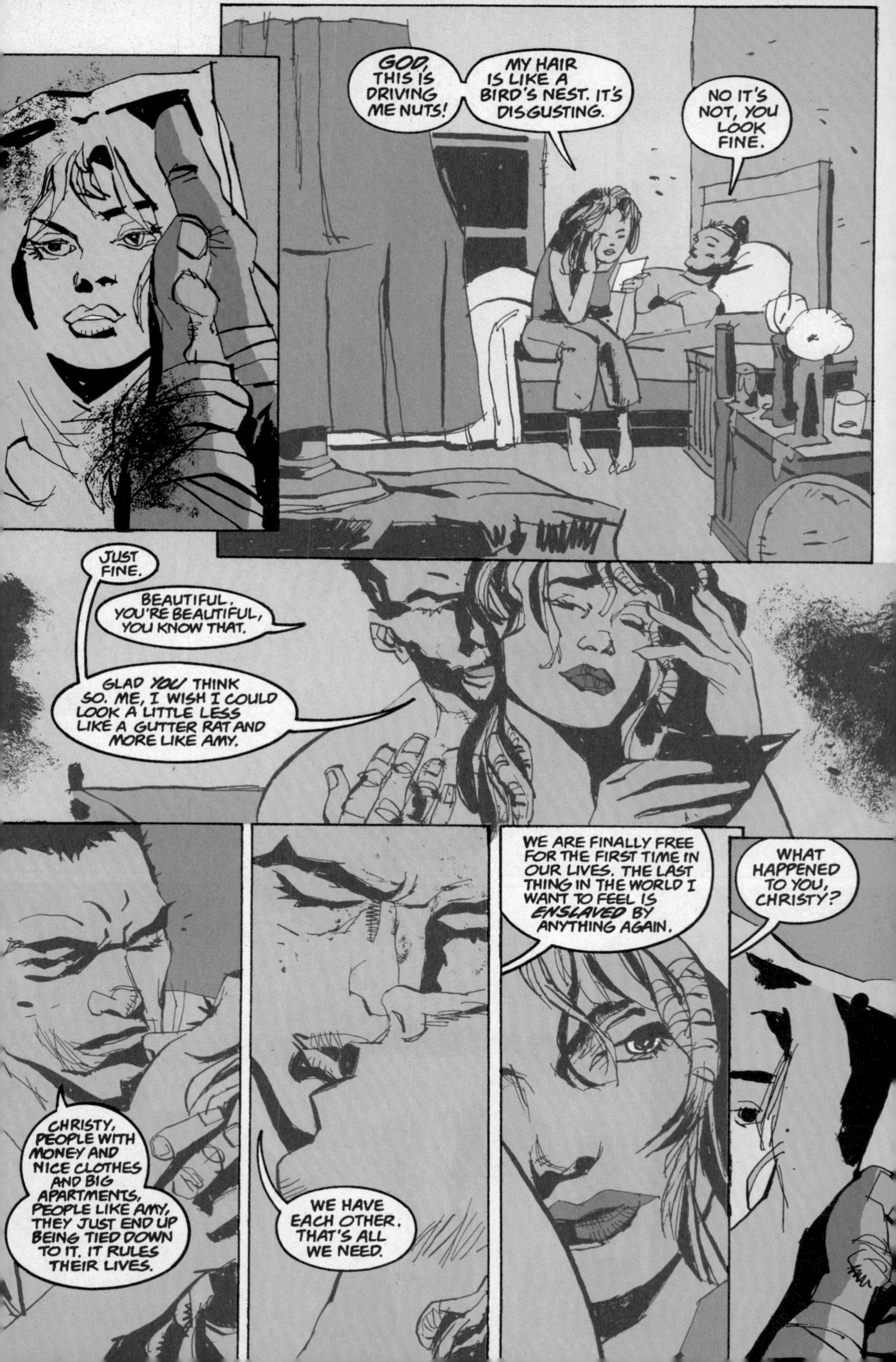
GOD, THIS IS DRIVING ME NUTS!
MY HAIR IS LIKE A BIRD'S NEST. IT'S DISGUSTING.
NO IT'S NOT, YOU LOOK FINE.
JUST FINE.
BEAUTIFUL. YOU'RE BEAUTIFUL, YOU KNOW THAT.
GLAD YOU THINK SO. ME, I WISH I COULD LOOK A LITTLE LESS LIKE A GUTTER RAT AND MORE LIKE AMY.
CHRISTY, PEOPLE WITH MONEY AND NICE CLOTHES AND BIG APARTMENTS, PEOPLE LIKE AMY, THEY JUST END UP BEING TIED DOWN TO IT. IT RULES THEIR LIVES.
WE HAVE EACH OTHER. THAT'S ALL WE NEED.
WE ARE FINALLY FREE FOR THE FIRST TIME IN OUR LIVES. THE LAST THING IN THE WORLD I WANT TO FEEL IS ENSLAVED BY ANYTHING AGAIN.
WHAT HAPPENED TO YOU, CHRISTY?

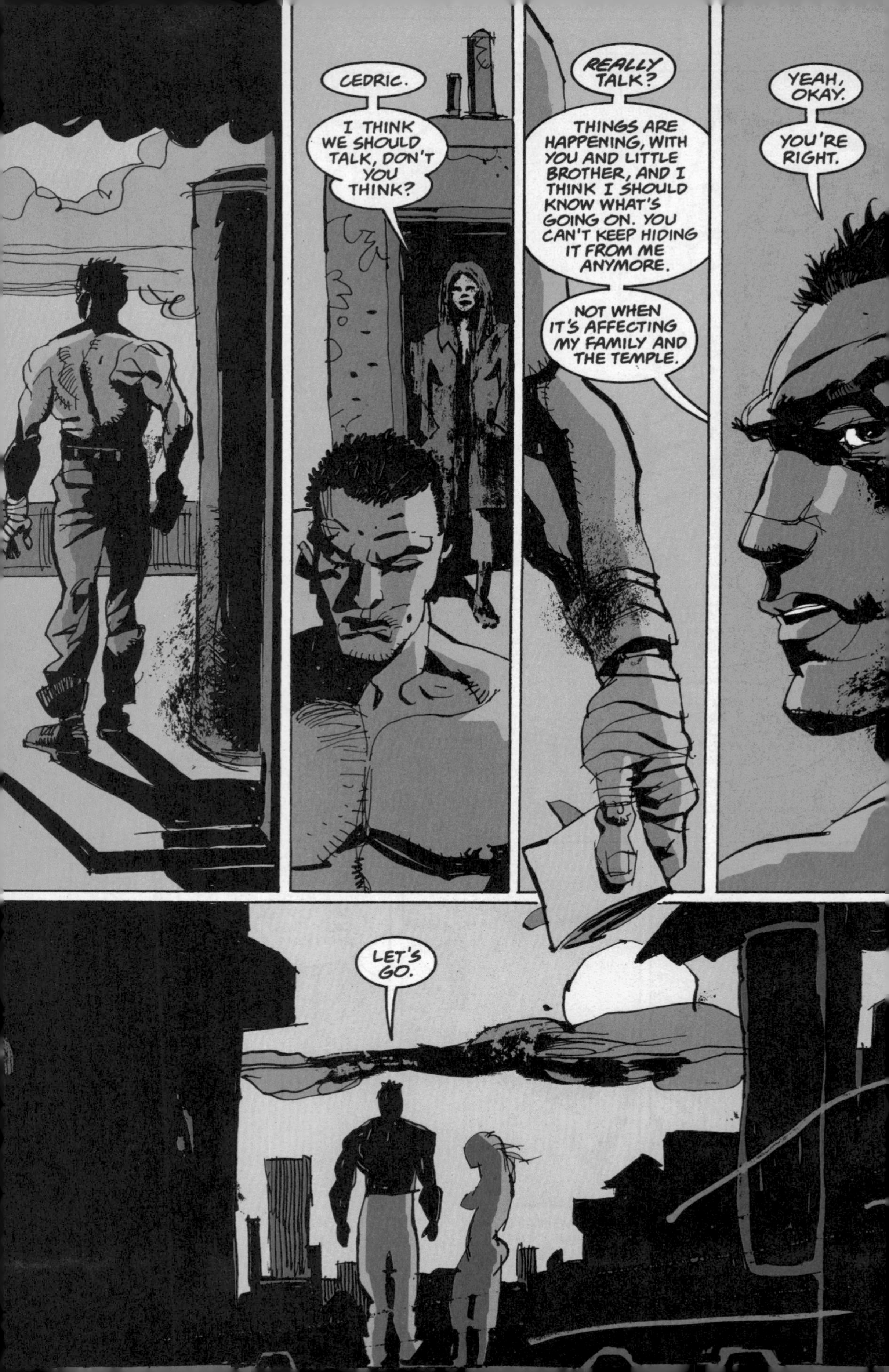
CEDRIC.
I THINK WE SHOULD TALK, DON'T YOU THINK?
REALLY TALK?
THINGS ARE HAPPENING, WITH YOU AND LITTLE BROTHER, AND I THINK I SHOULD KNOW WHAT'S GOING ON. YOU CAN'T KEEP HIDING IT FROM ME ANYMORE.
NOT WHEN IT'S AFFECTING MY FAMILY AND THE TEMPLE.
YEAH, OKAY.
YOU'RE RIGHT.
LET'S GO.

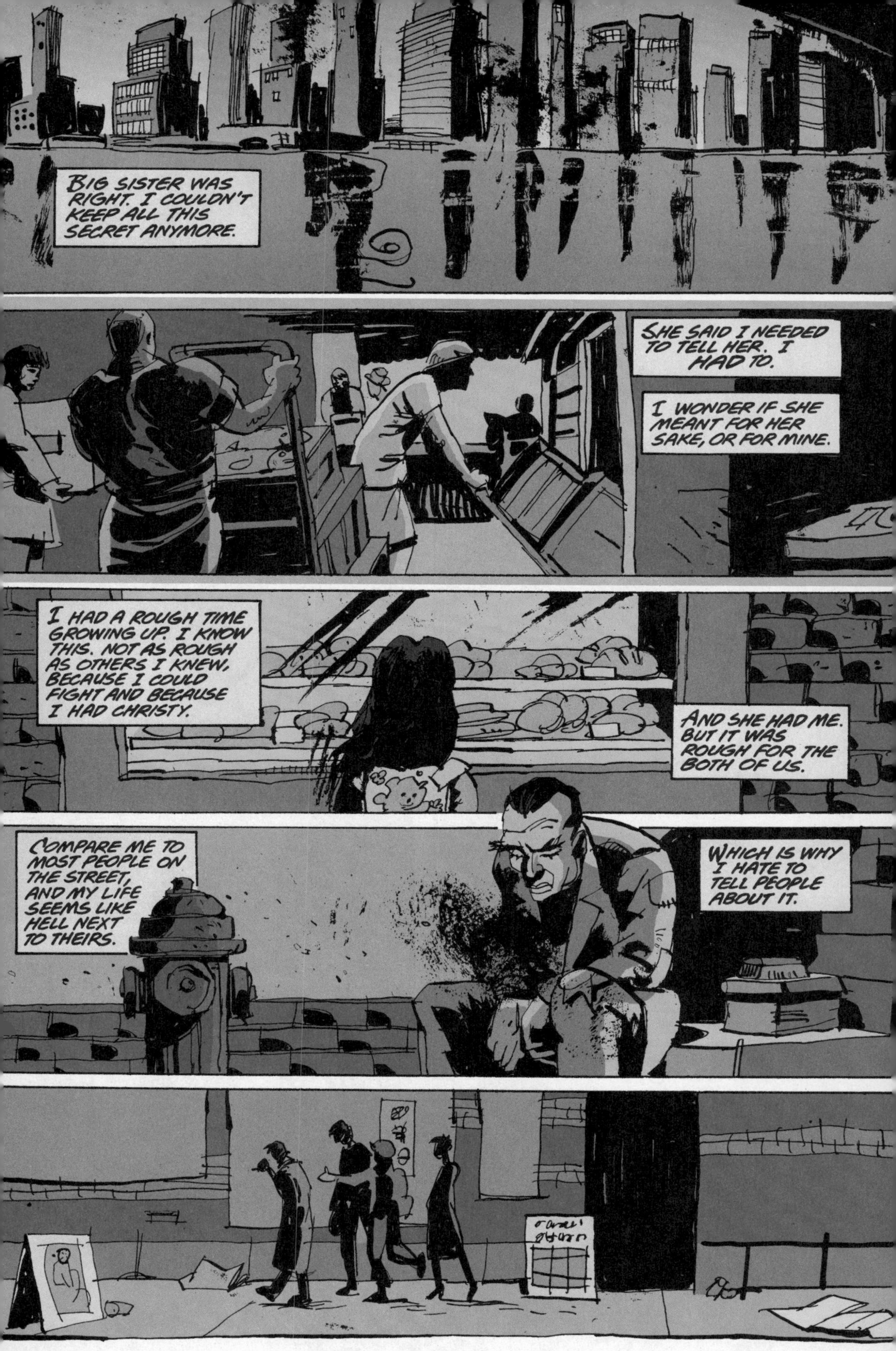
BIG SISTER WAS RIGHT. I COULDN'T KEEP ALL THIS SECRET ANYMORE.
SHE SAID I NEEDED TO TELL HER. I HAD TO.
I WONDER IF SHE MEANT FOR HER SAKE, OR FOR MINE.
I HAD A ROUGH TIME GROWING UP. I KNOW THIS. NOT AS ROUGH AS OTHERS I KNEW, BECAUSE I COULD FIGHT AND BECAUSE I HAD CHRISTY.
AND SHE HAD ME. BUT IT WAS ROUGH FOR THE BOTH OF US.
COMPARE ME TO MOST PEOPLE ON THE STREET, AND MY LIFE SEEMS LIKE HELL NEXT TO THEIRS.
WHICH IS WHY I HATE TO TELL PEOPLE ABOUT IT.

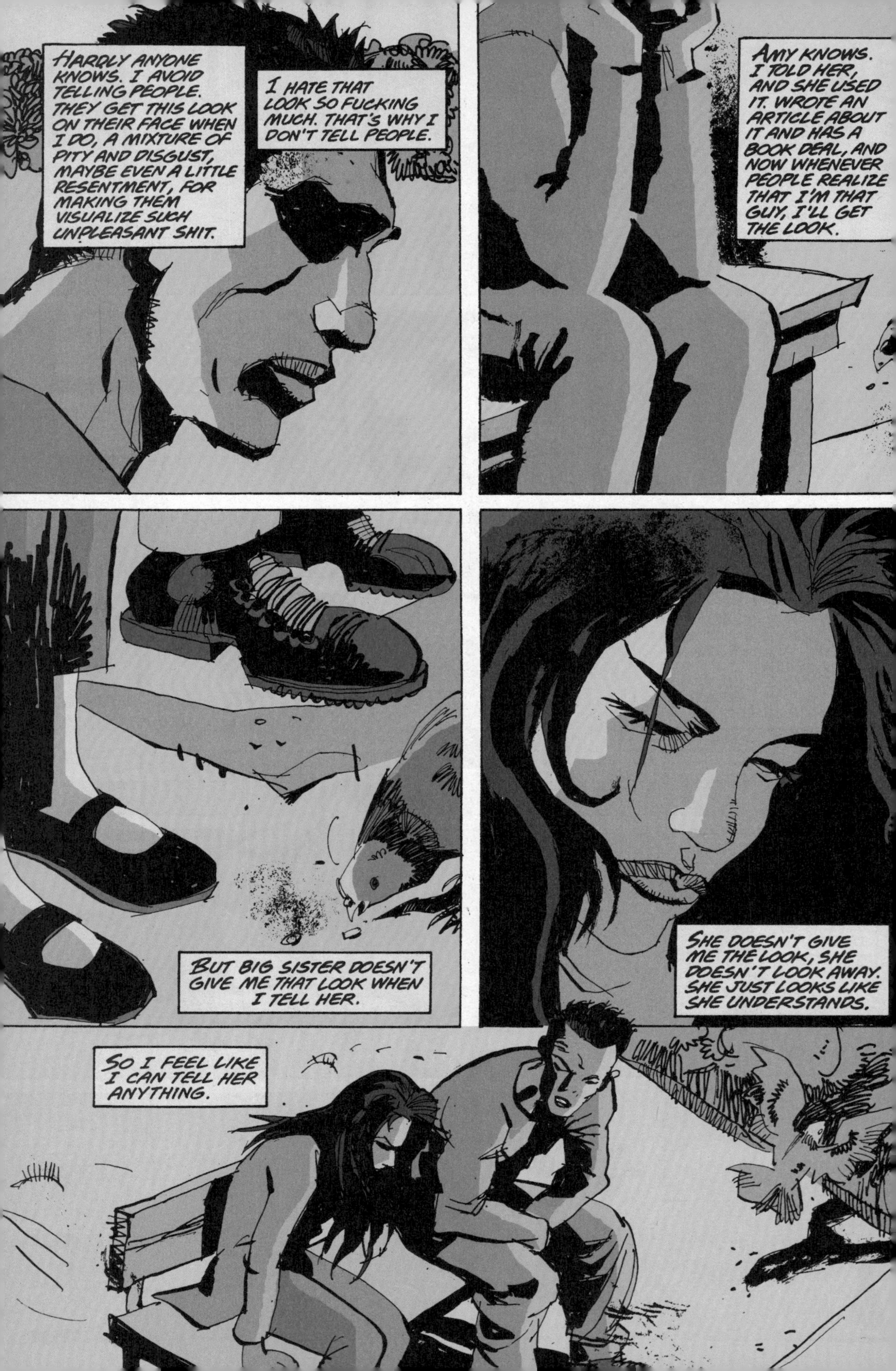
HARDLY ANYONE KNOWS. I AVOID TELLING PEOPLE. THEY GET THIS LOOK ON THEIR FACE WHEN I DO, A MIXTURE OF PITY AND DISGUST, MAYBE EVEN A LITTLE RESENTMENT, FOR MAKING THEM VISUALIZE SUCH UNPLEASANT SHIT.
I HATE THAT LOOK SO FUCKING MUCH. THAT'S WHY I DON'T TELL PEOPLE.
AMY KNOWS. I TOLD HER, AND SHE USED IT. WROTE AN ARTICLE ABOUT IT AND HAS A BOOK DEAL, AND NOW WHENEVER PEOPLE REALIZE THAT I'M THAT GUY, I'LL GET THE LOOK.
BUT BIG SISTER DOESN'T GIVE ME THAT LOOK WHEN I TELL HER.
SHE DOESN'T GIVE ME THE LOOK, SHE DOESN'T LOOK AWAY. SHE JUST LOOKS LIKE SHE UNDERSTANDS.
SO I FEEL LIKE I CAN TELL HER ANYTHING.

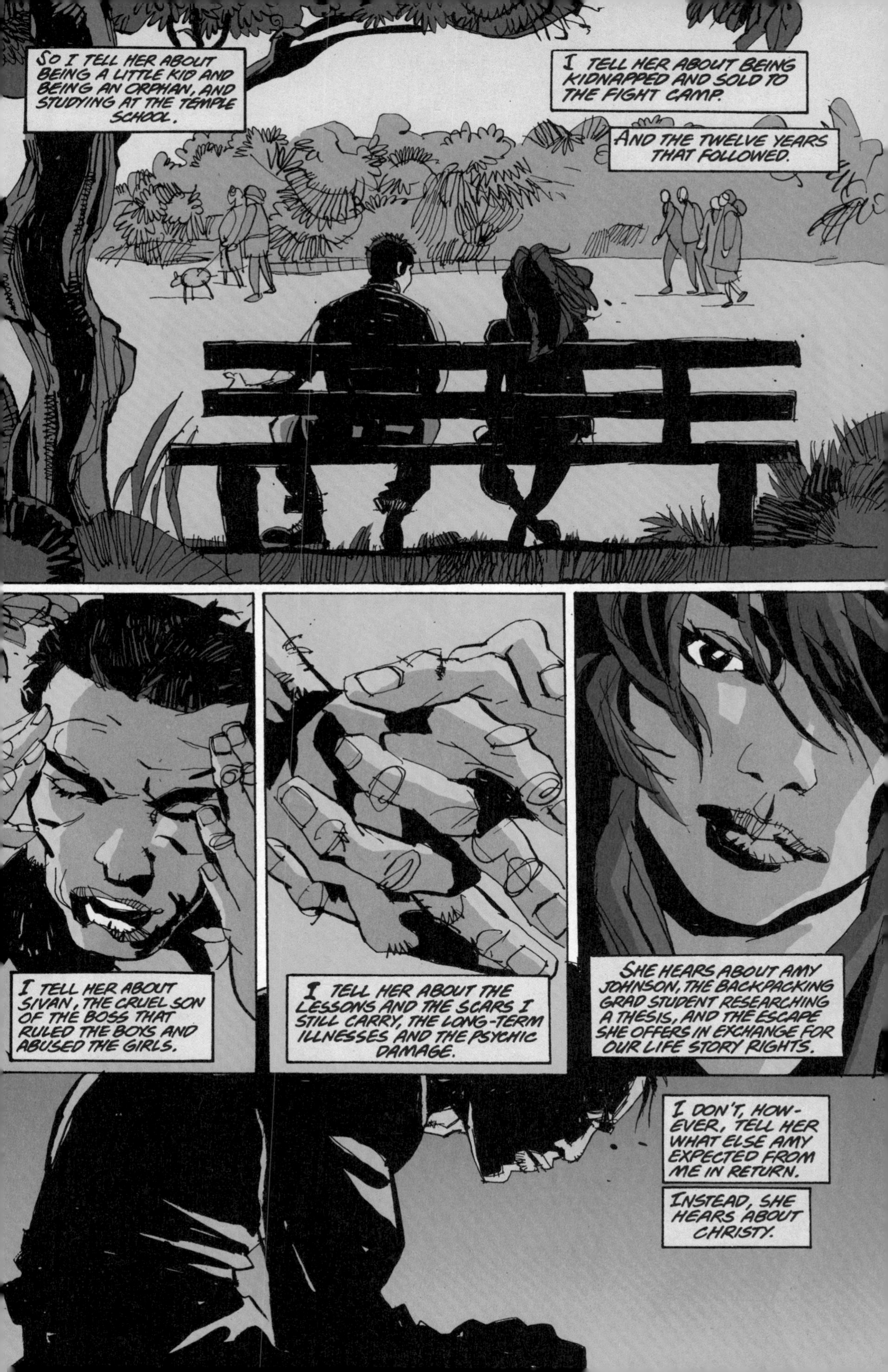
SO I TELL HER ABOUT BEING A LITTLE KID AND BEING AN ORPHAN, AND STUDYING AT THE TEMPLE SCHOOL.
I TELL HER ABOUT BEING KIDNAPPED AND SOLD TO THE FIGHT CAMP.
AND THE TWELVE YEARS THAT FOLLOWED.
I TELL HER ABOUT SIVAN, THE CRUEL SON OF THE BOSS THAT RULED THE BOYS AND ABUSED THE GIRLS.
I TELL HER ABOUT THE LESSONS AND THE SCARS I STILL CARRY, THE LONG-TERM ILLNESSES AND THE PSYCHIC DAMAGE.
SHE HEARS ABOUT AMY JOHNSON, THE BACKPACKING GRAD STUDENT RESEARCHING A THESIS, AND THE ESCAPE SHE OFFERS IN EXCHANGE FOR OUR LIFE STORY RIGHTS.
I DON'T, HOW-EVER, TELL HER WHAT ELSE AMY EXPECTED FROM ME IN RETURN.
INSTEAD, SHE HEARS ABOUT CHRISTY.

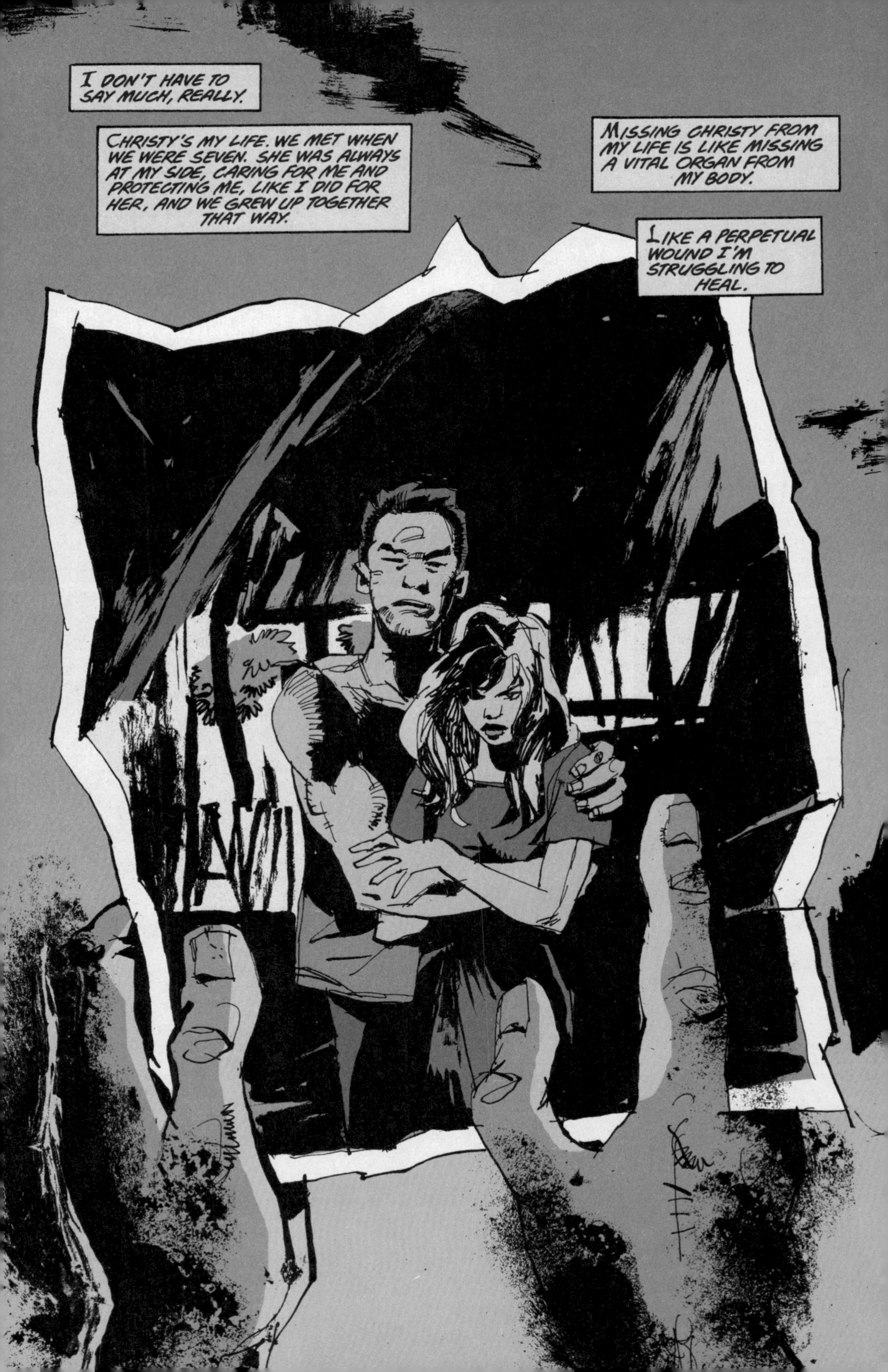
I DON'T HAVE TO SAY MUCH, REALLY.
CHRISTY'S MY LIFE. WE MET WHEN WE WERE SEVEN. SHE WAS ALWAYS AT MY SIDE, CARING FOR ME AND PROTECTING ME, LIKE I DID FOR HER, AND WE GREW UP TOGETHER THAT WAY.
MISSING CHRISTY FROM MY LIFE IS LIKE MISSING A VITAL ORGAN FROM MY BODY.
LIKE A PERPETUAL WOUND I'M STRUGGLING TO HEAL.

I'M SORRY, CED.

HOW DOES LITTLE BROTHER FIT INTO ALL OF THIS?

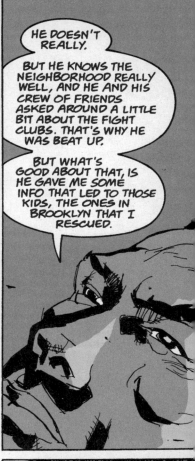

HE DOESN'T REALLY.

BUT HE KNOWS THE NEIGHBORHOOD REALLY WELL, AND HE AND HIS CREW OF FRIENDS ASKED AROUND A LITTLE BIT ABOUT THE FIGHT CLUBS. THAT'S WHY HE WAS BEAT UP.

BUT WHAT'S GOOD ABOUT THAT, IS HE GAVE ME SOME INFO THAT LED TO THOSE KIDS, THE ONES IN BROOKLYN THAT I RESCUED.

DID HE REALLY HELP WITH THAT?

YEAH. THOSE KIDS WERE DOOMED TO THE SAME LIFE I HAD, BUT WE STOPPED IT, LITTLE BROTHER AND I.

I DIDN'T KNOW. HE DIDN'T SAY ANYTHING ABOUT THAT.

I KNOW I'M STRICT ABOUT HIM, AND TOUGH ON YOU ABOUT KEEPING HIM OUT OF TROUBLE...

...BUT IF HE CAN HELP YOU WITH THIS, IT'S A GOOD THING.

THAT'S GOOD, BECAUSE I CAN'T STOP THIS.

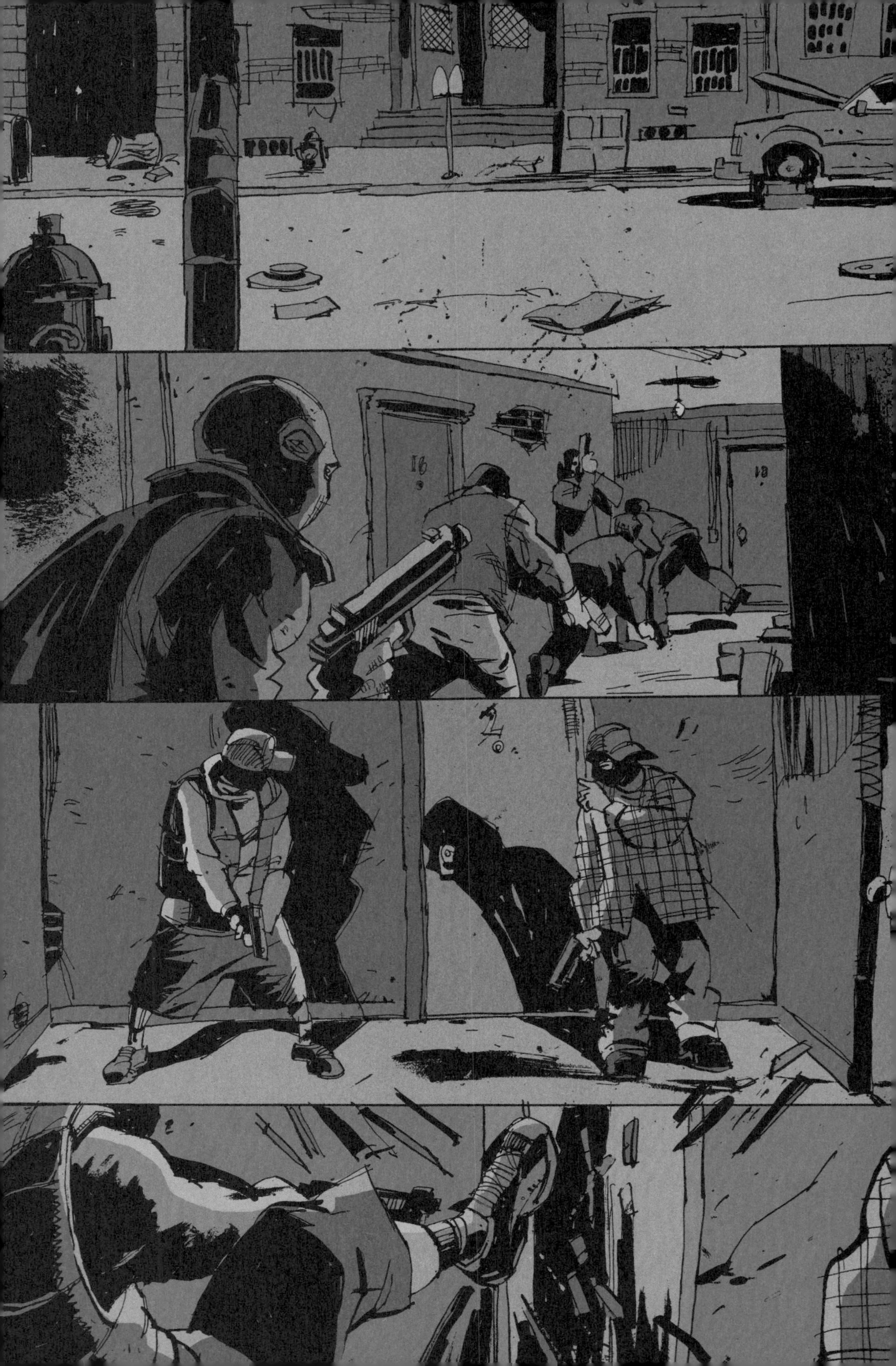

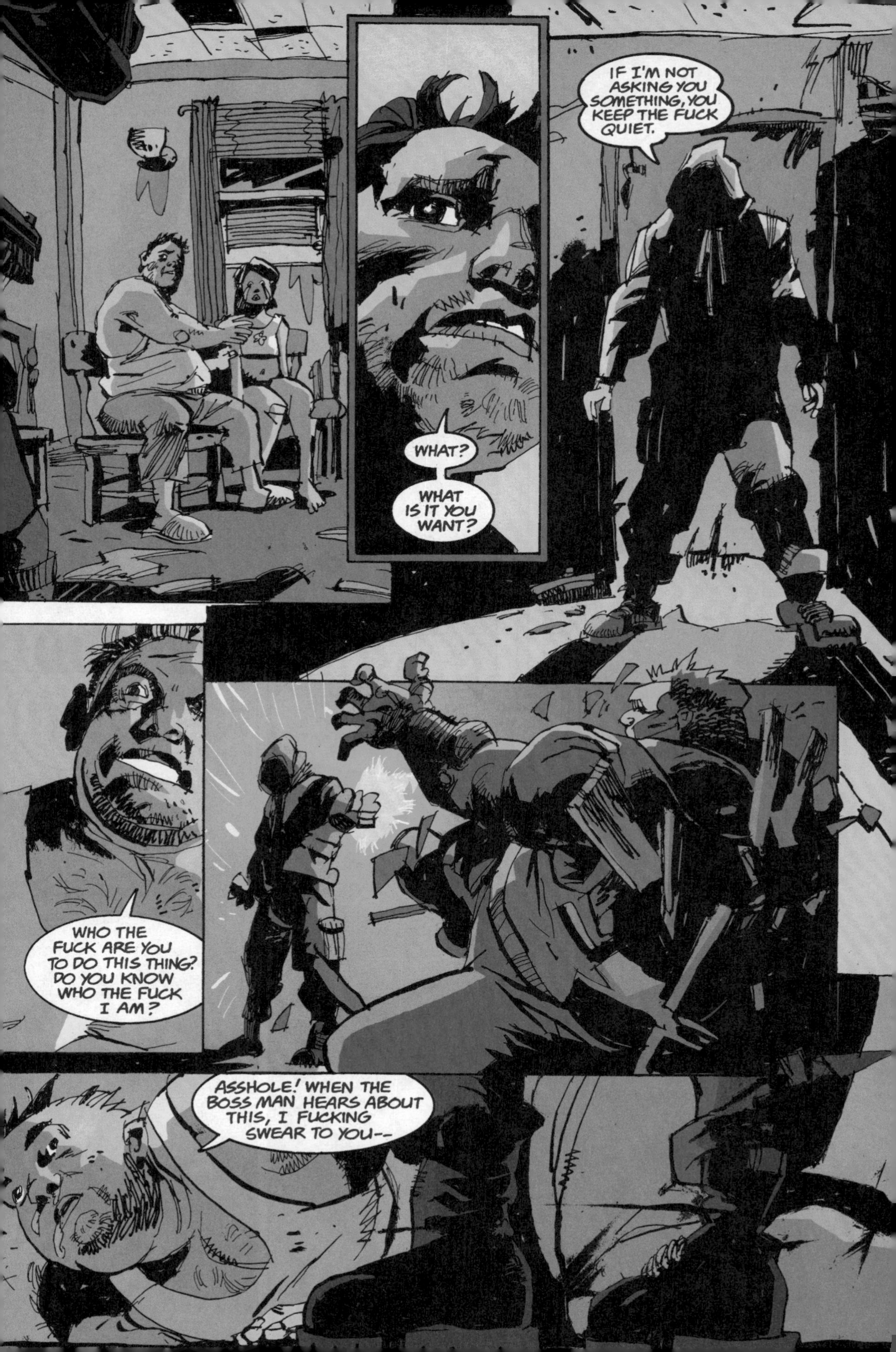
IF I'M NOT ASKING YOU SOMETHING, YOU KEEP THE FUCK QUIET.
WHAT?
WHAT IS IT YOU WANT?
WHO THE FUCK ARE YOU TO DO THIS THING? DO YOU KNOW WHO THE FUCK I AM?
ASSHOLE! WHEN THE BOSS MAN HEARS ABOUT THIS, I FUCKING SWEAR TO YOU--

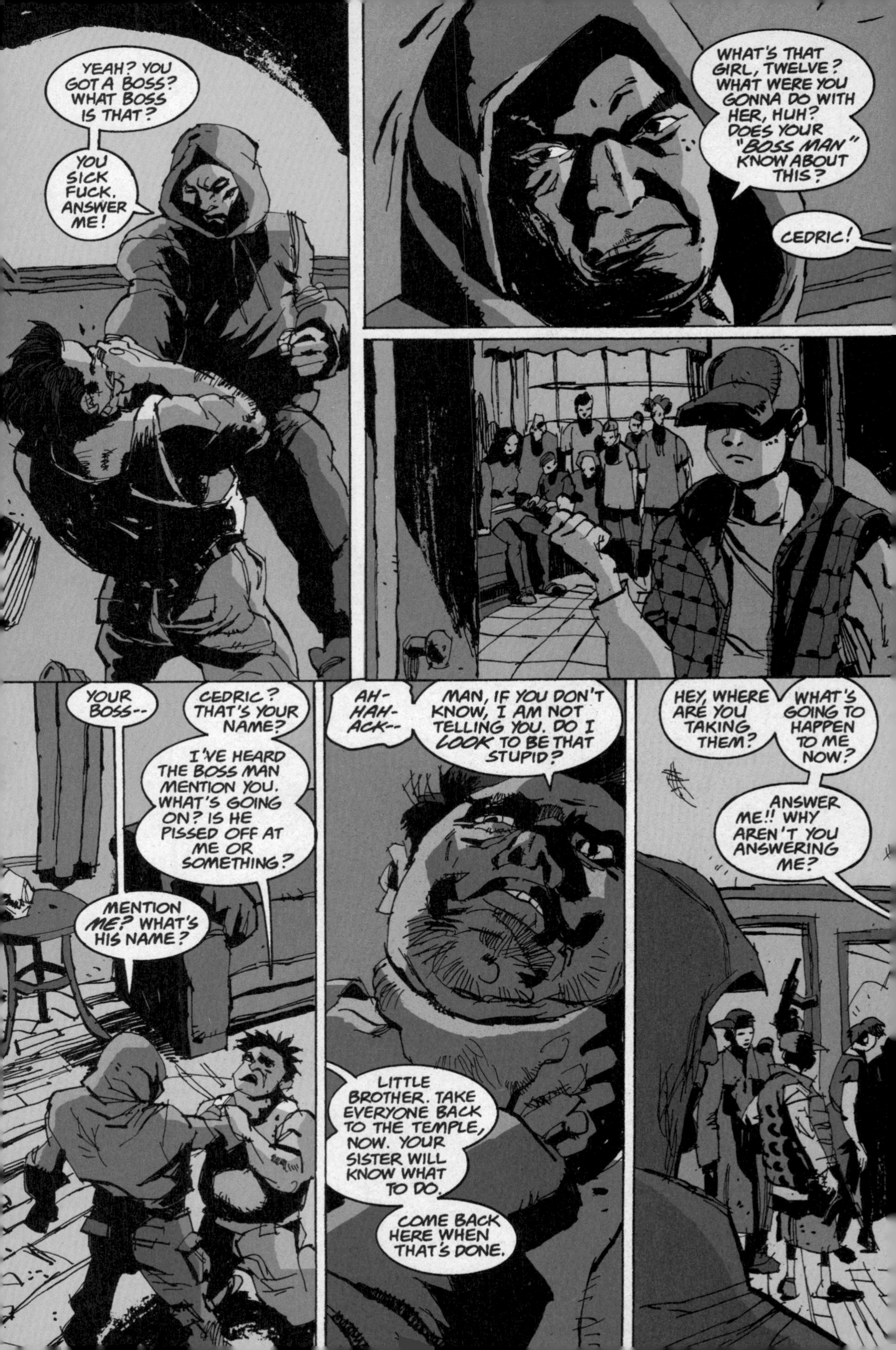
YEAH? YOU GOT A BOSS? WHAT BOSS IS THAT?
YOU SICK FUCK. ANSWER ME!
WHAT'S THAT GIRL, TWELVE? WHAT WERE YOU GONNA DO WITH HER, HUH? DOES YOUR "BOSS MAN" KNOW ABOUT THIS?
CEDRIC!
YOUR BOSS--
CEDRIC? THAT'S YOUR NAME?
I'VE HEARD THE BOSS MAN MENTION YOU. WHAT'S GOING ON? IS HE PISSED OFF AT ME OR SOMETHING?
MENTION ME? WHAT'S HIS NAME?
AH-HAH-ACK--
MAN, IF YOU DON'T KNOW, I AM NOT TELLING YOU. DO I LOOK TO BE THAT STUPID?
LITTLE BROTHER. TAKE EVERYONE BACK TO THE TEMPLE, NOW. YOUR SISTER WILL KNOW WHAT TO DO.
COME BACK HERE WHEN THAT'S DONE.
HEY, WHERE ARE YOU TAKING THEM?
WHAT'S GOING TO HAPPEN TO ME NOW?
ANSWER ME!! WHY AREN'T YOU ANSWERING ME?

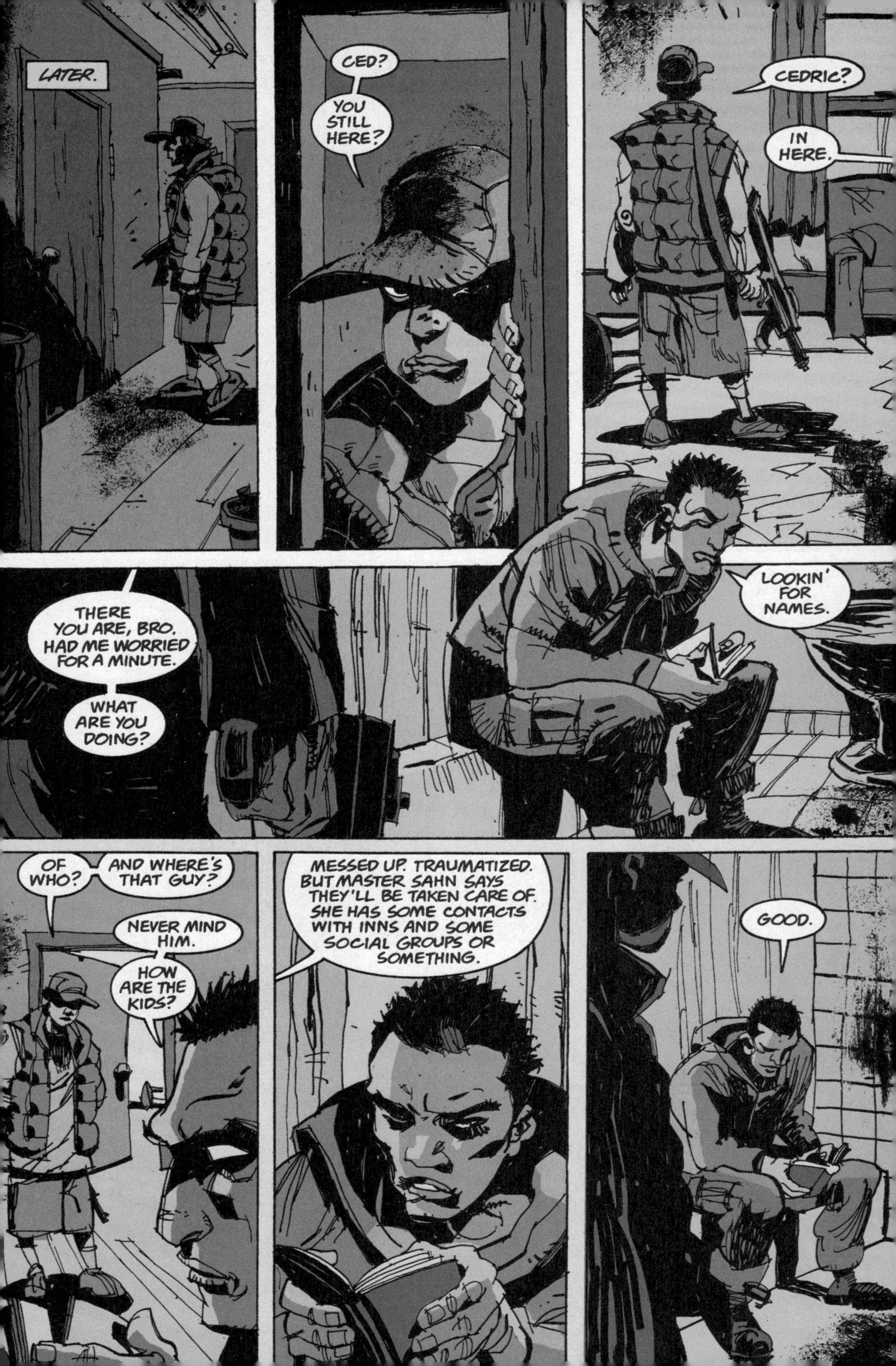
LATER.
CED?
YOU STILL HERE?
CEDRIC?
IN HERE.
THERE YOU ARE, BRO. HAD ME WORRIED FOR A MINUTE.
WHAT ARE YOU DOING?
LOOKIN' FOR NAMES.
OF WHO?
AND WHERE'S THAT GUY?
NEVER MIND HIM.
HOW ARE THE KIDS?
MESSED UP. TRAUMATIZED. BUT MASTER SAHN SAYS THEY'LL BE TAKEN CARE OF. SHE HAS SOME CONTACTS WITH INNS AND SOME SOCIAL GROUPS OR SOMETHING.
GOOD.

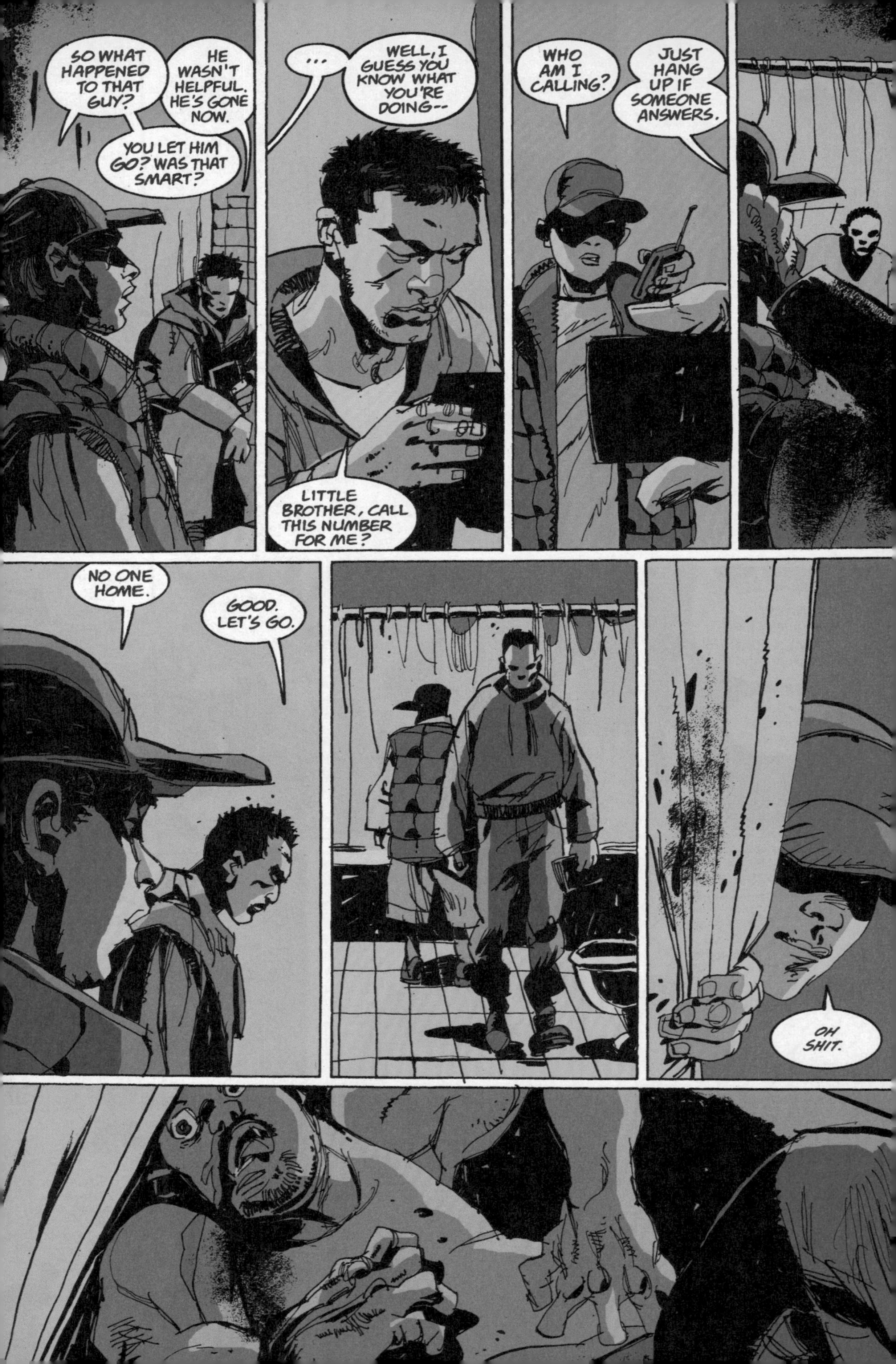
SO WHAT HAPPENED TO THAT GUY?
HE WASN'T HELPFUL. HE'S GONE NOW.
YOU LET HIM GO? WAS THAT SMART?
...
WELL, I GUESS YOU KNOW WHAT YOU'RE DOING--
LITTLE BROTHER, CALL THIS NUMBER FOR ME?
WHO AM I CALLING?
JUST HANG UP IF SOMEONE ANSWERS.
NO ONE HOME.
GOOD. LET'S GO.
OH SHIT.

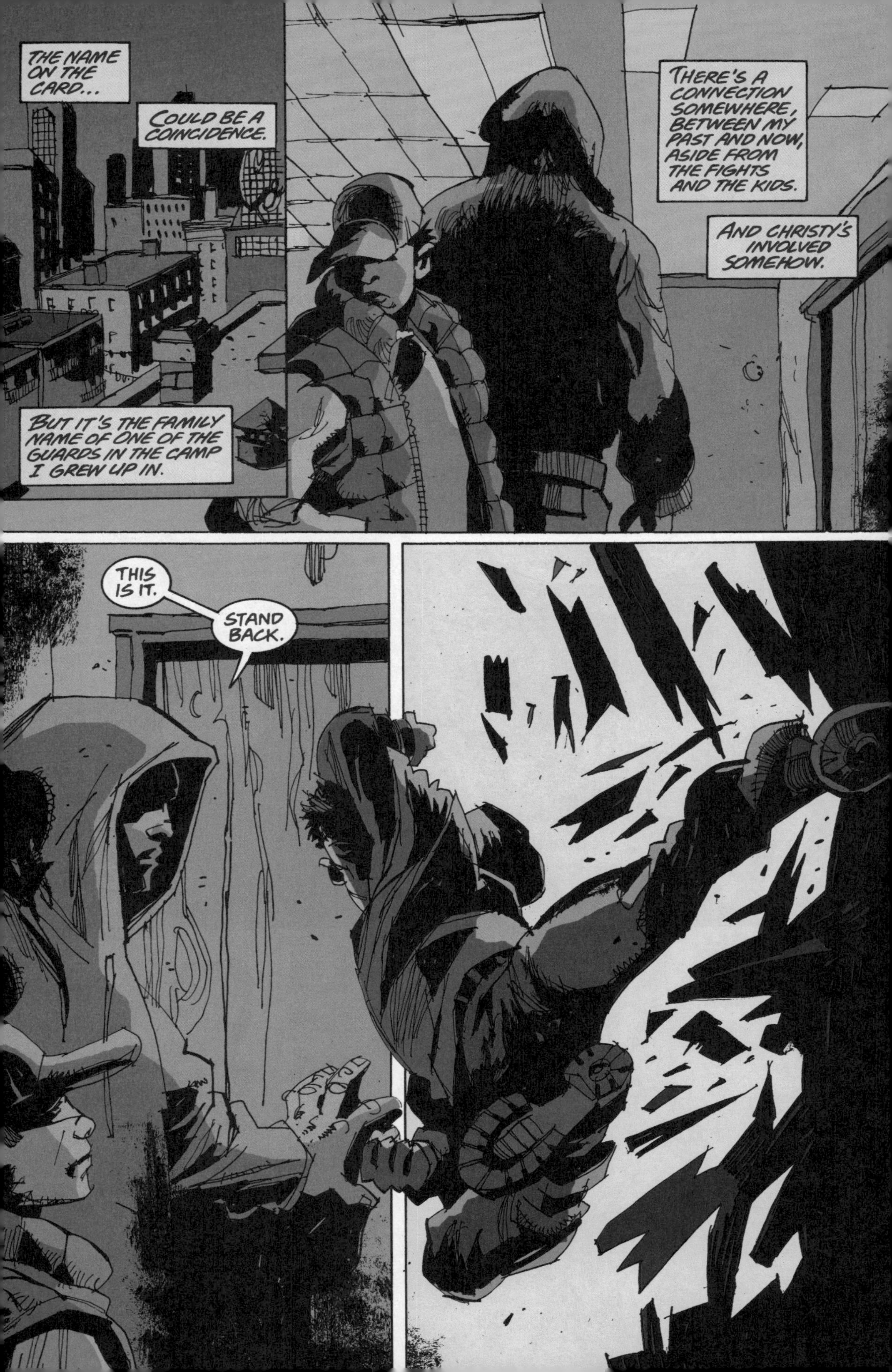
THE NAME ON THE CARD...
COULD BE A COINCIDENCE.
BUT IT'S THE FAMILY NAME OF ONE OF THE GUARDS IN THE CAMP I GREW UP IN.
THERE'S A CONNECTION SOMEWHERE, BETWEEN MY PAST AND NOW, ASIDE FROM THE FIGHTS AND THE KIDS.
AND CHRISTY'S INVOLVED SOMEHOW.
THIS IS IT.
STAND BACK.

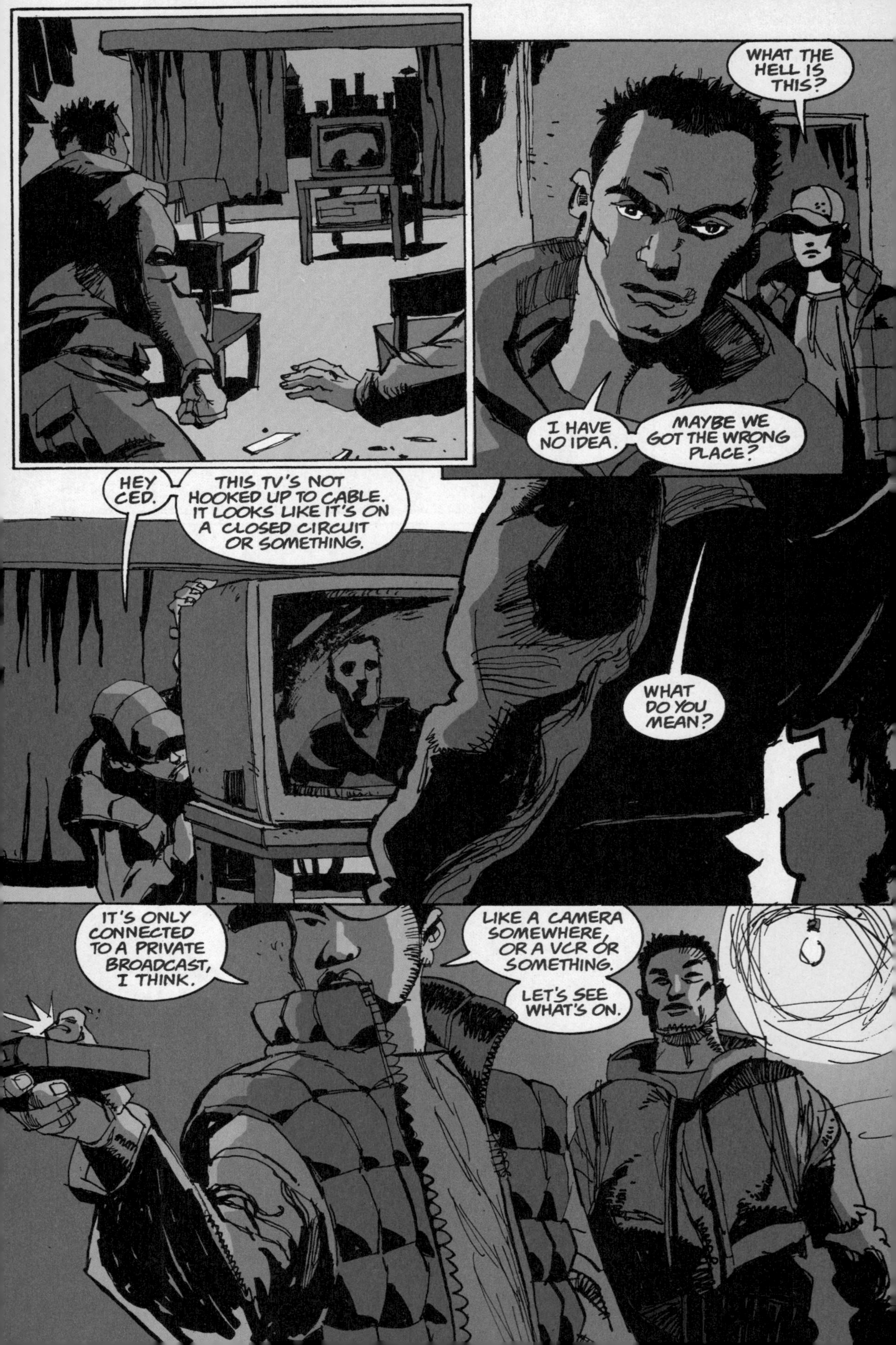
WHAT THE HELL IS THIS?
I HAVE NO IDEA.
MAYBE WE GOT THE WRONG PLACE?
HEY CED.
THIS TV'S NOT HOOKED UP TO CABLE. IT LOOKS LIKE IT'S ON A CLOSED CIRCUIT OR SOMETHING.
WHAT DO YOU MEAN?
IT'S ONLY CONNECTED TO A PRIVATE BROADCAST, I THINK.
LIKE A CAMERA SOMEWHERE, OR A VCR OR SOMETHING.
LET'S SEE WHAT'S ON.

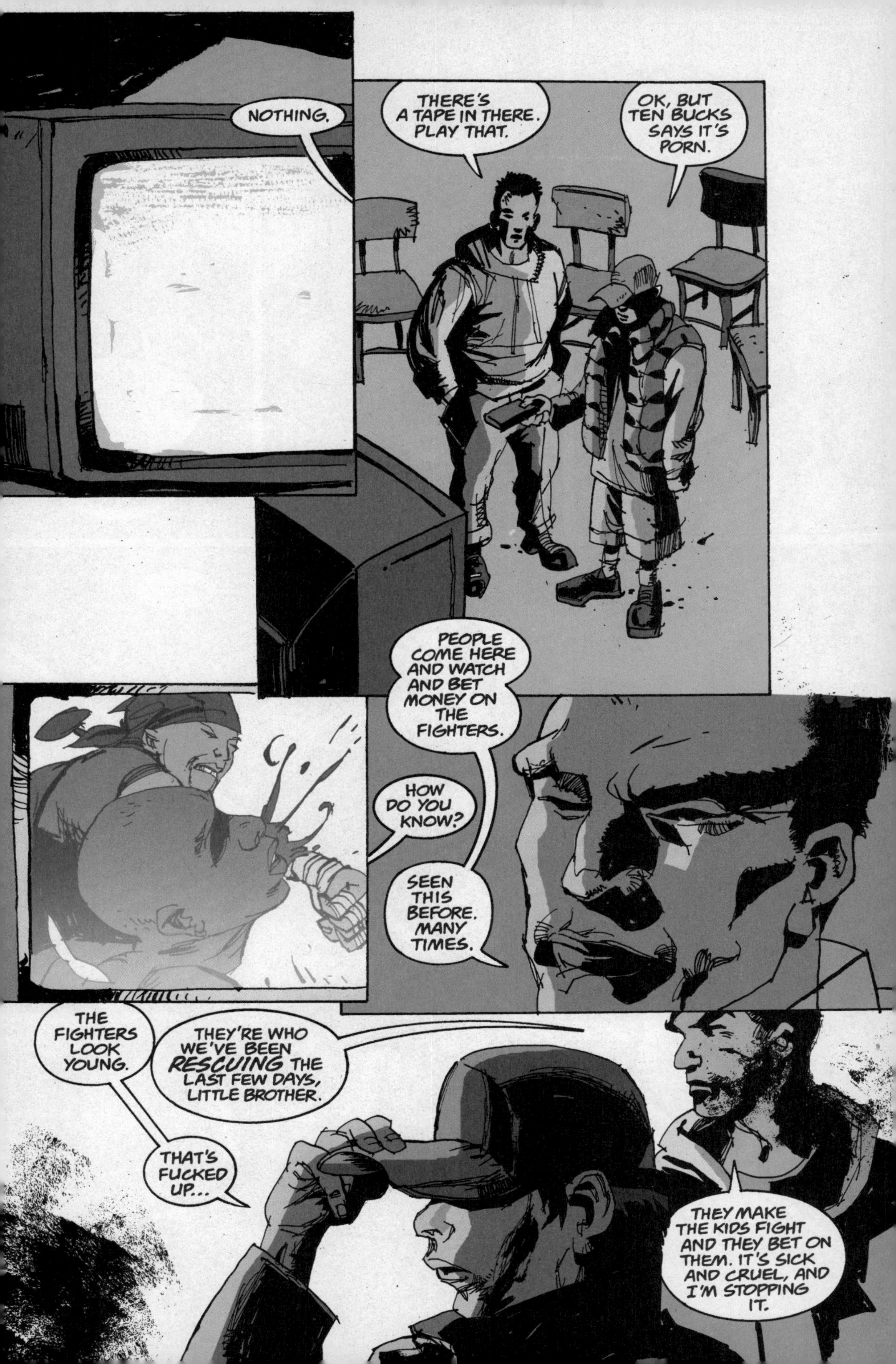
NOTHING.
THERE'S A TAPE IN THERE. PLAY THAT.
OK, BUT TEN BUCKS SAYS IT'S PORN.
PEOPLE COME HERE AND WATCH AND BET MONEY ON THE FIGHTERS.
HOW DO YOU KNOW?
SEEN THIS BEFORE. MANY TIMES.
THE FIGHTERS LOOK YOUNG.
THEY'RE WHO WE'VE BEEN RESCUING THE LAST FEW DAYS, LITTLE BROTHER.
THAT'S FUCKED UP...
THEY MAKE THE KIDS FIGHT AND THEY BET ON THEM. IT'S SICK AND CRUEL, AND I'M STOPPING IT.

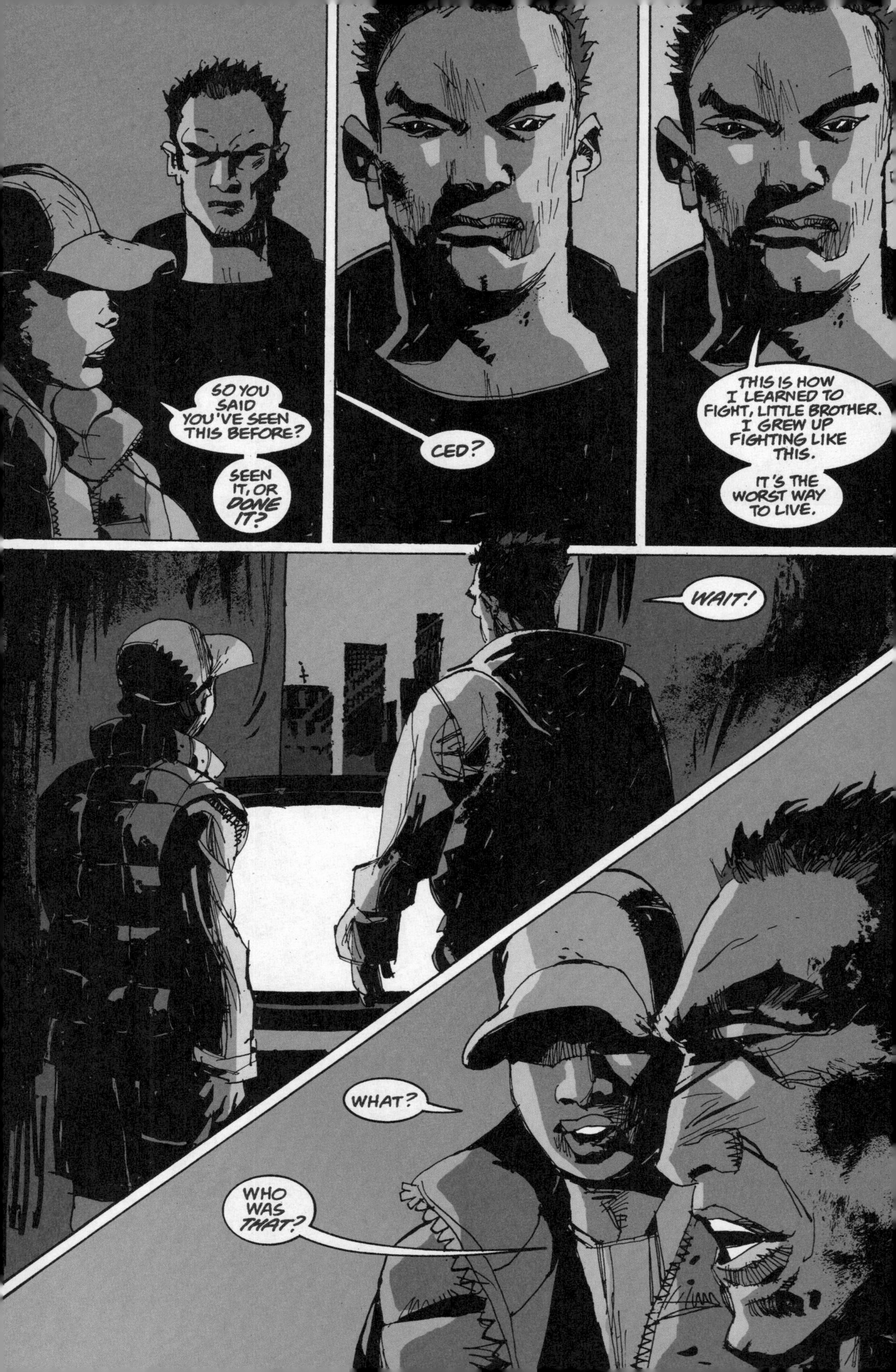
SO YOU SAID YOU'VE SEEN THIS BEFORE?
SEEN IT, OR *DONE IT?*
CED?
THIS IS HOW I LEARNED TO FIGHT, LITTLE BROTHER. I GREW UP FIGHTING LIKE THIS.
IT'S THE WORST WAY TO LIVE.
WAIT!
WHAT?
WHO WAS *THAT?*

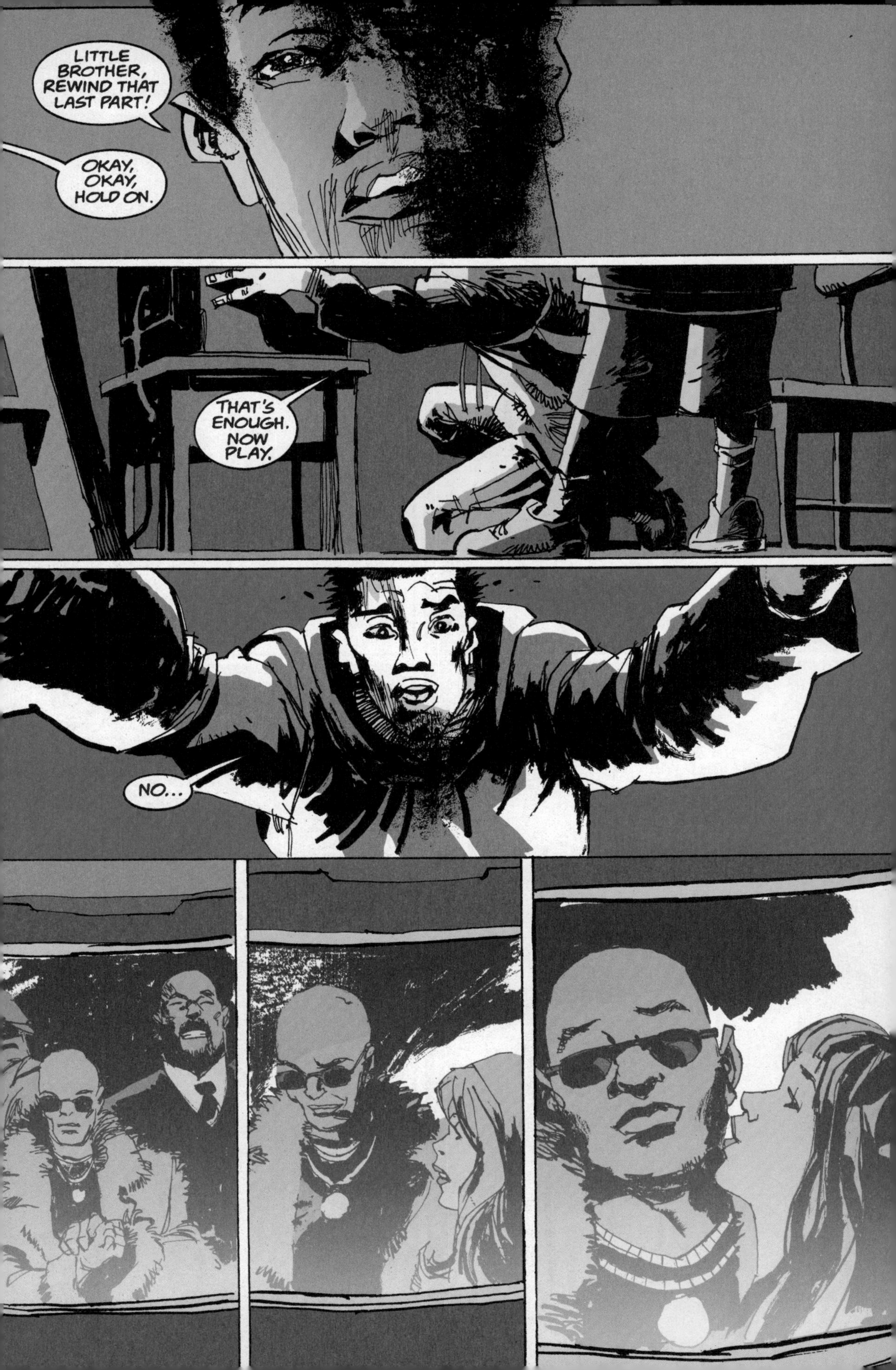
LITTLE BROTHER, REWIND THAT LAST PART!
OKAY, OKAY, HOLD ON.
THAT'S ENOUGH. NOW PLAY.
NO...

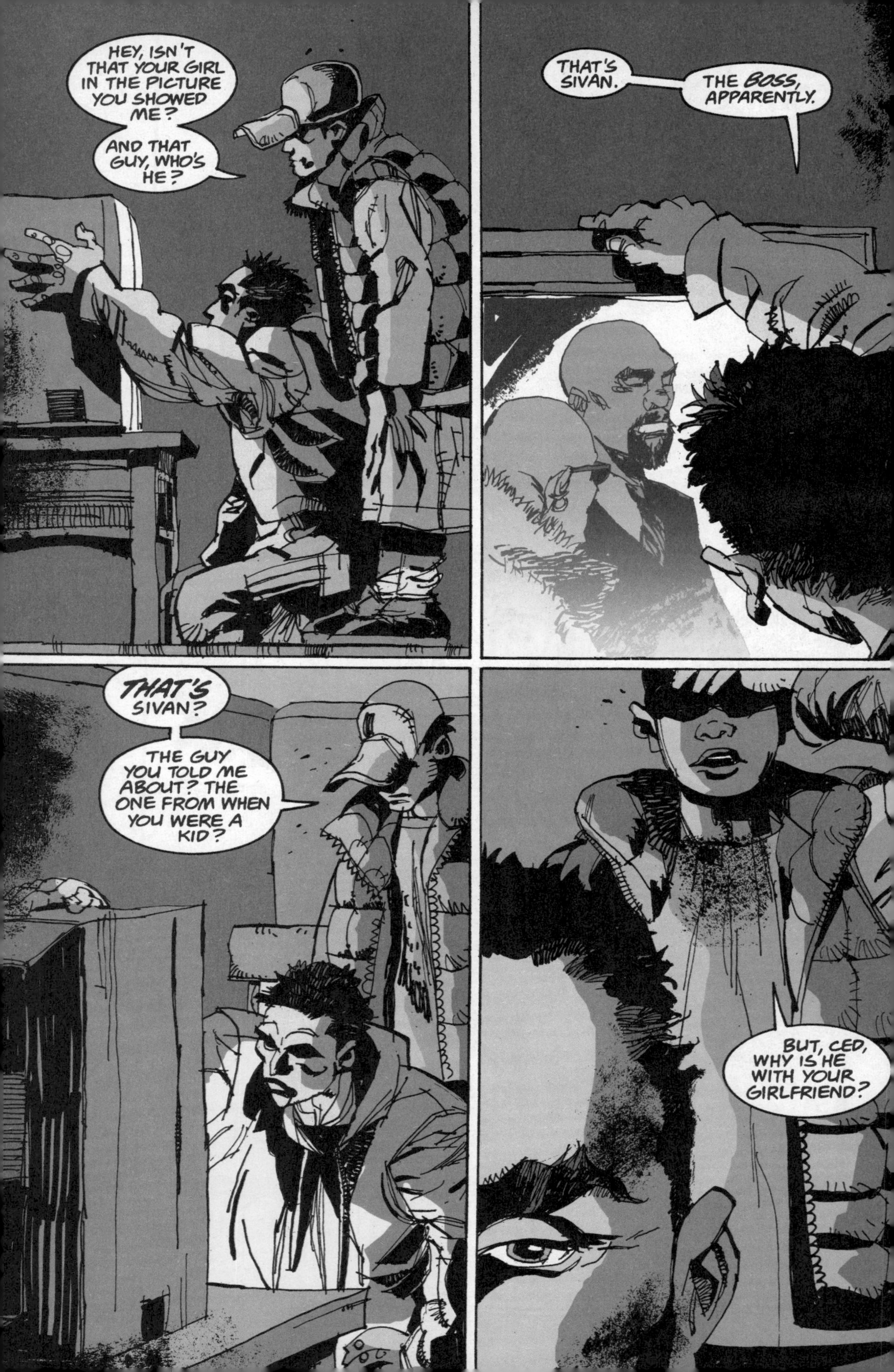
HEY, ISN'T THAT YOUR GIRL IN THE PICTURE YOU SHOWED ME?
AND THAT GUY, WHO'S HE?
THAT'S SIVAN.
THE *BOSS*, APPARENTLY.
THAT'S SIVAN?
THE GUY YOU TOLD ME ABOUT? THE ONE FROM WHEN YOU WERE A KID?
BUT, CED, WHY IS HE WITH YOUR GIRLFRIEND?

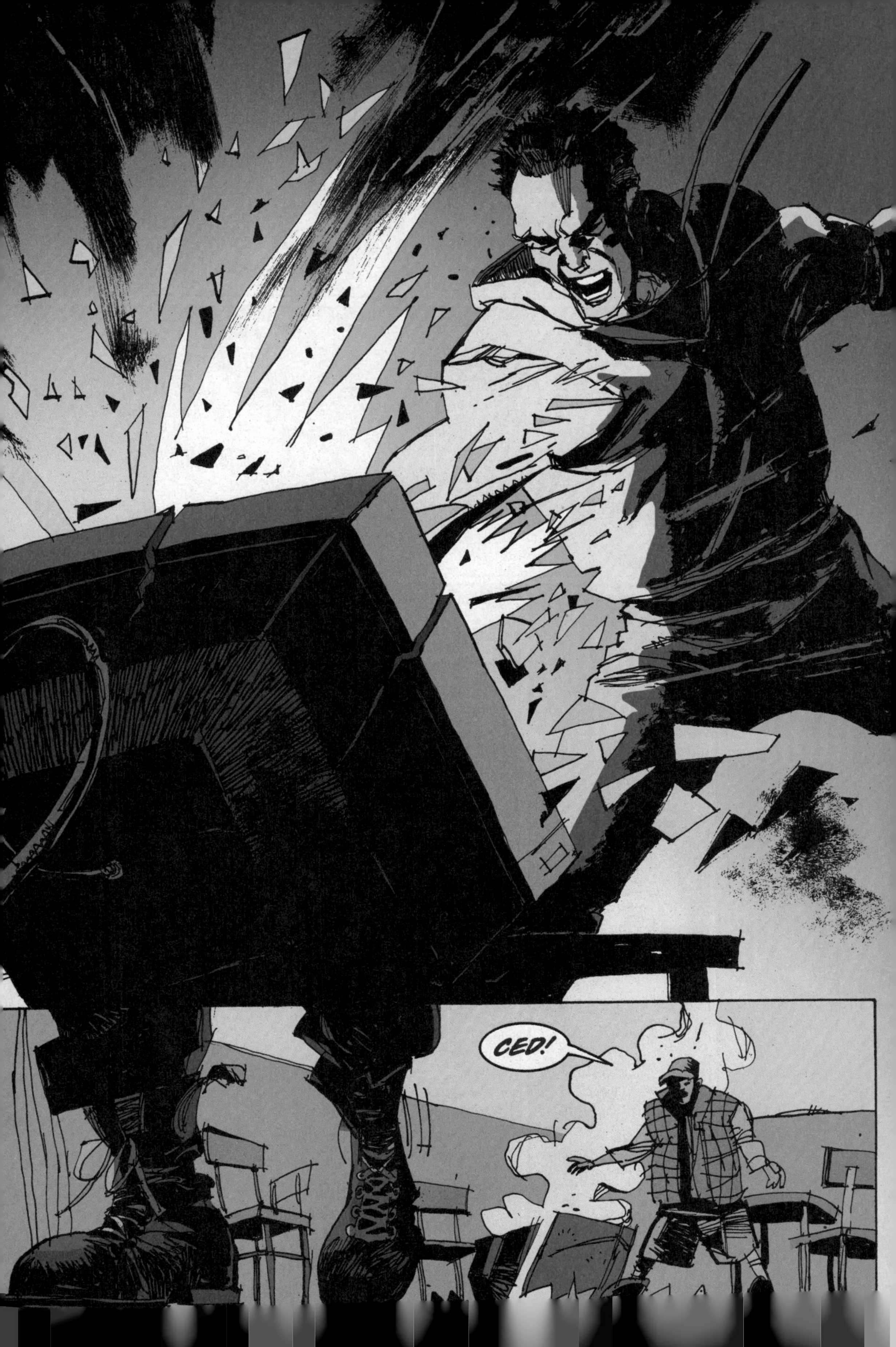
CED!

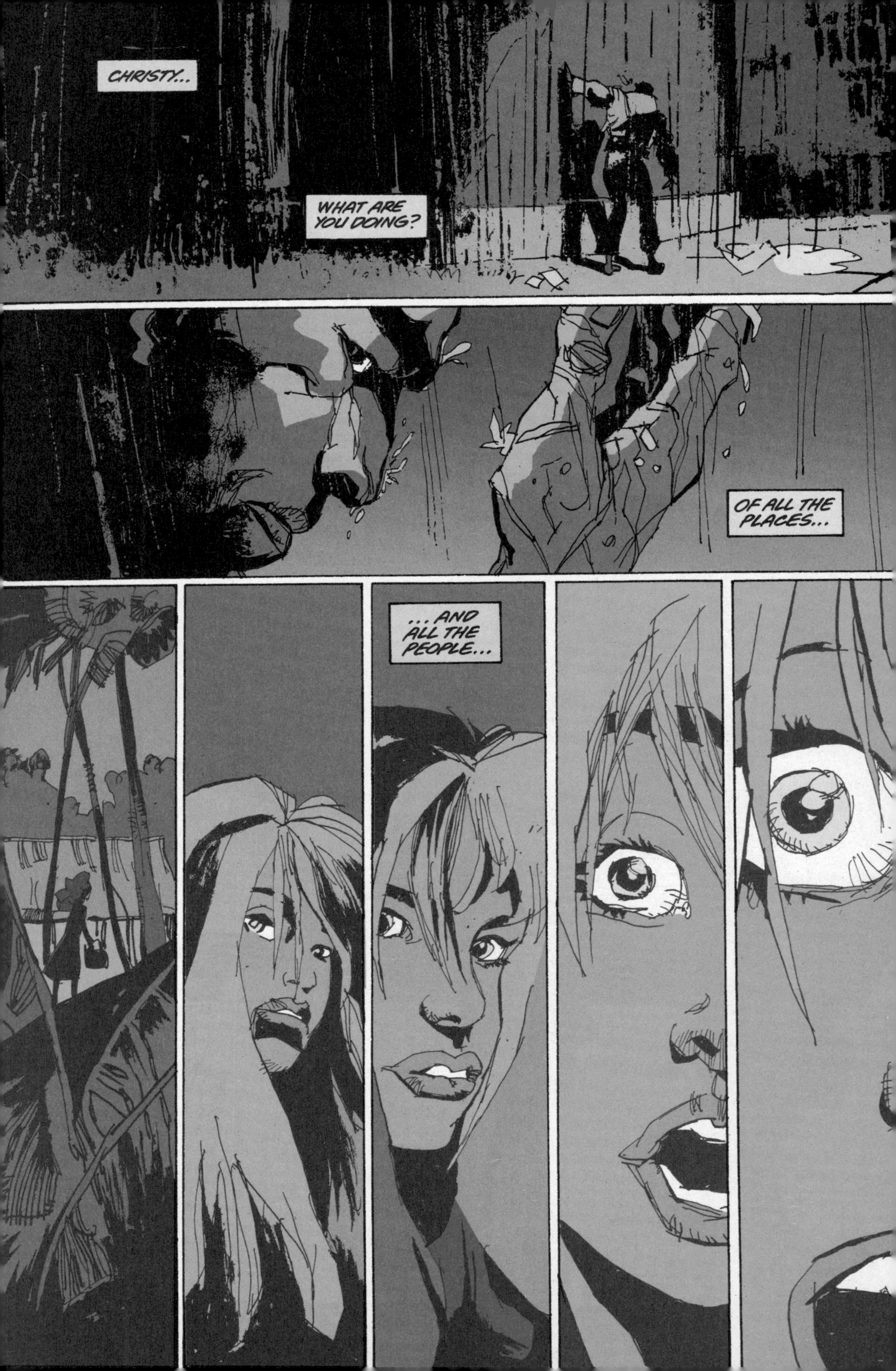
CHRISTY...
WHAT ARE YOU DOING?
OF ALL THE PLACES...
...AND ALL THE PEOPLE...

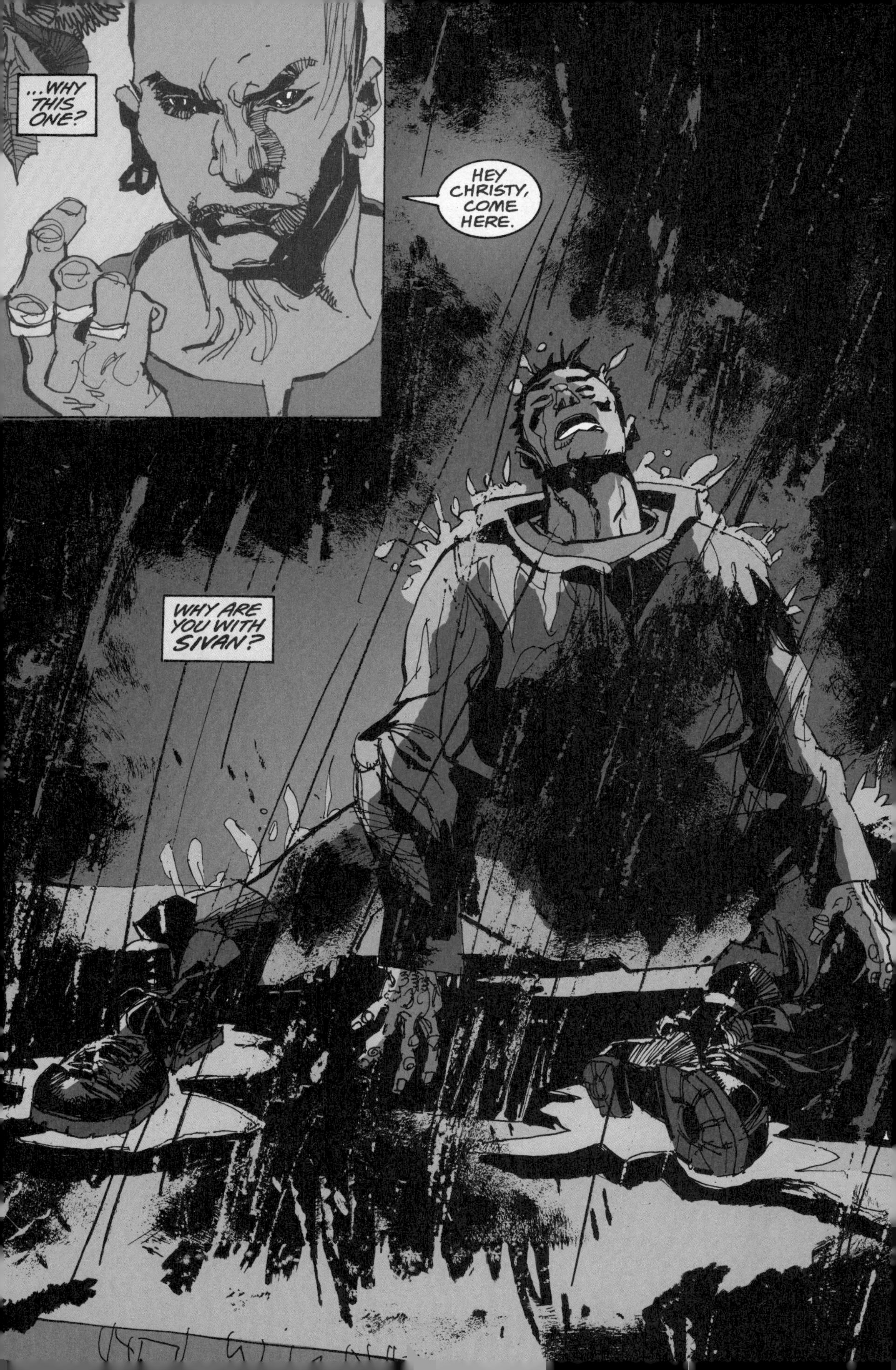
...WHY THIS ONE?
HEY CHRISTY, COME HERE.
WHY ARE YOU WITH SIVAN?

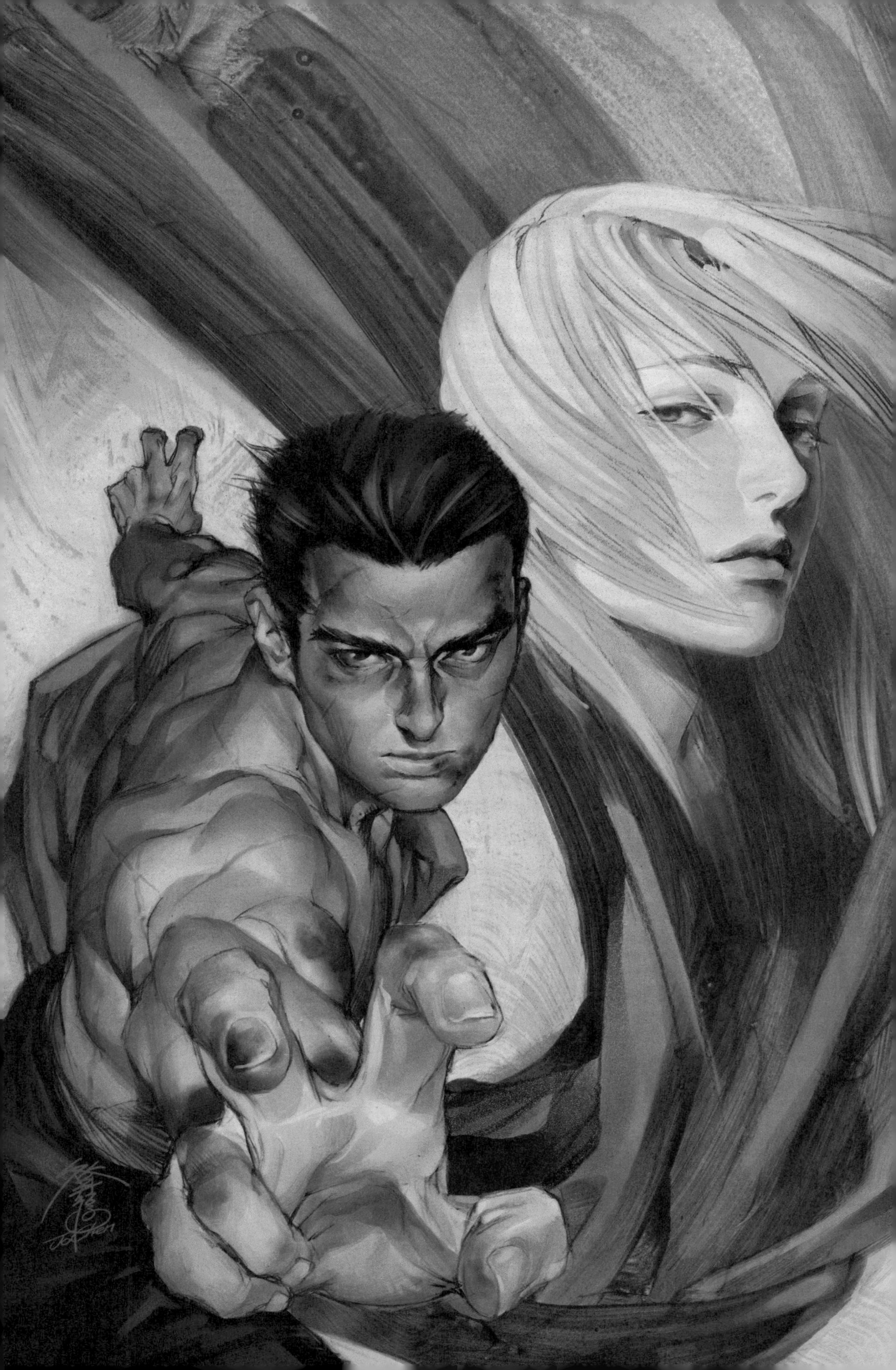

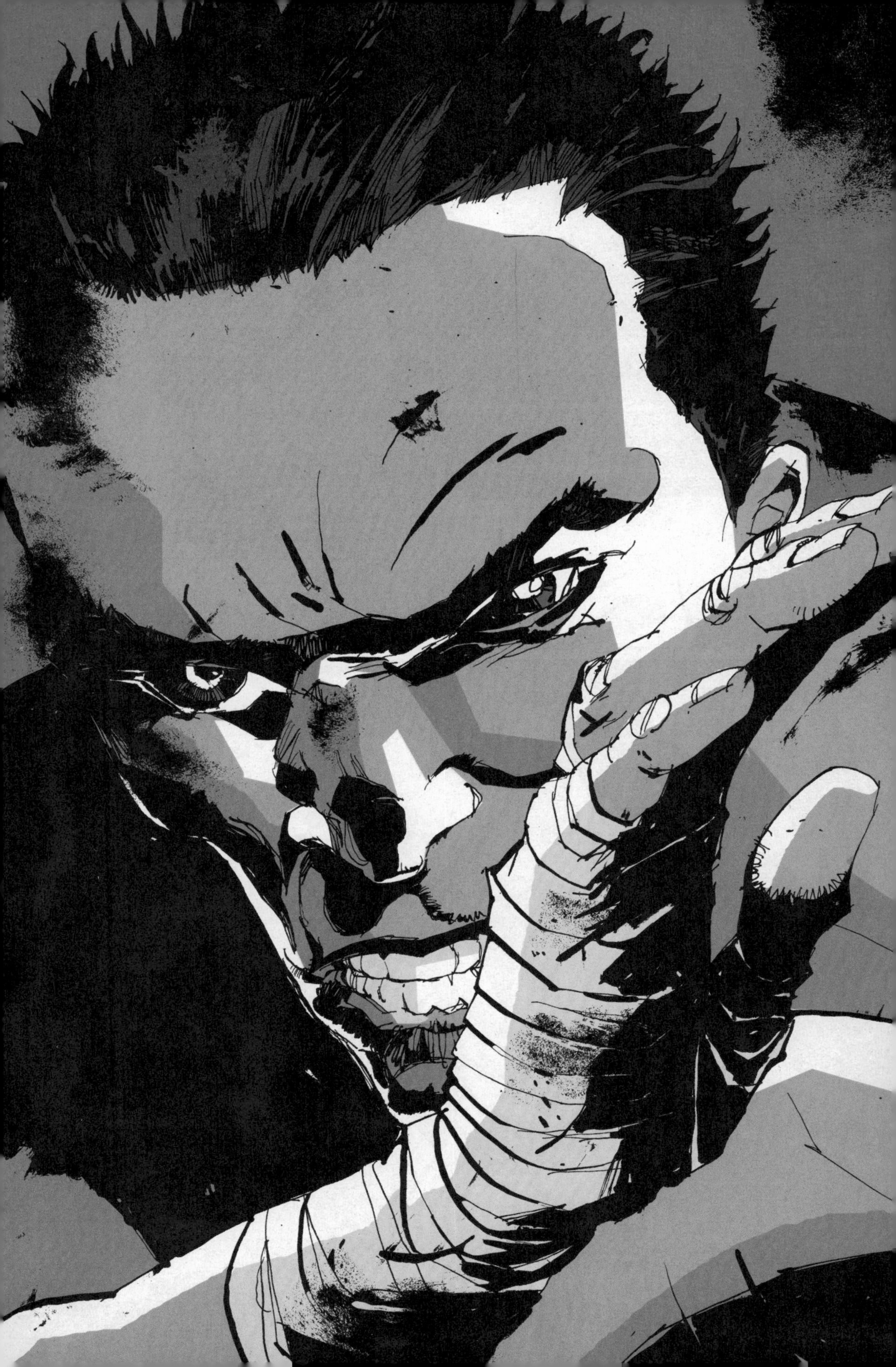

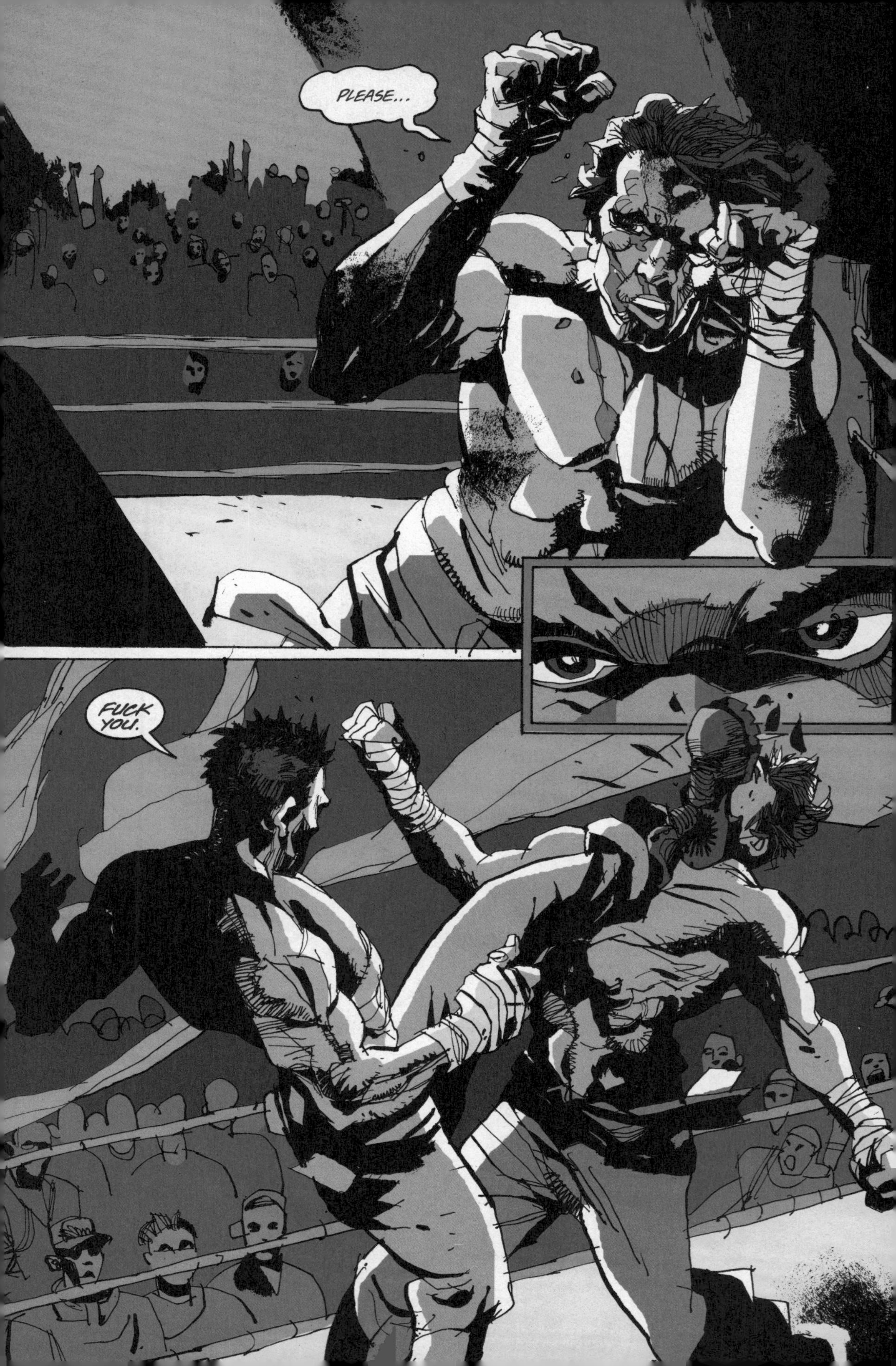
PLEASE...
FUCK YOU.

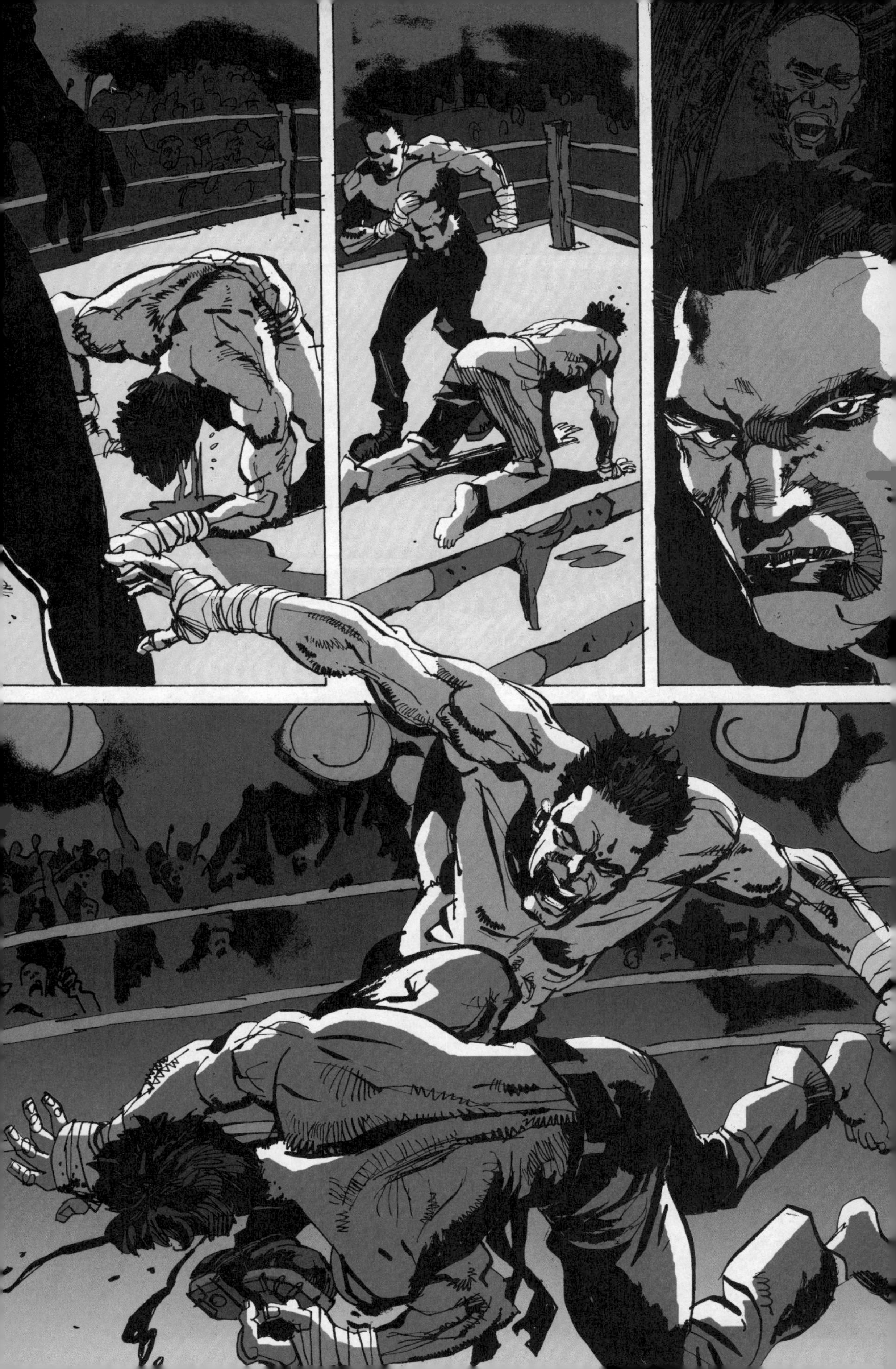

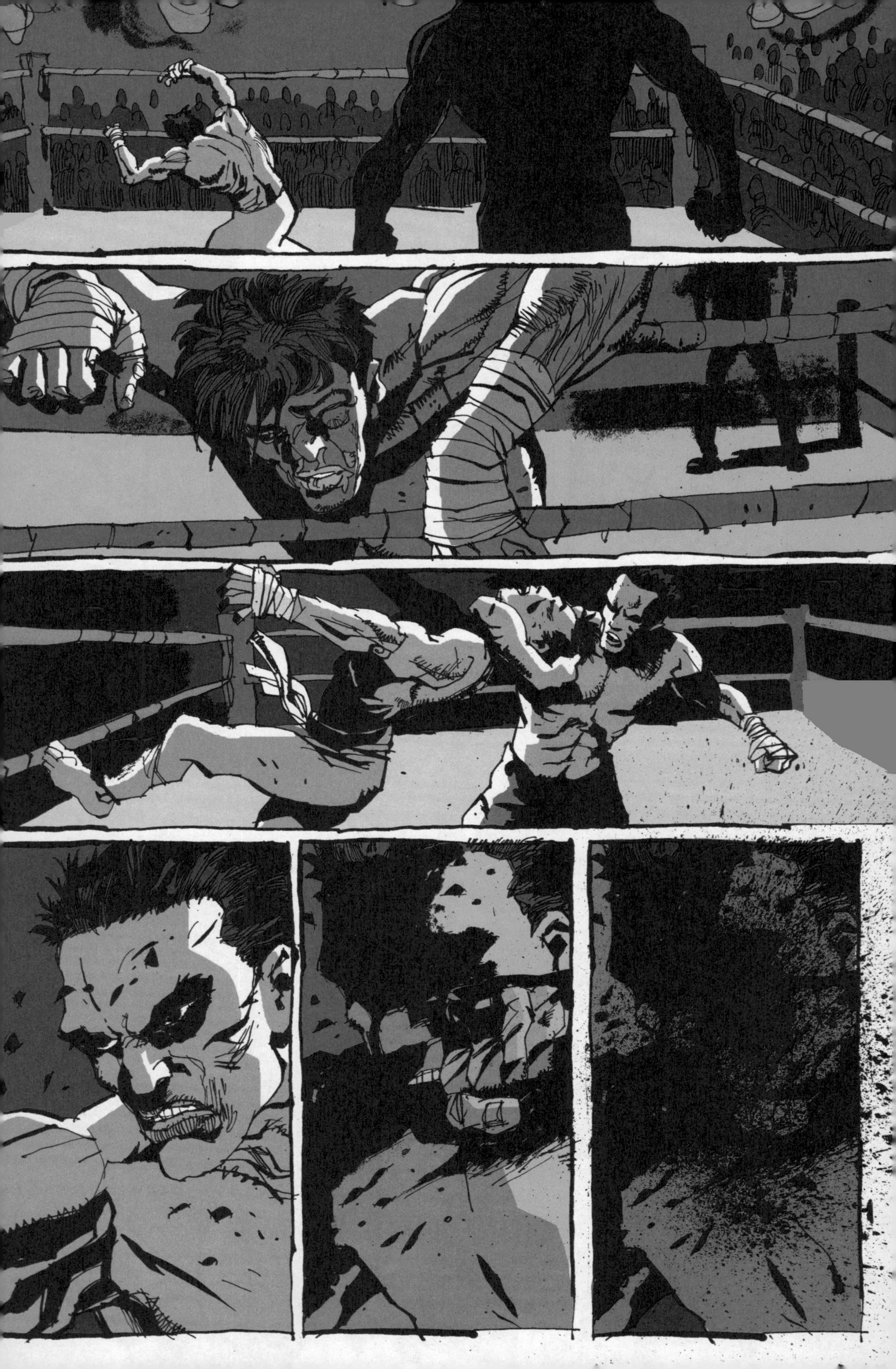

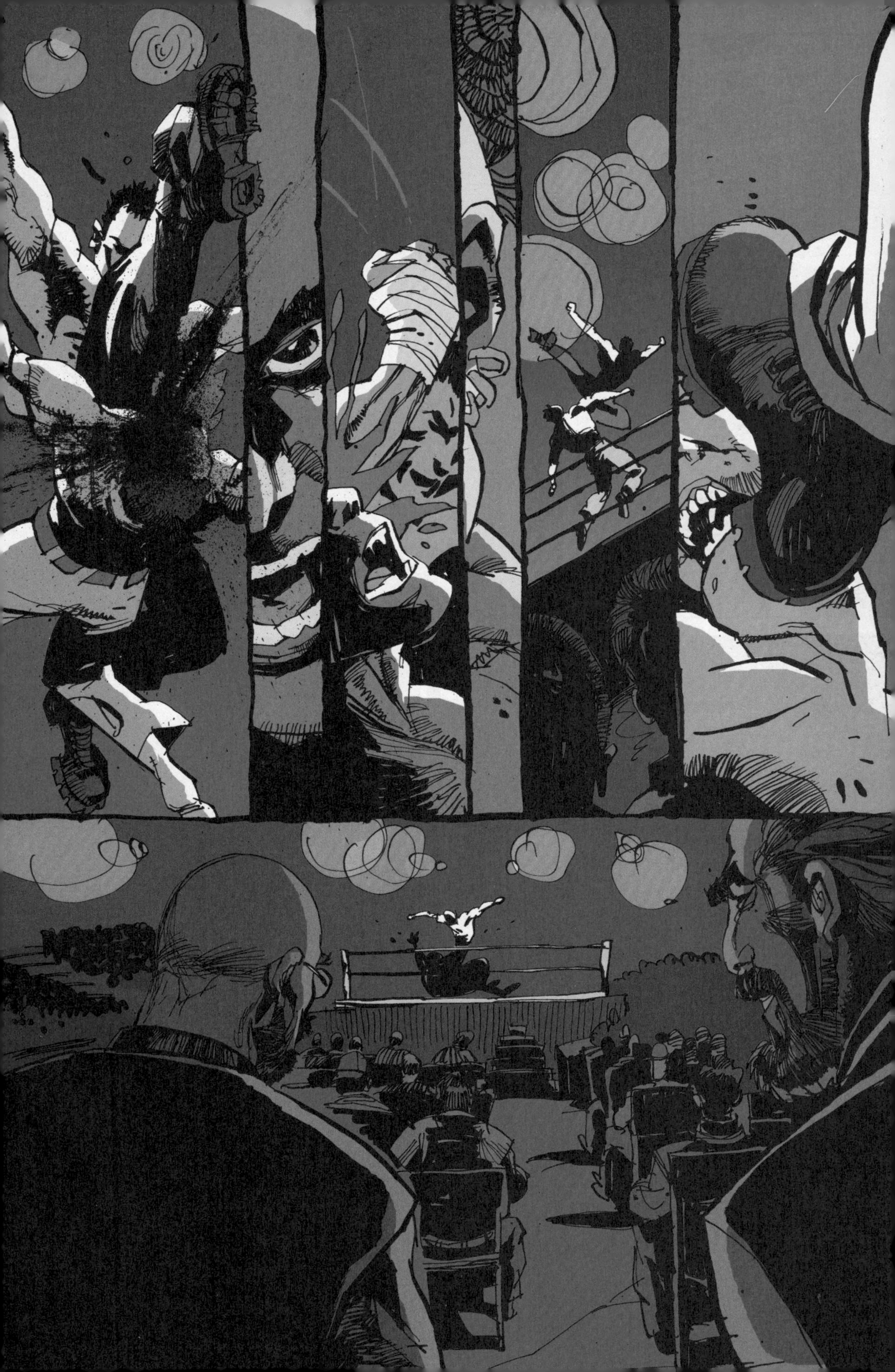

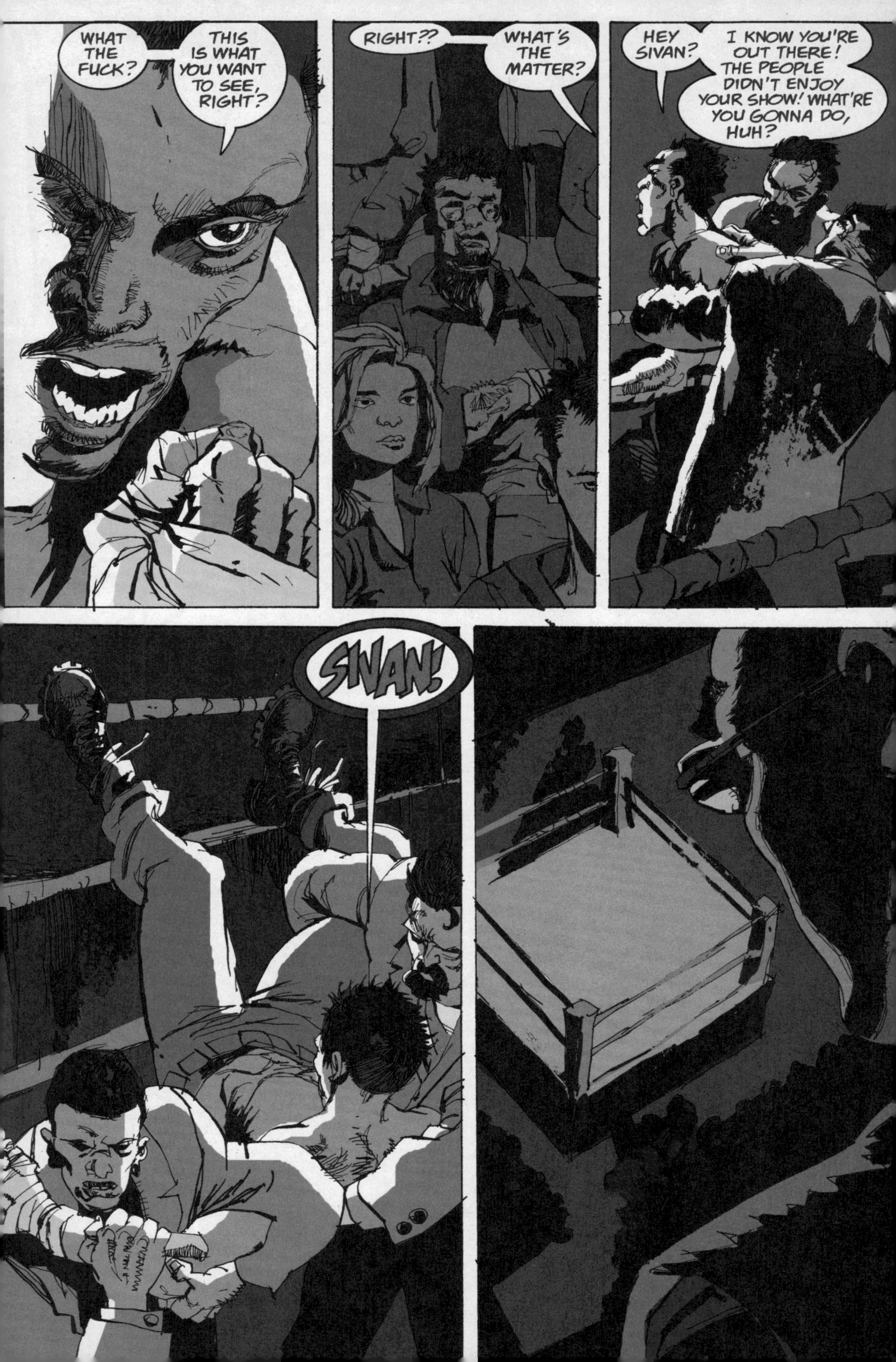
WHAT THE FUCK?
THIS IS WHAT YOU WANT TO SEE, RIGHT?
RIGHT??
WHAT'S THE MATTER?
HEY SIVAN?
I KNOW YOU'RE OUT THERE! THE PEOPLE DIDN'T ENJOY YOUR SHOW! WHAT'RE YOU GONNA DO, HUH?
SIVAN!

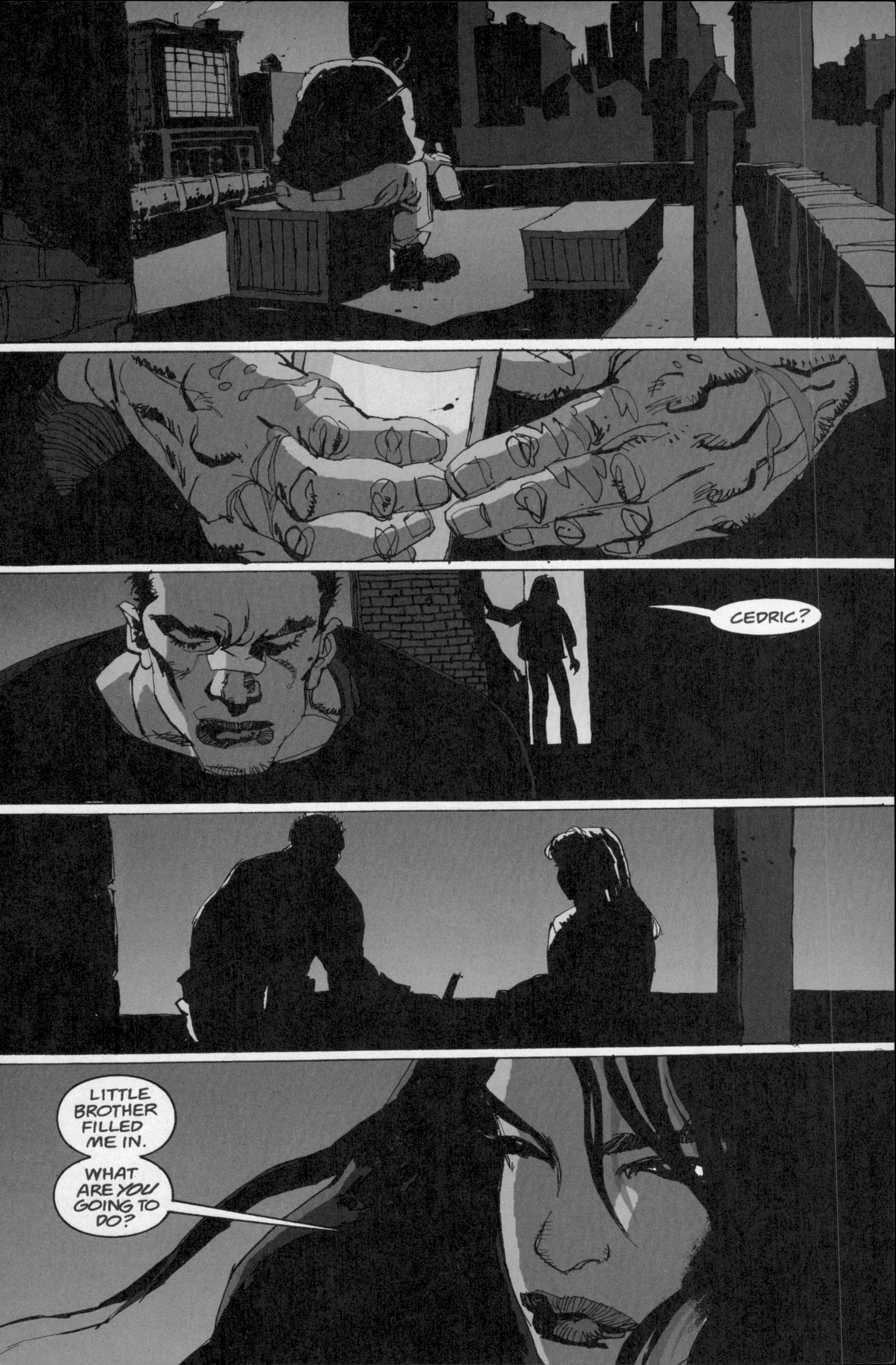
CEDRIC?
LITTLE BROTHER FILLED ME IN.
WHAT ARE YOU GOING TO DO?

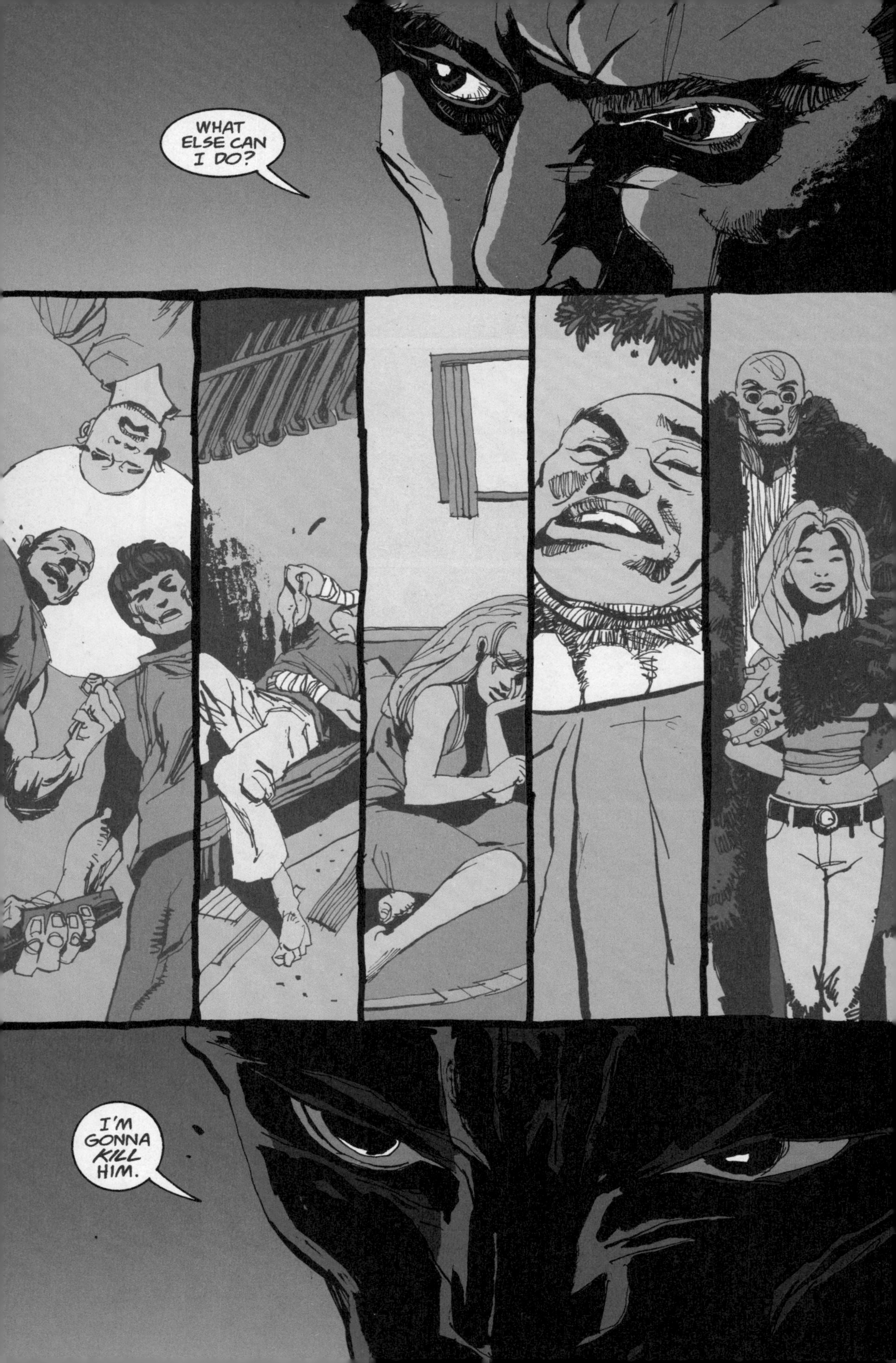
WHAT ELSE CAN I DO?
I'M GONNA KILL HIM.

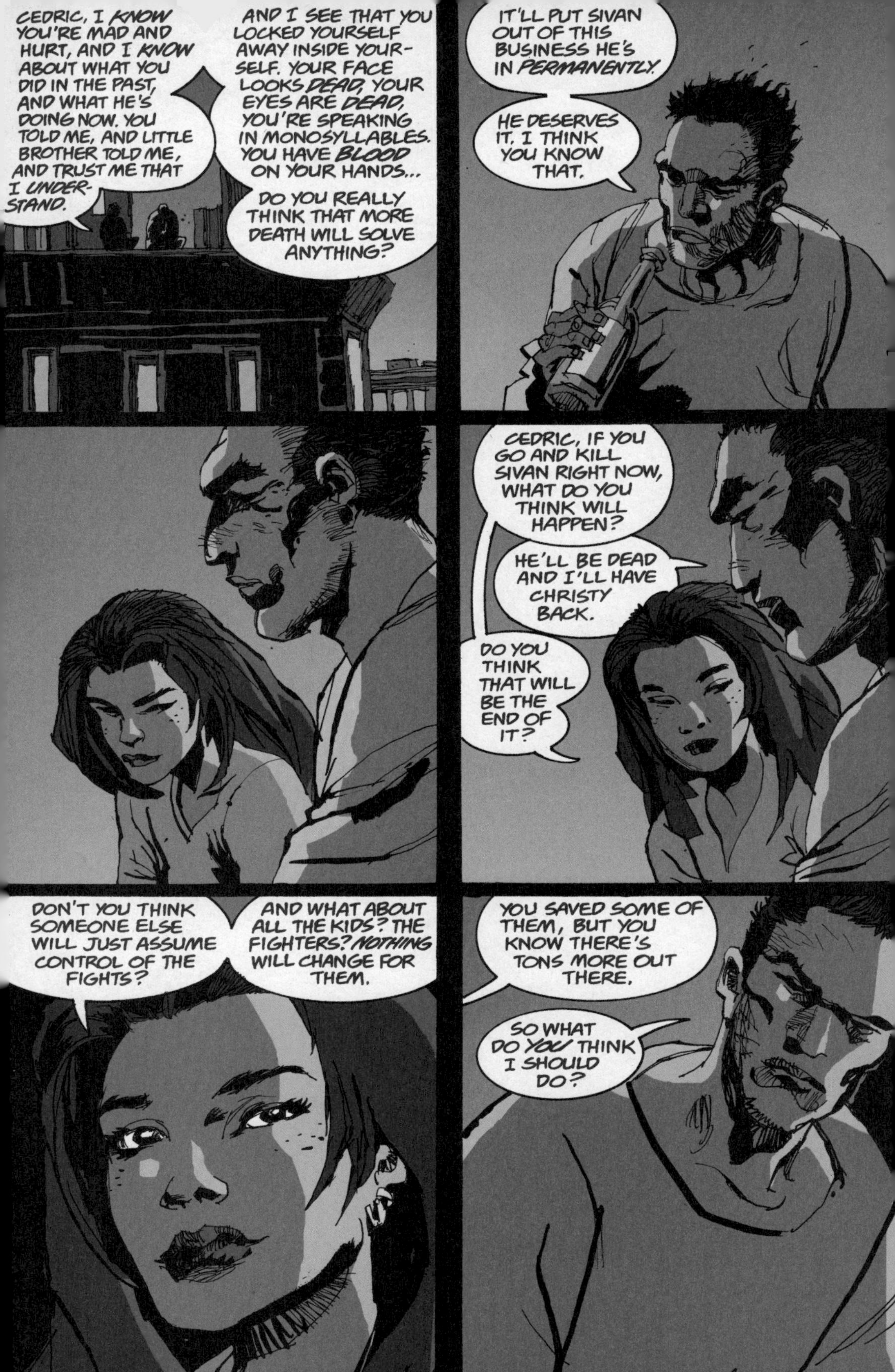
CEDRIC, I KNOW YOU'RE MAD AND HURT, AND I KNOW ABOUT WHAT YOU DID IN THE PAST, AND WHAT HE'S DOING NOW. YOU TOLD ME, AND LITTLE BROTHER TOLD ME, AND TRUST ME THAT I UNDERSTAND.
AND I SEE THAT YOU LOCKED YOURSELF AWAY INSIDE YOURSELF. YOUR FACE LOOKS DEAD, YOUR EYES ARE DEAD, YOU'RE SPEAKING IN MONOSYLLABLES. YOU HAVE BLOOD ON YOUR HANDS...
DO YOU REALLY THINK THAT MORE DEATH WILL SOLVE ANYTHING?
IT'LL PUT SIVAN OUT OF THIS BUSINESS HE'S IN PERMANENTLY.
HE DESERVES IT. I THINK YOU KNOW THAT.
CEDRIC, IF YOU GO AND KILL SIVAN RIGHT NOW, WHAT DO YOU THINK WILL HAPPEN?
HE'LL BE DEAD AND I'LL HAVE CHRISTY BACK.
DO YOU THINK THAT WILL BE THE END OF IT?
DON'T YOU THINK SOMEONE ELSE WILL JUST ASSUME CONTROL OF THE FIGHTS?
AND WHAT ABOUT ALL THE KIDS? THE FIGHTERS? NOTHING WILL CHANGE FOR THEM.
YOU SAVED SOME OF THEM, BUT YOU KNOW THERE'S TONS MORE OUT THERE.
SO WHAT DO YOU THINK I SHOULD DO?

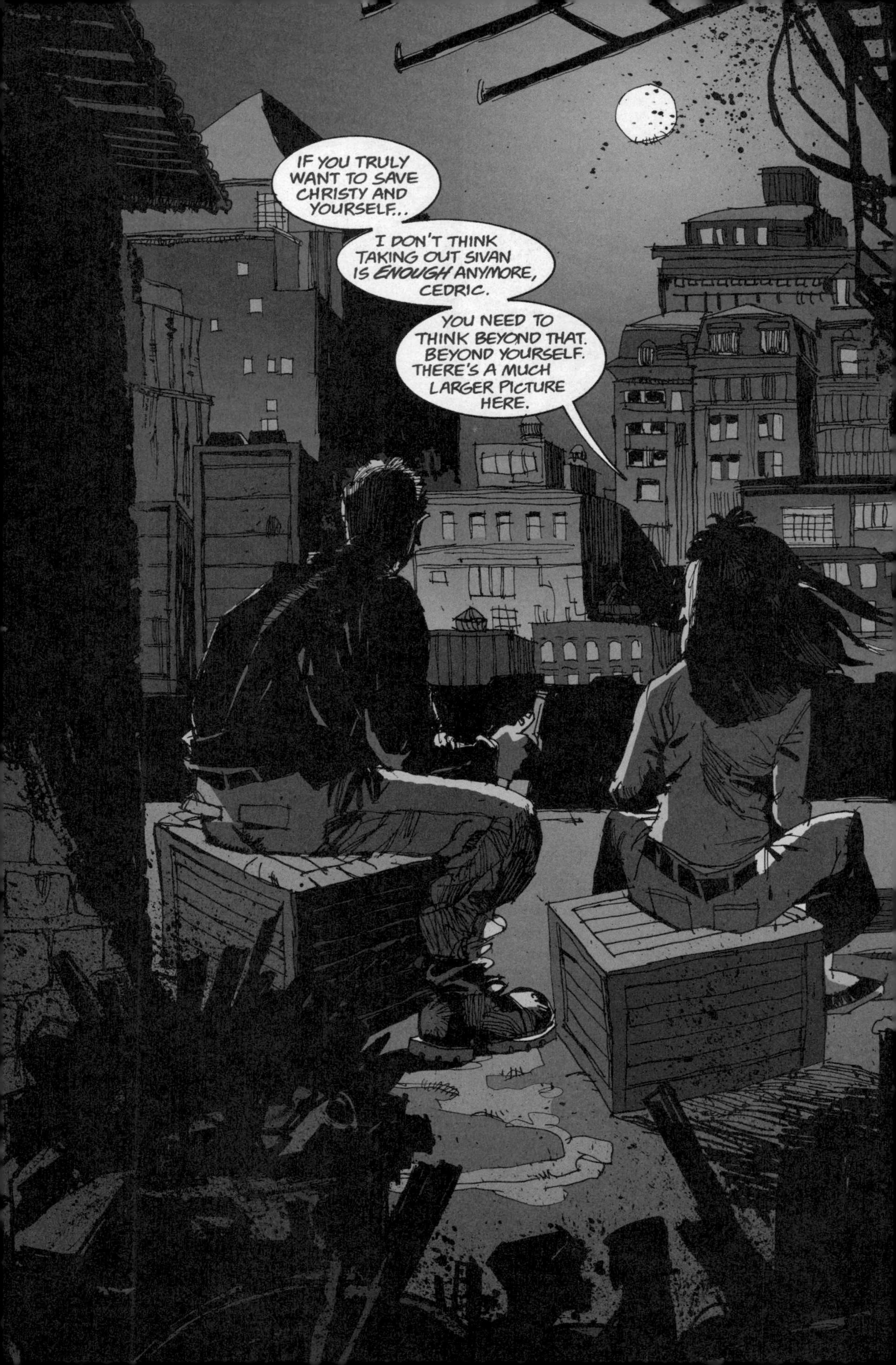
IF YOU TRULY WANT TO SAVE CHRISTY AND YOURSELF...
I DON'T THINK TAKING OUT SIVAN IS *ENOUGH* ANYMORE, CEDRIC.
YOU NEED TO THINK BEYOND THAT. BEYOND YOURSELF. THERE'S A MUCH LARGER PICTURE HERE.

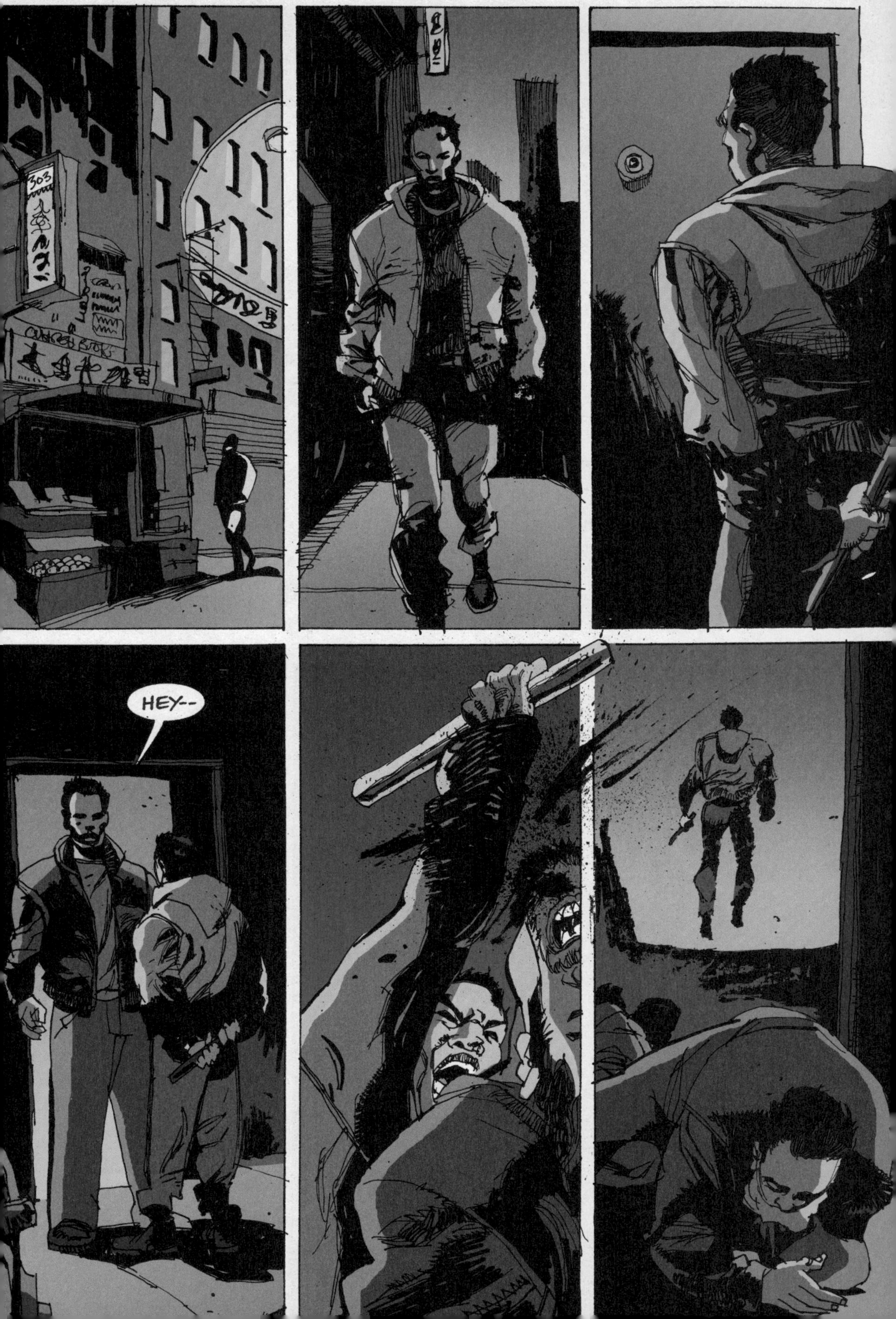
HEY--

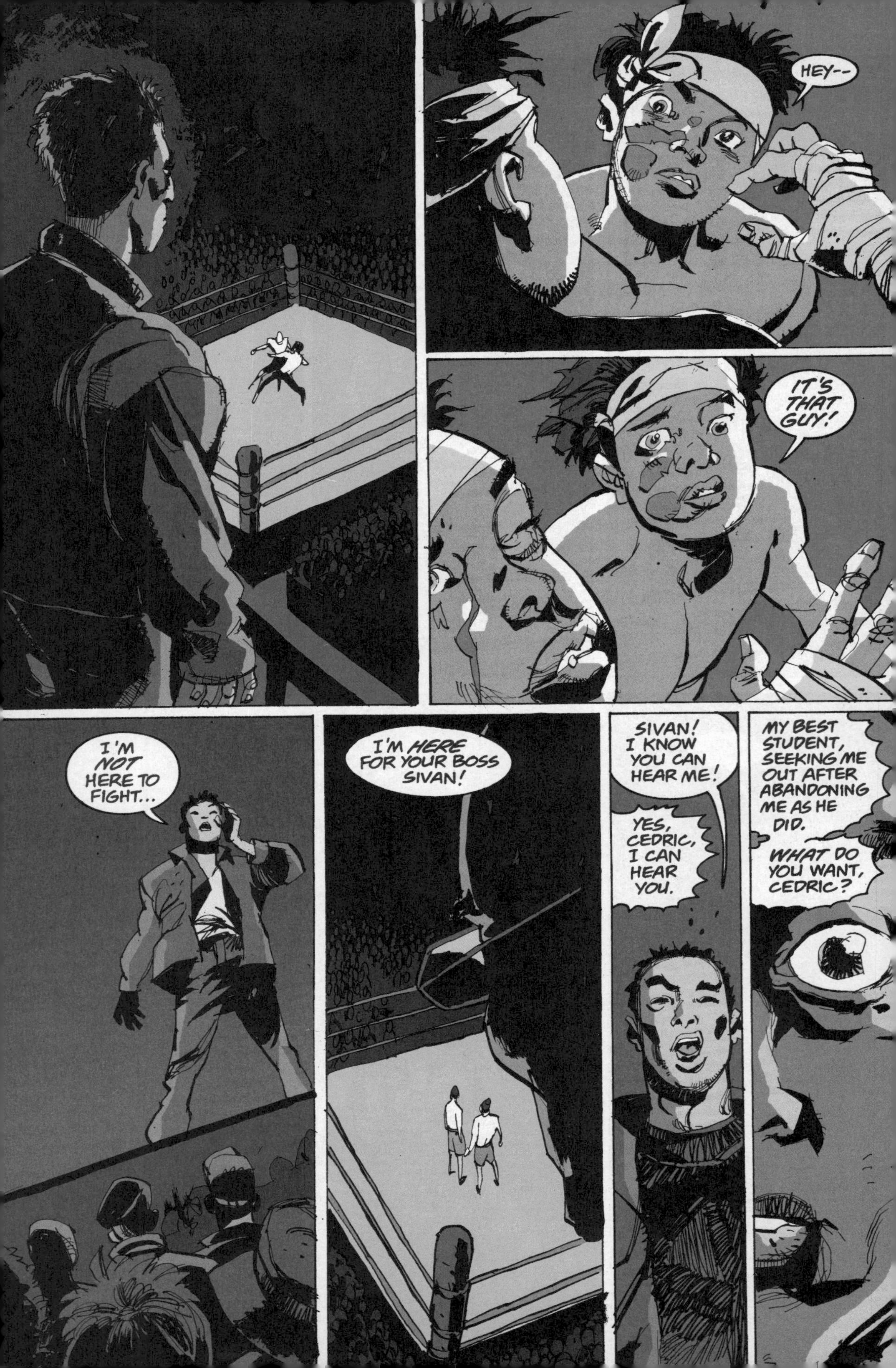
HEY--
IT'S THAT GUY!
I'M NOT HERE TO FIGHT...
I'M HERE FOR YOUR BOSS SIVAN!
SIVAN! I KNOW YOU CAN HEAR ME!
YES, CEDRIC, I CAN HEAR YOU.
MY BEST STUDENT, SEEKING ME OUT AFTER ABANDONING ME AS HE DID.
WHAT DO YOU WANT, CEDRIC?

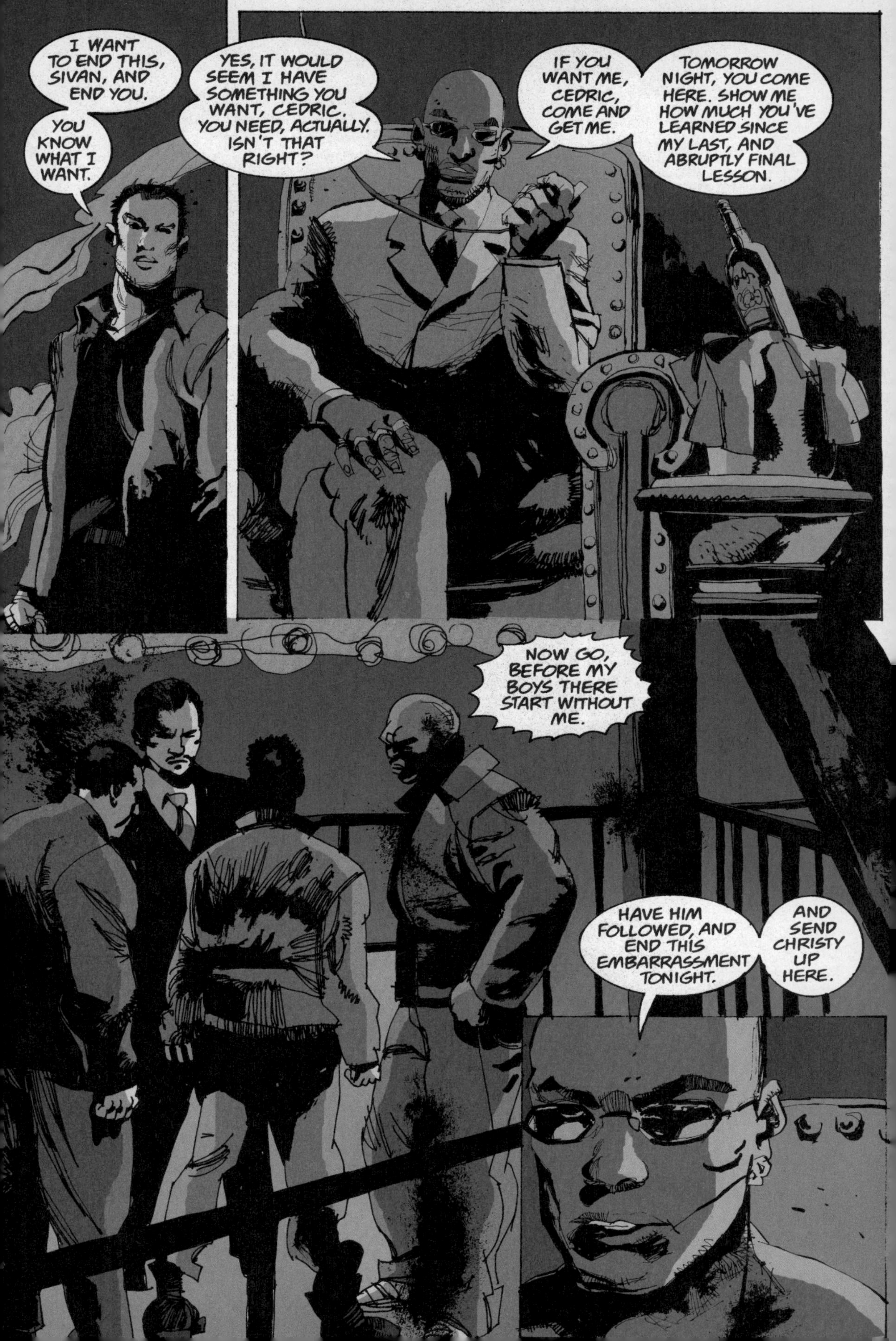
I WANT TO END THIS, SIVAN, AND END YOU.
YOU KNOW WHAT I WANT.
YES, IT WOULD SEEM I HAVE SOMETHING YOU WANT, CEDRIC. YOU NEED, ACTUALLY. ISN'T THAT RIGHT?
IF YOU WANT ME, CEDRIC, COME AND GET ME.
TOMORROW NIGHT, YOU COME HERE. SHOW ME HOW MUCH YOU'VE LEARNED SINCE MY LAST, AND ABRUPTLY FINAL LESSON.
NOW GO, BEFORE MY BOYS THERE START WITHOUT ME.
HAVE HIM FOLLOWED, AND END THIS EMBARRASSMENT TONIGHT.
AND SEND CHRISTY UP HERE.

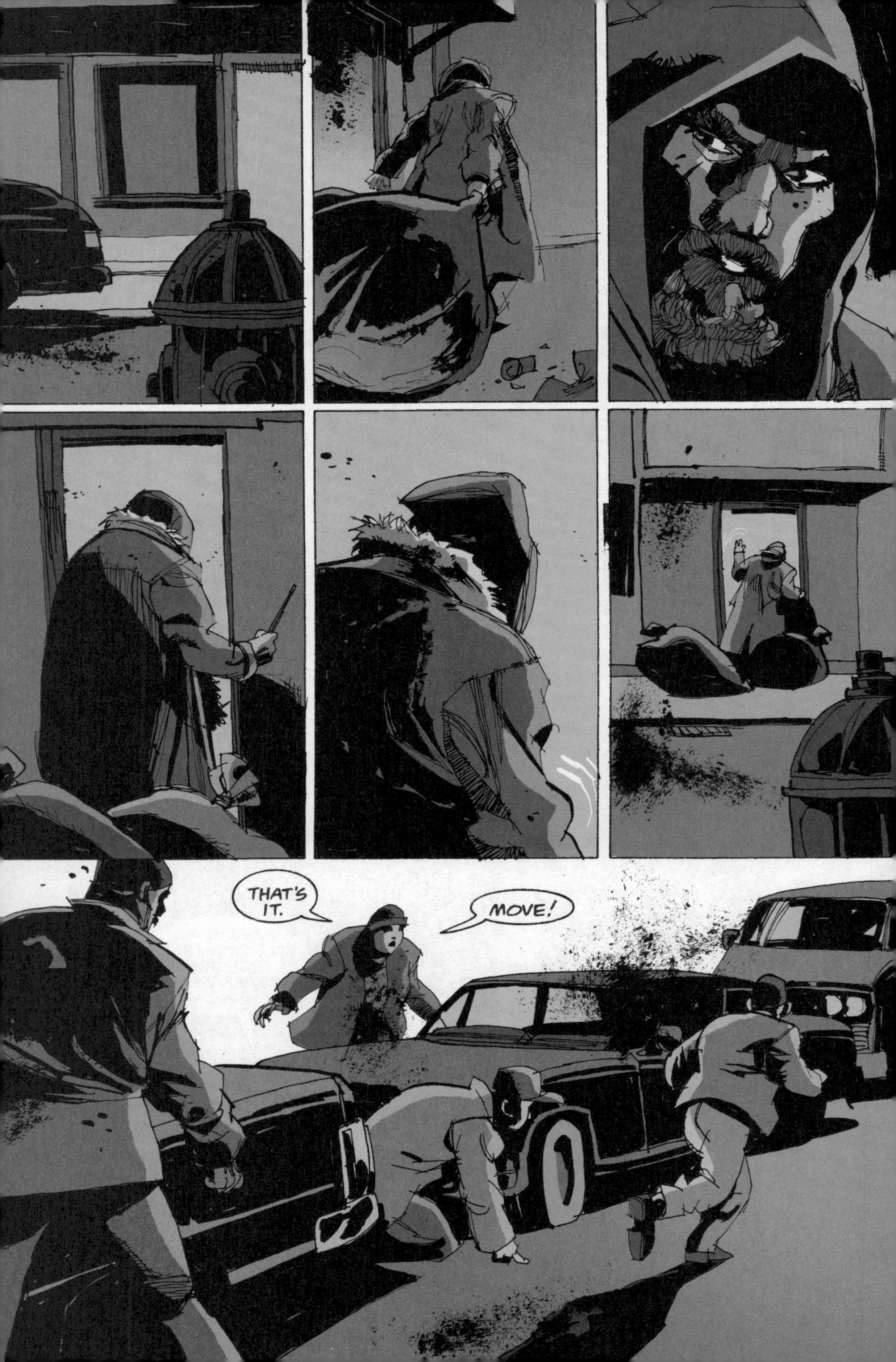
THAT'S IT.
MOVE!

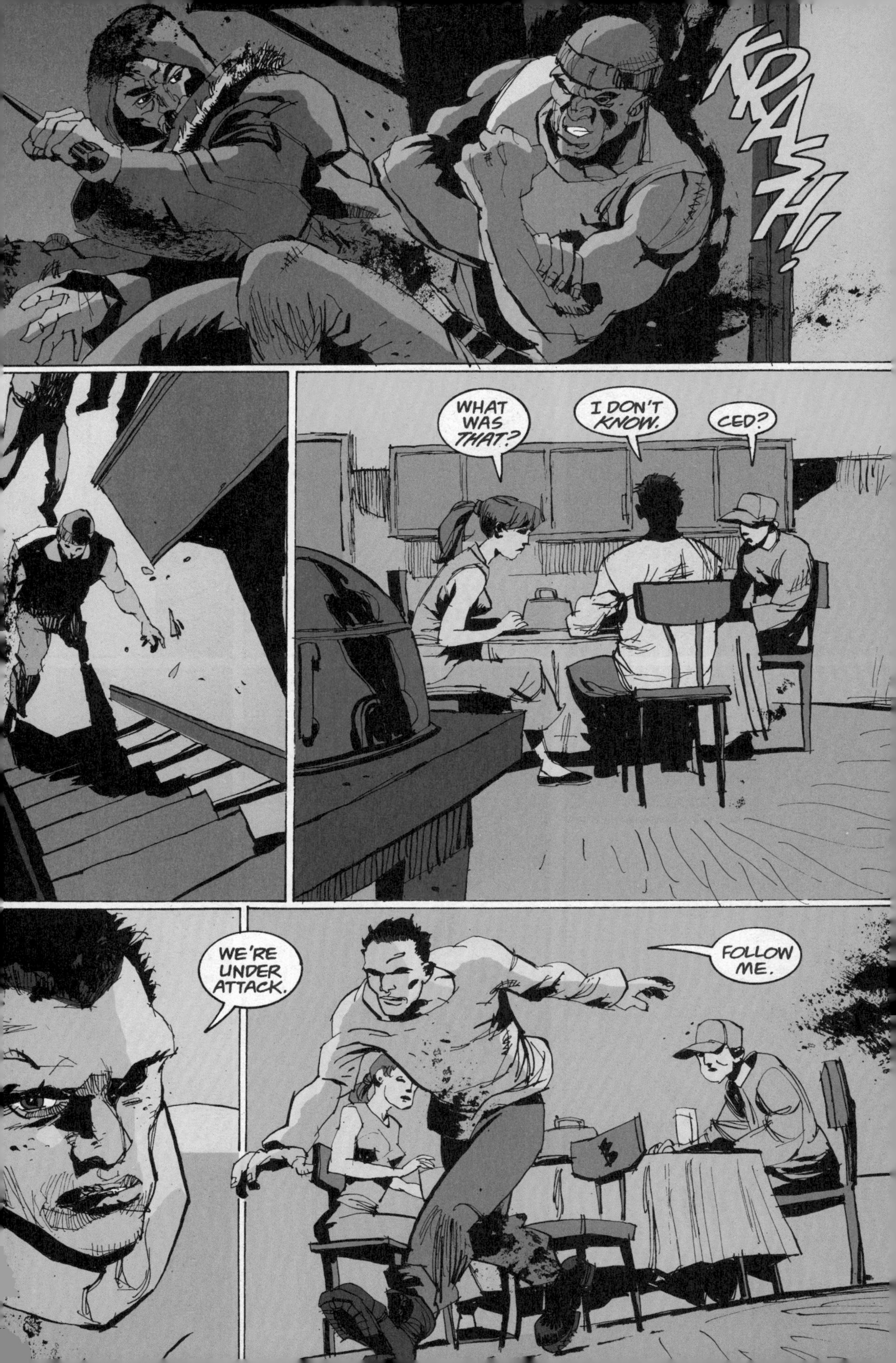
KRASH!!
WHAT WAS THAT?
I DON'T KNOW.
CED?
WE'RE UNDER ATTACK.
FOLLOW ME.

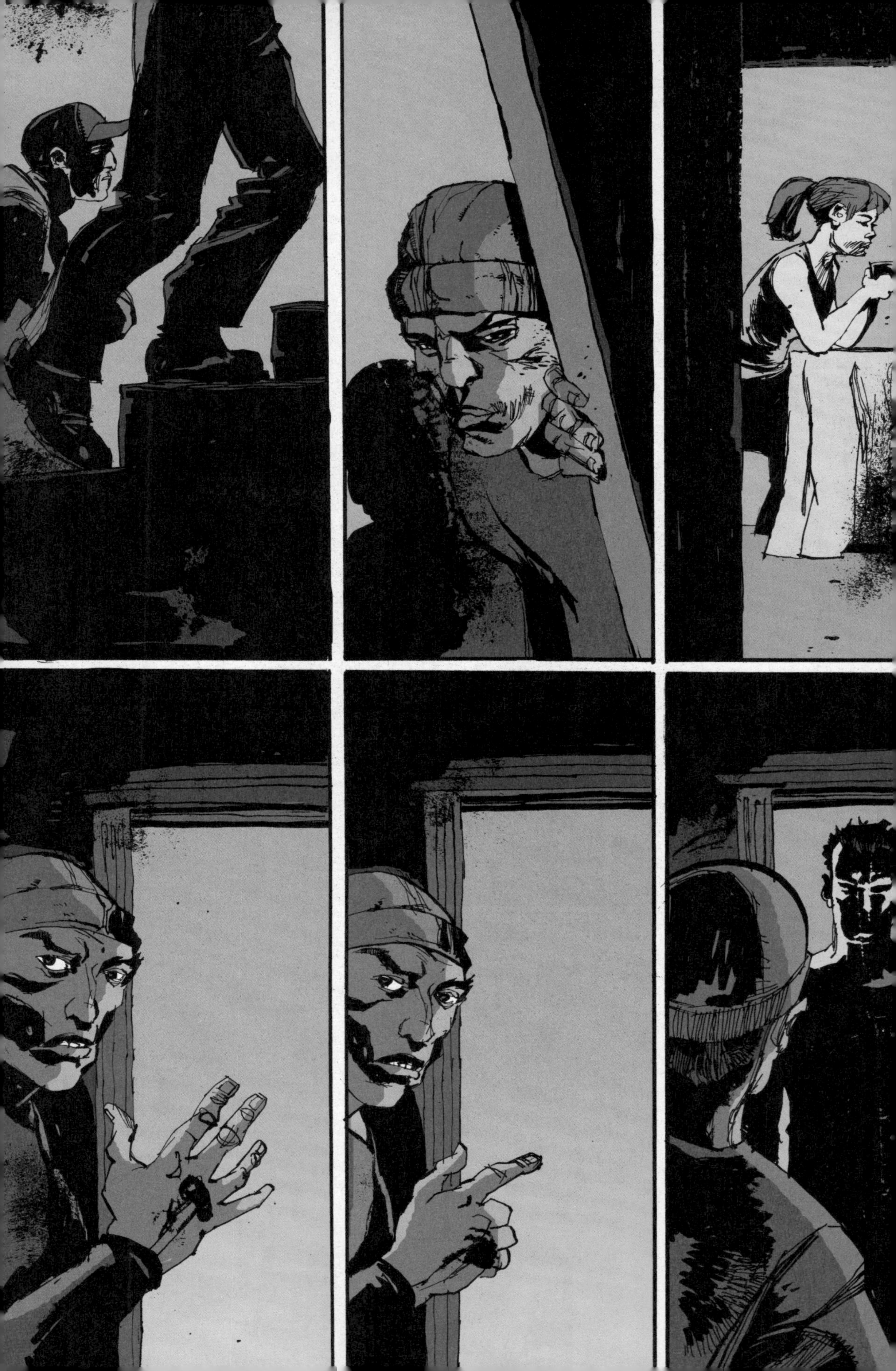

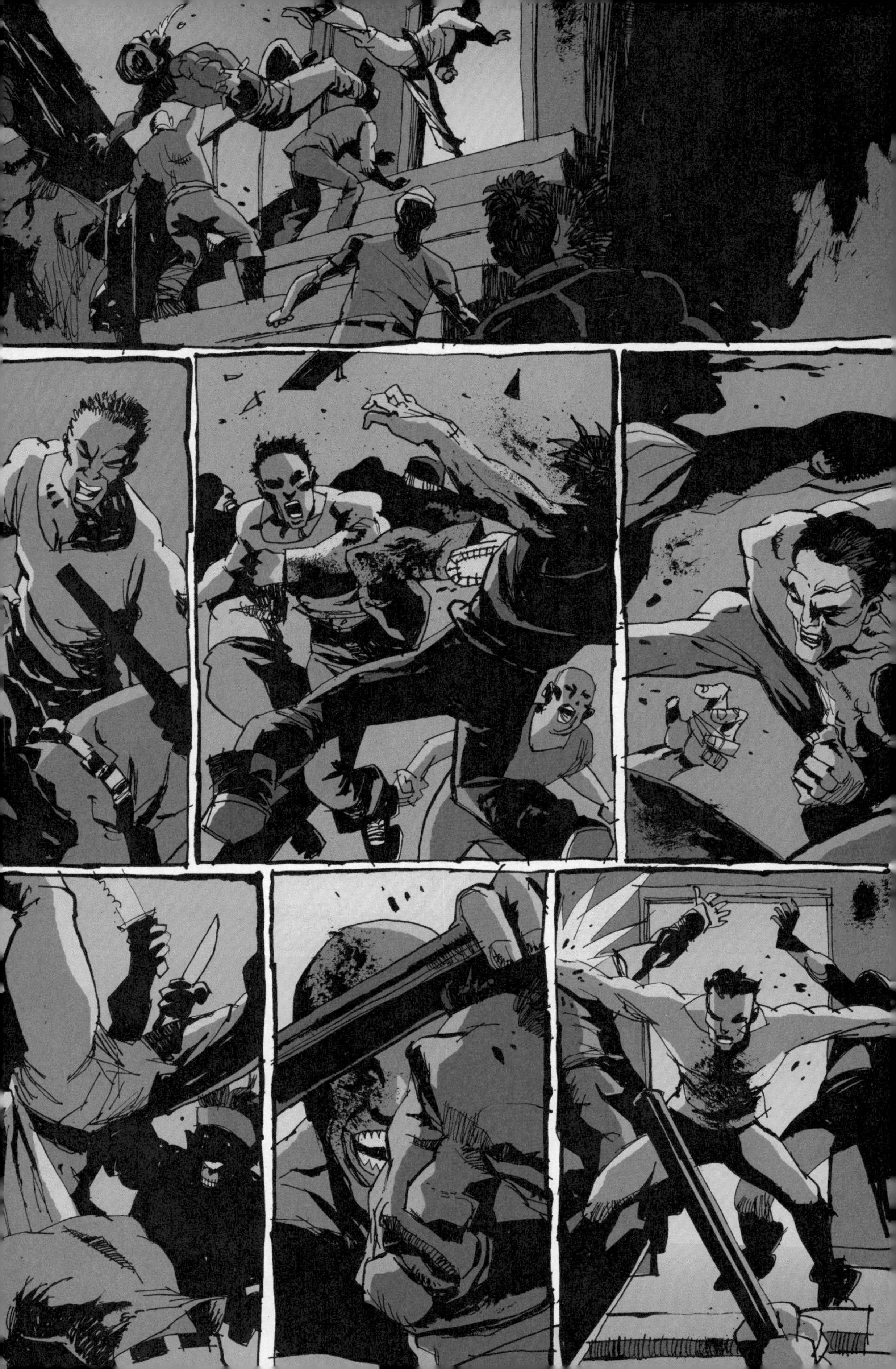

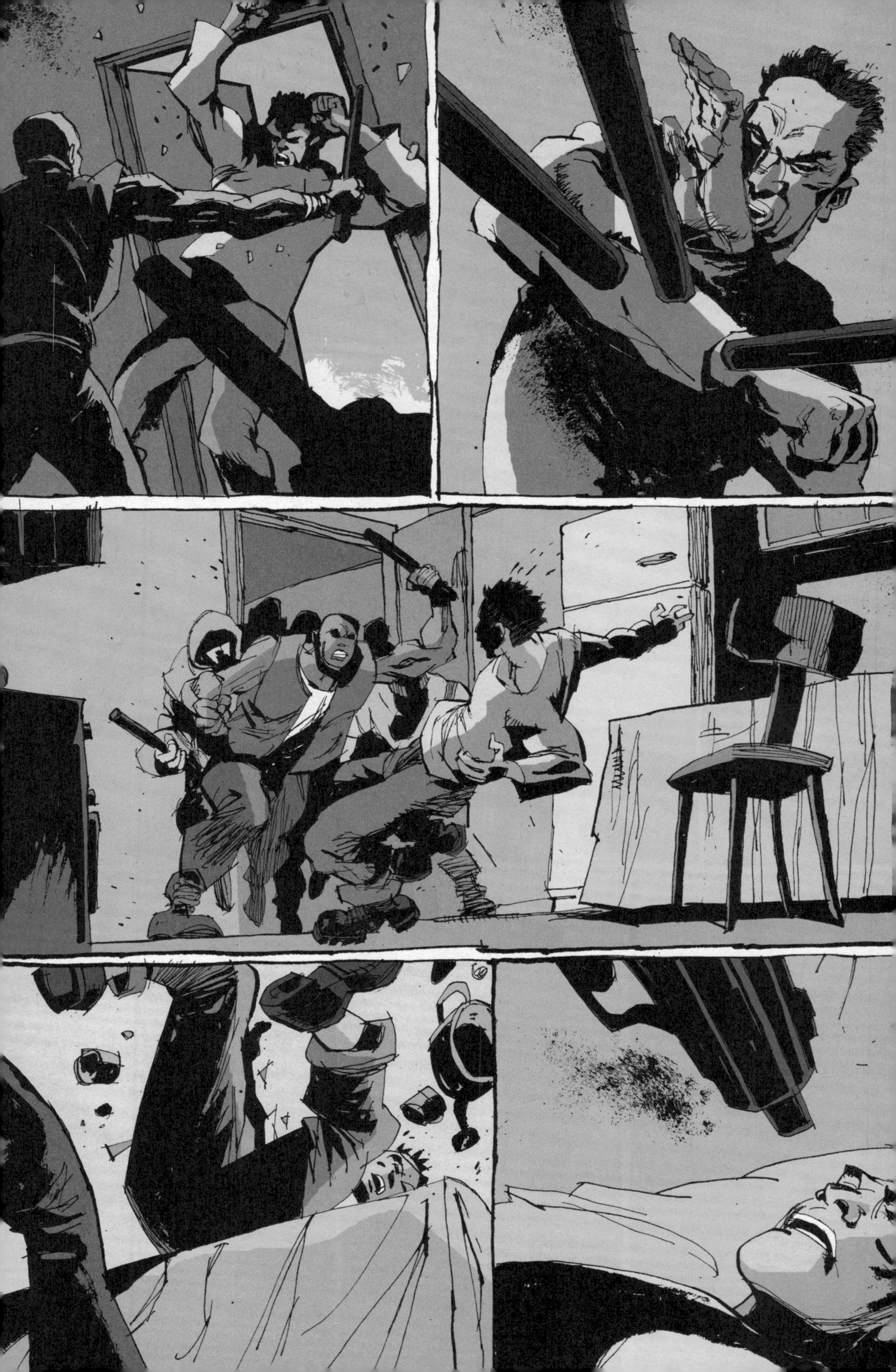

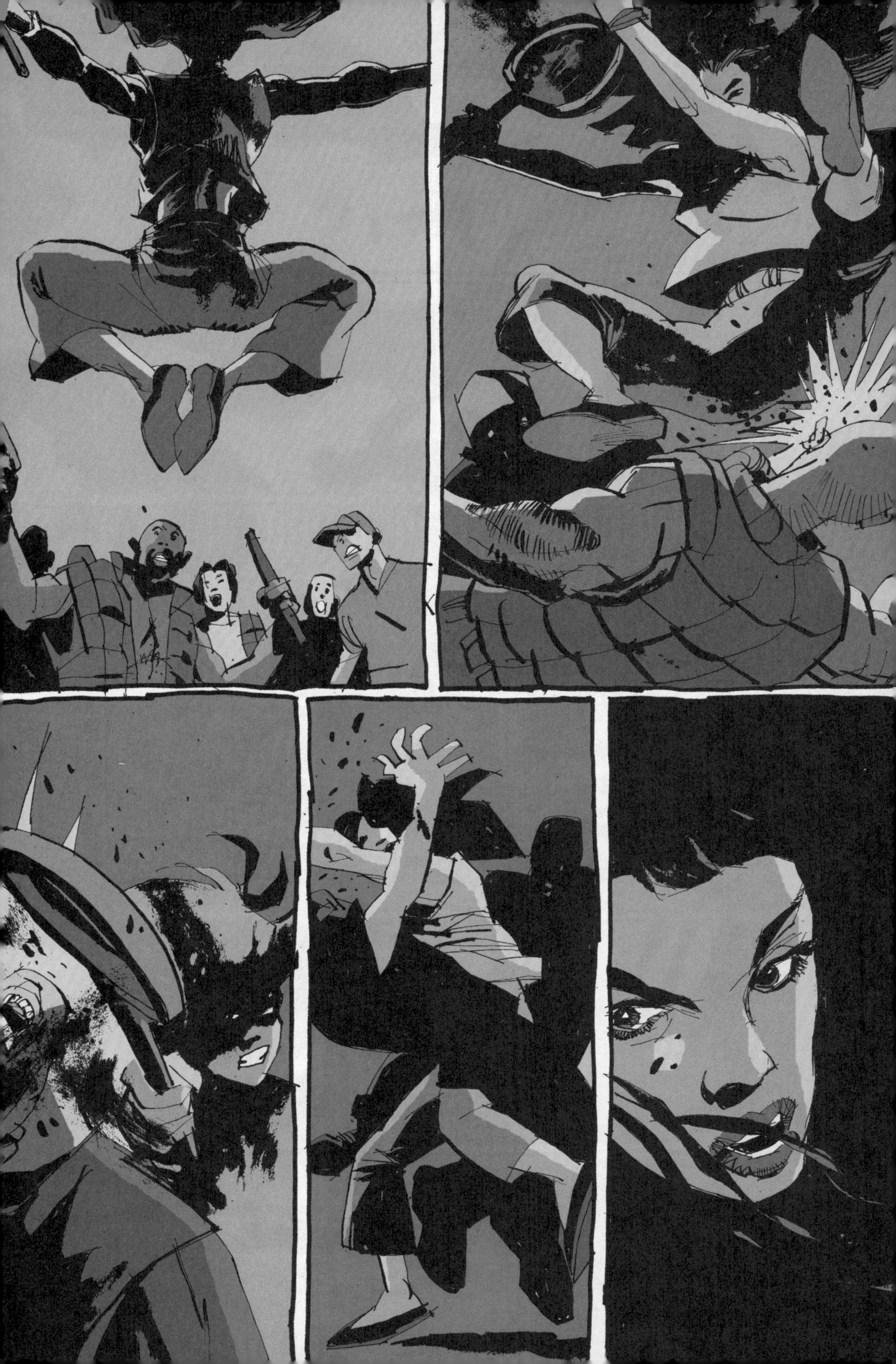

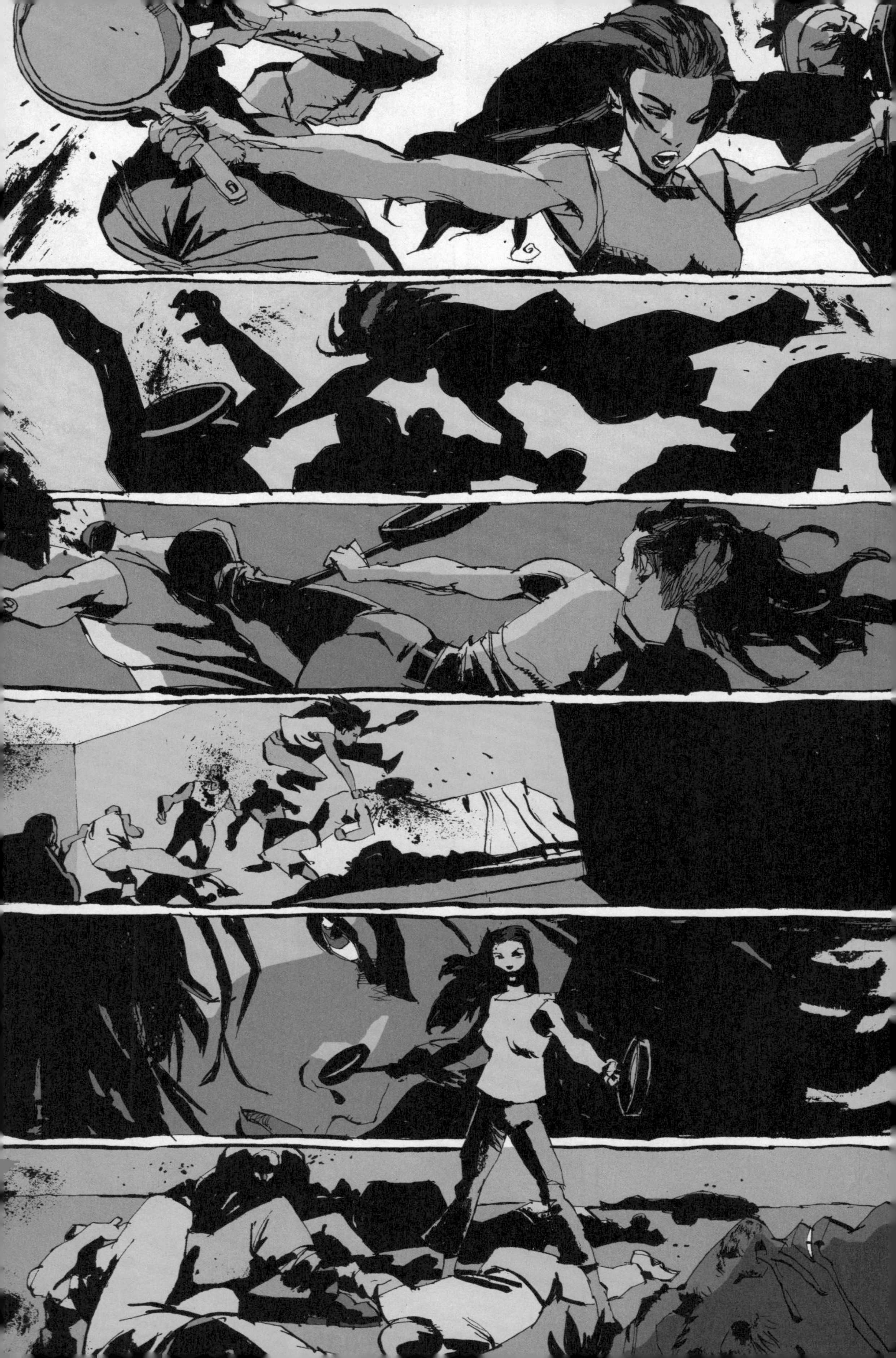

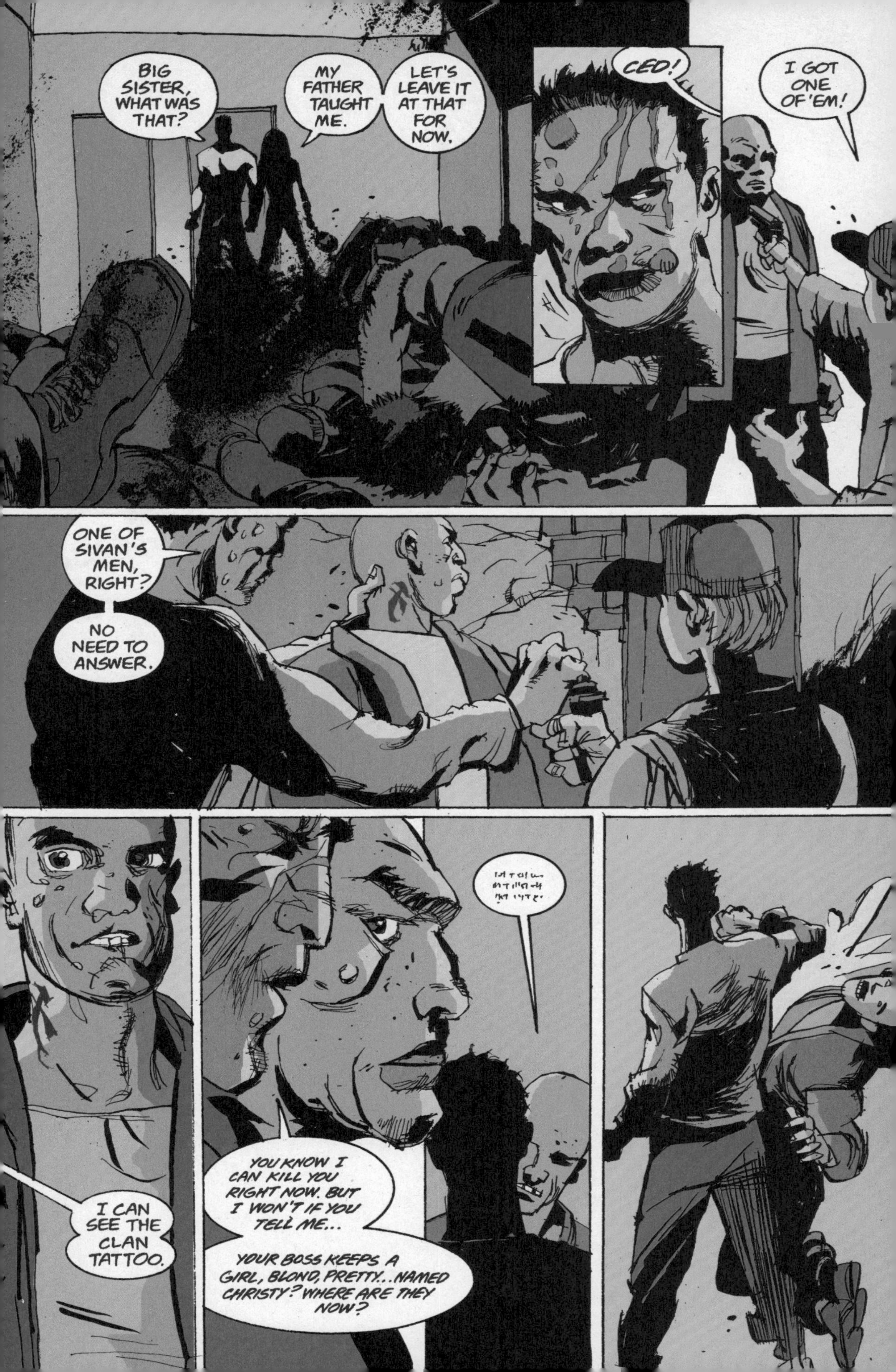
BIG SISTER, WHAT WAS THAT?
MY FATHER TAUGHT ME.
LET'S LEAVE IT AT THAT FOR NOW.
CED!
I GOT ONE OF 'EM!
ONE OF SIVAN'S MEN, RIGHT?
NO NEED TO ANSWER.
I CAN SEE THE CLAN TATTOO.
YOU KNOW I CAN KILL YOU RIGHT NOW. BUT I WON'T IF YOU TELL ME...
YOUR BOSS KEEPS A GIRL, BLOND, PRETTY... NAMED CHRISTY? WHERE ARE THEY NOW?

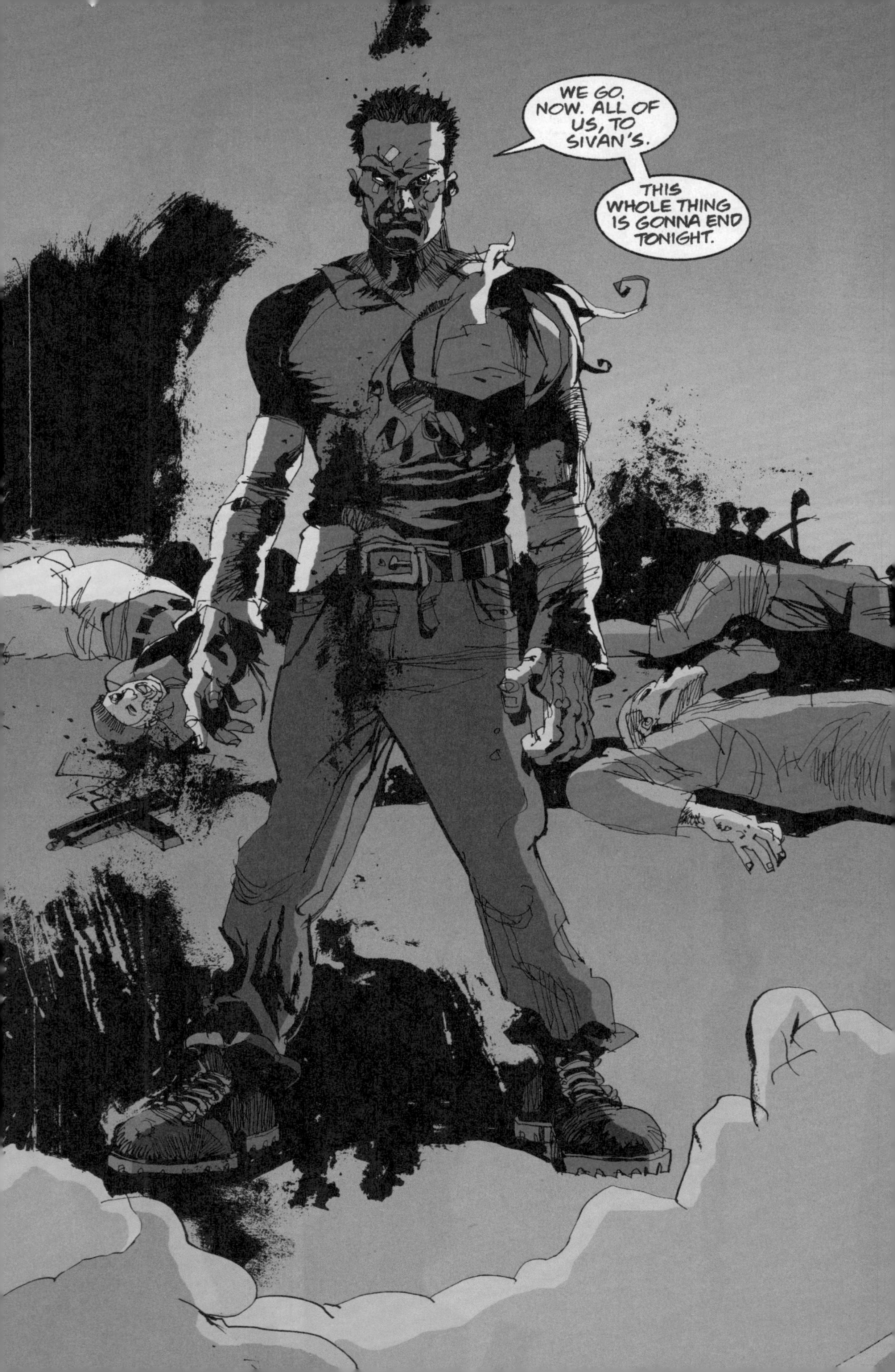
WE GO. NOW. ALL OF US, TO SIVAN'S.
THIS WHOLE THING IS GONNA END TONIGHT.

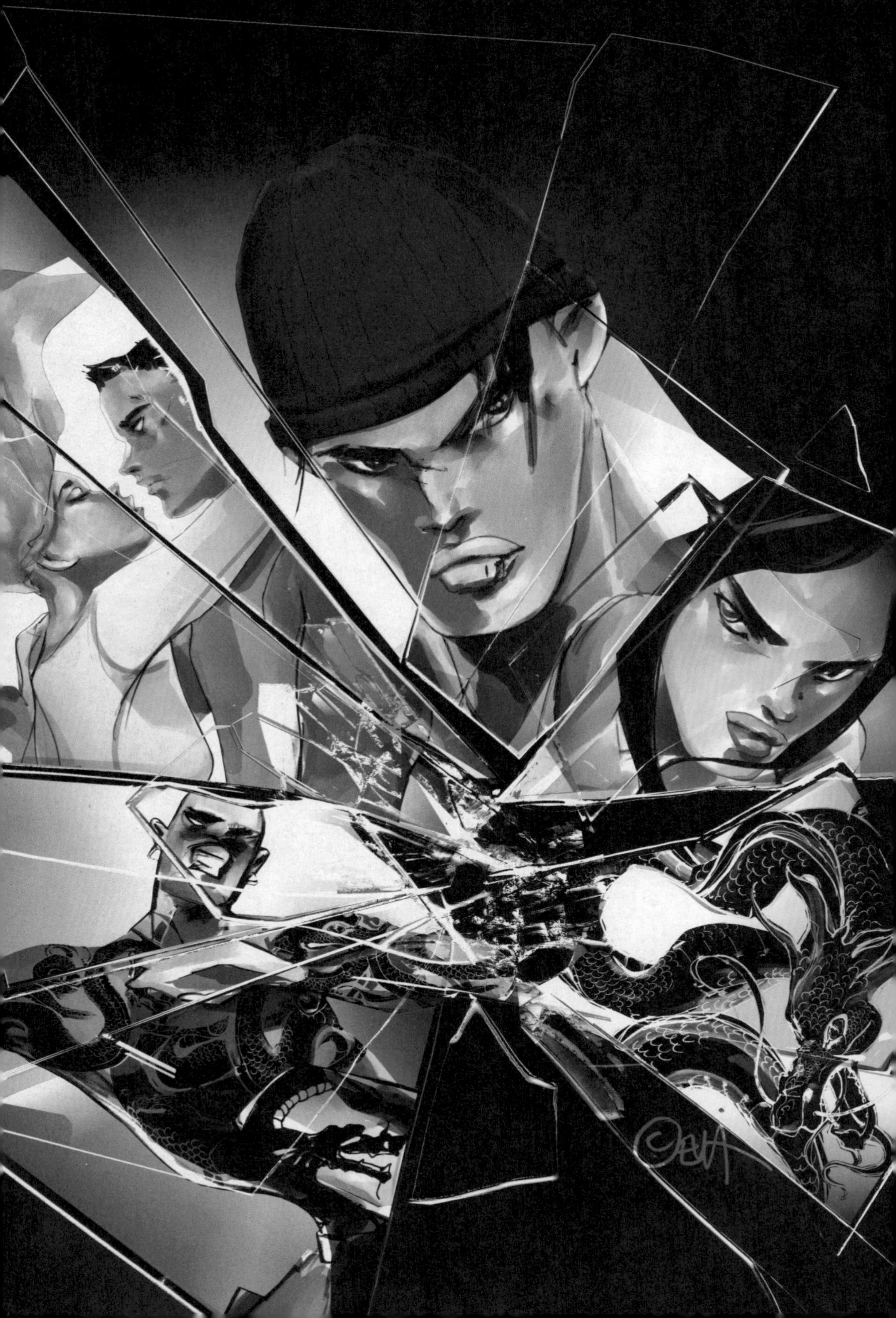

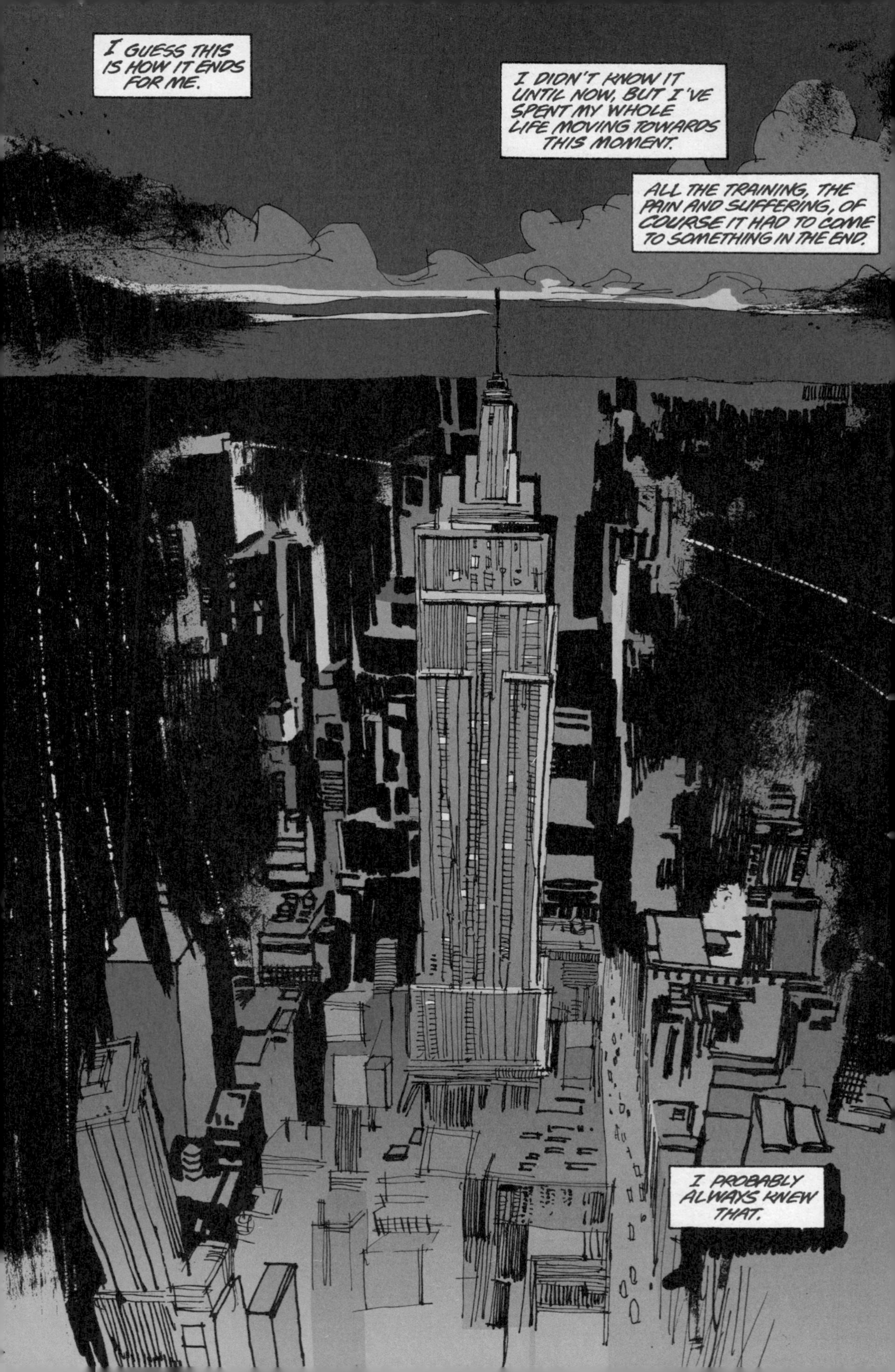

I GUESS THIS IS HOW IT ENDS FOR ME.
I DIDN'T KNOW IT UNTIL NOW, BUT I'VE SPENT MY WHOLE LIFE MOVING TOWARDS THIS MOMENT.
ALL THE TRAINING, THE PAIN AND SUFFERING, OF COURSE IT HAD TO COME TO SOMETHING IN THE END.
I PROBABLY ALWAYS KNEW THAT.

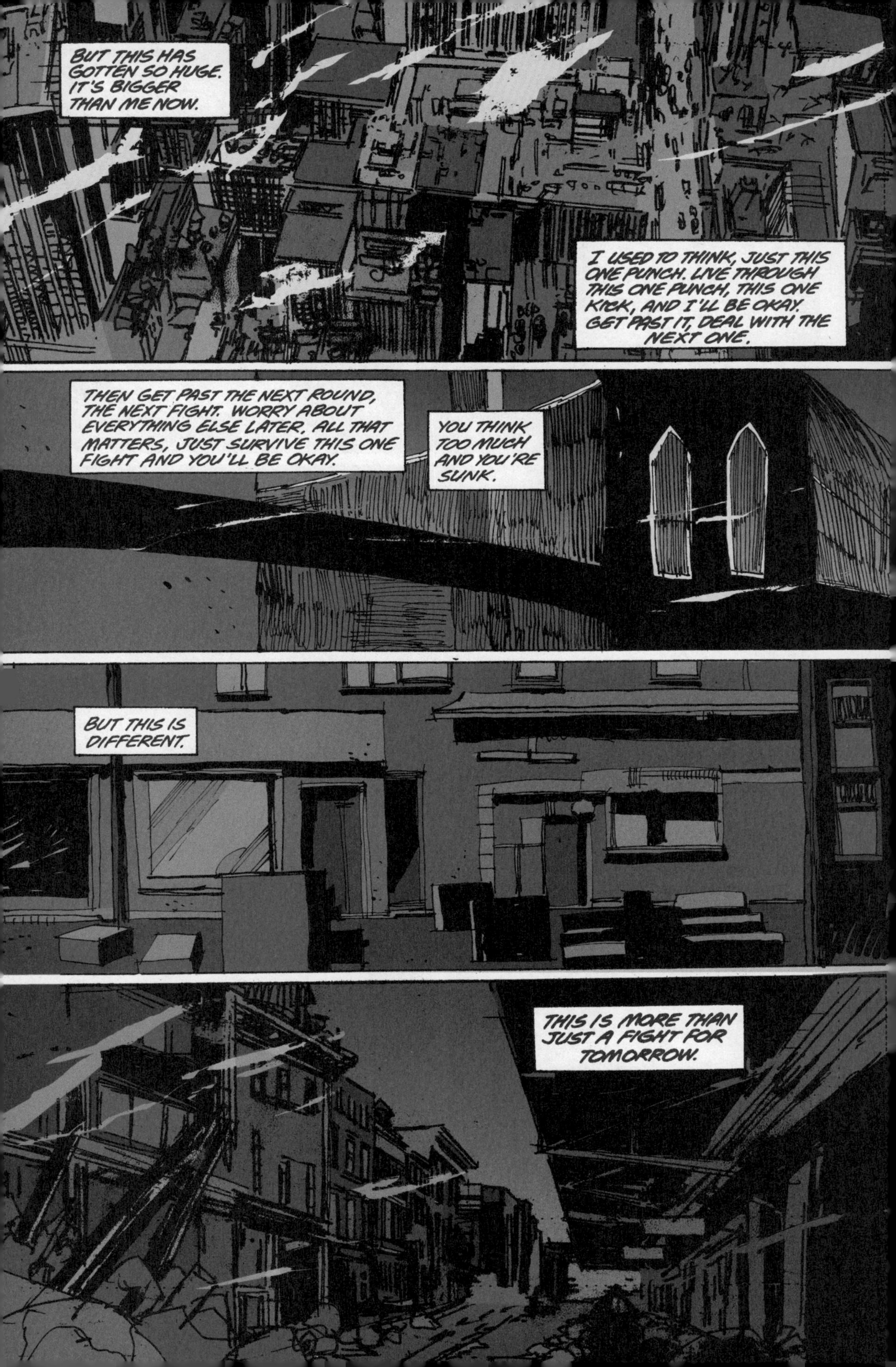
BUT THIS HAS GOTTEN SO HUGE. IT'S BIGGER THAN ME NOW.
I USED TO THINK, JUST THIS ONE PUNCH. LIVE THROUGH THIS ONE PUNCH, THIS ONE KICK, AND I'LL BE OKAY. GET PAST IT, DEAL WITH THE NEXT ONE.
THEN GET PAST THE NEXT ROUND, THE NEXT FIGHT. WORRY ABOUT EVERYTHING ELSE LATER. ALL THAT MATTERS, JUST SURVIVE THIS ONE FIGHT AND YOU'LL BE OKAY.
YOU THINK TOO MUCH AND YOU'RE SUNK.
BUT THIS IS DIFFERENT.
THIS IS MORE THAN JUST A FIGHT FOR TOMORROW.

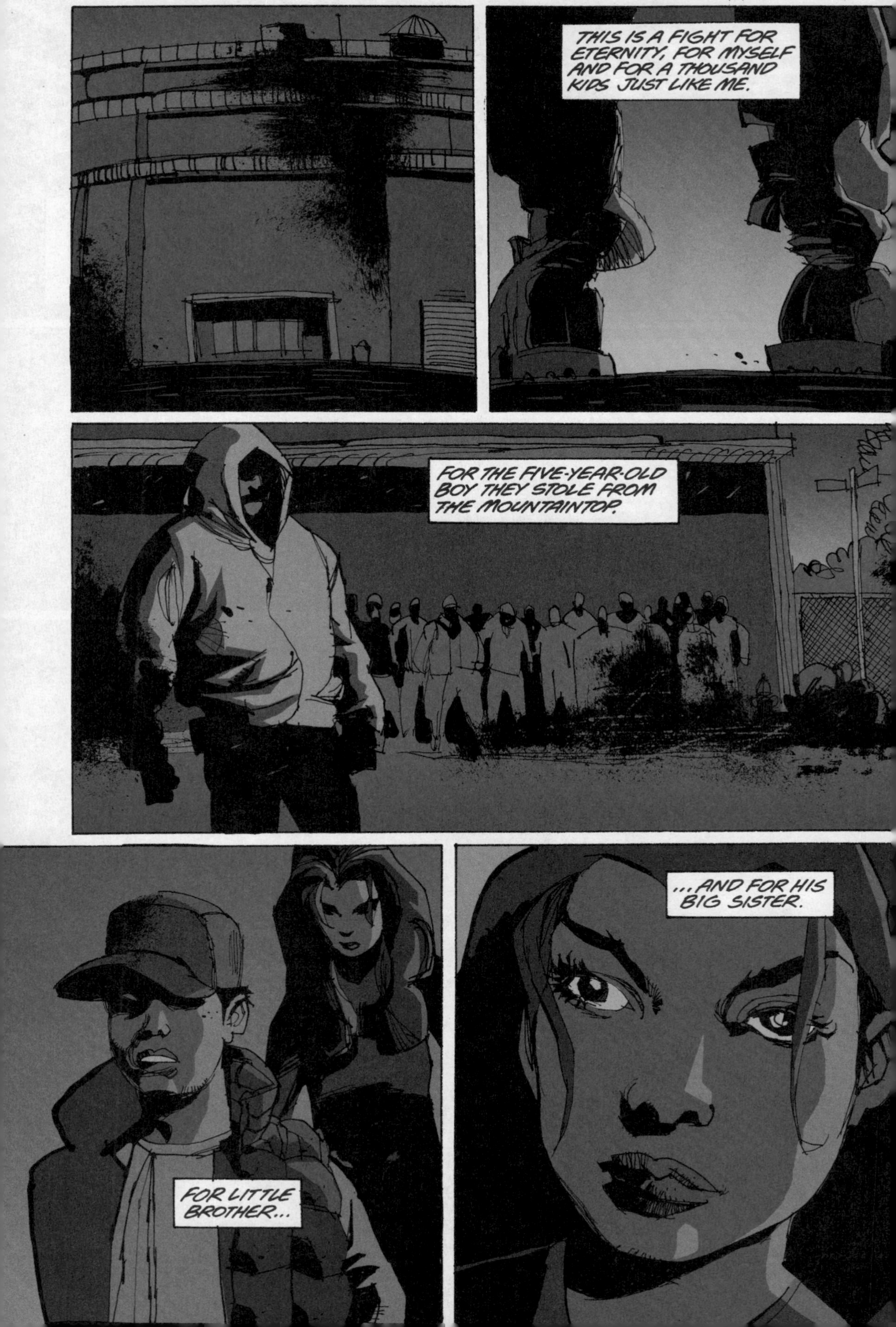
THIS IS A FIGHT FOR ETERNITY, FOR MYSELF AND FOR A THOUSAND KIDS JUST LIKE ME.
FOR THE FIVE-YEAR-OLD BOY THEY STOLE FROM THE MOUNTAINTOP.
FOR LITTLE BROTHER...
...AND FOR HIS BIG SISTER.

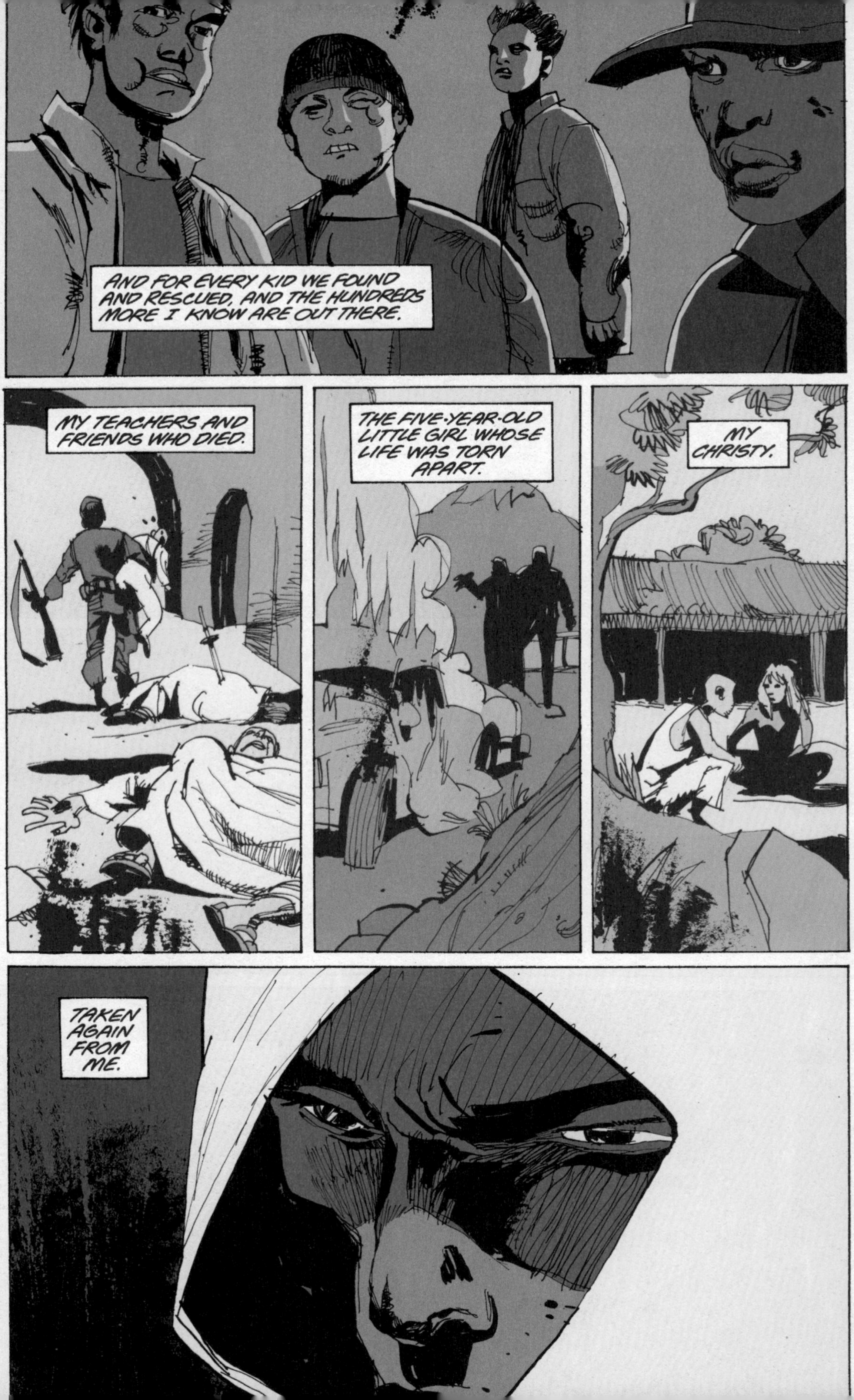
AND FOR EVERY KID WE FOUND AND RESCUED, AND THE HUNDREDS MORE I KNOW ARE OUT THERE.
MY TEACHERS AND FRIENDS WHO DIED.
THE FIVE-YEAR-OLD LITTLE GIRL WHOSE LIFE WAS TORN APART.
MY CHRISTY.
TAKEN AGAIN FROM ME.

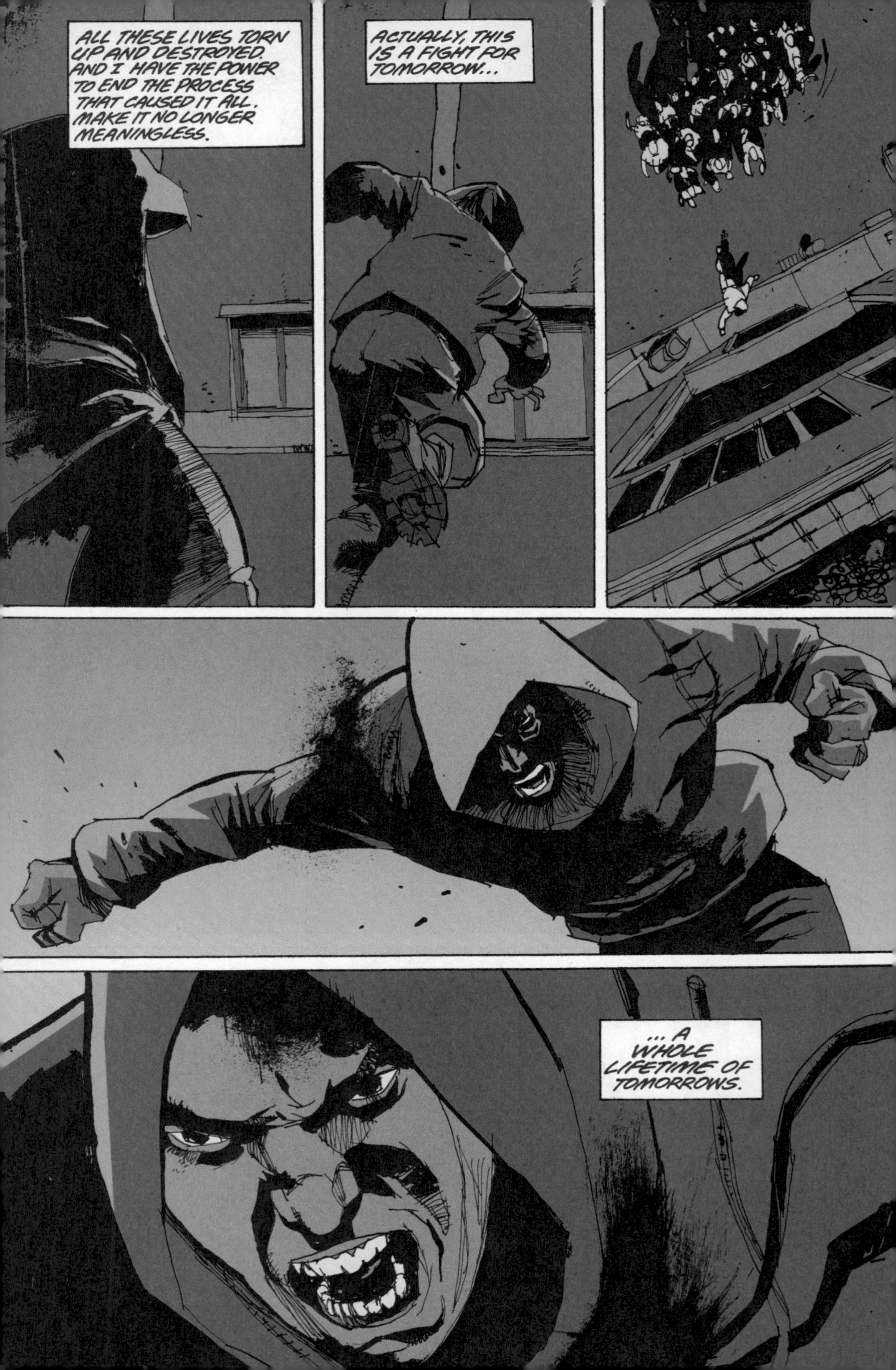
ALL THESE LIVES TORN UP AND DESTROYED. AND I HAVE THE POWER TO END THE PROCESS THAT CAUSED IT ALL. MAKE IT NO LONGER MEANINGLESS.
ACTUALLY, THIS IS A FIGHT FOR TOMORROW...
...A WHOLE LIFETIME OF TOMORROWS.

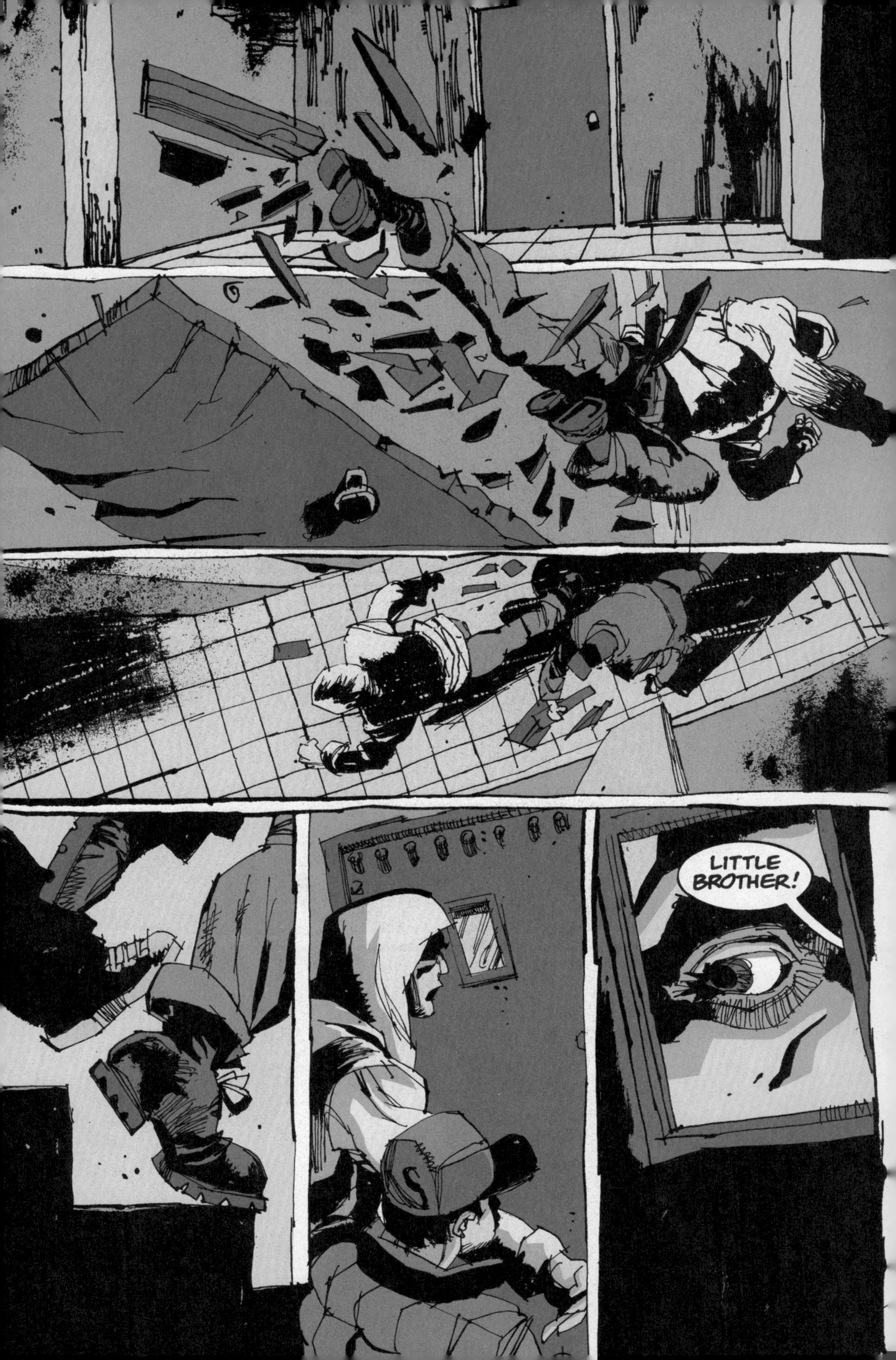
LITTLE BROTHER!

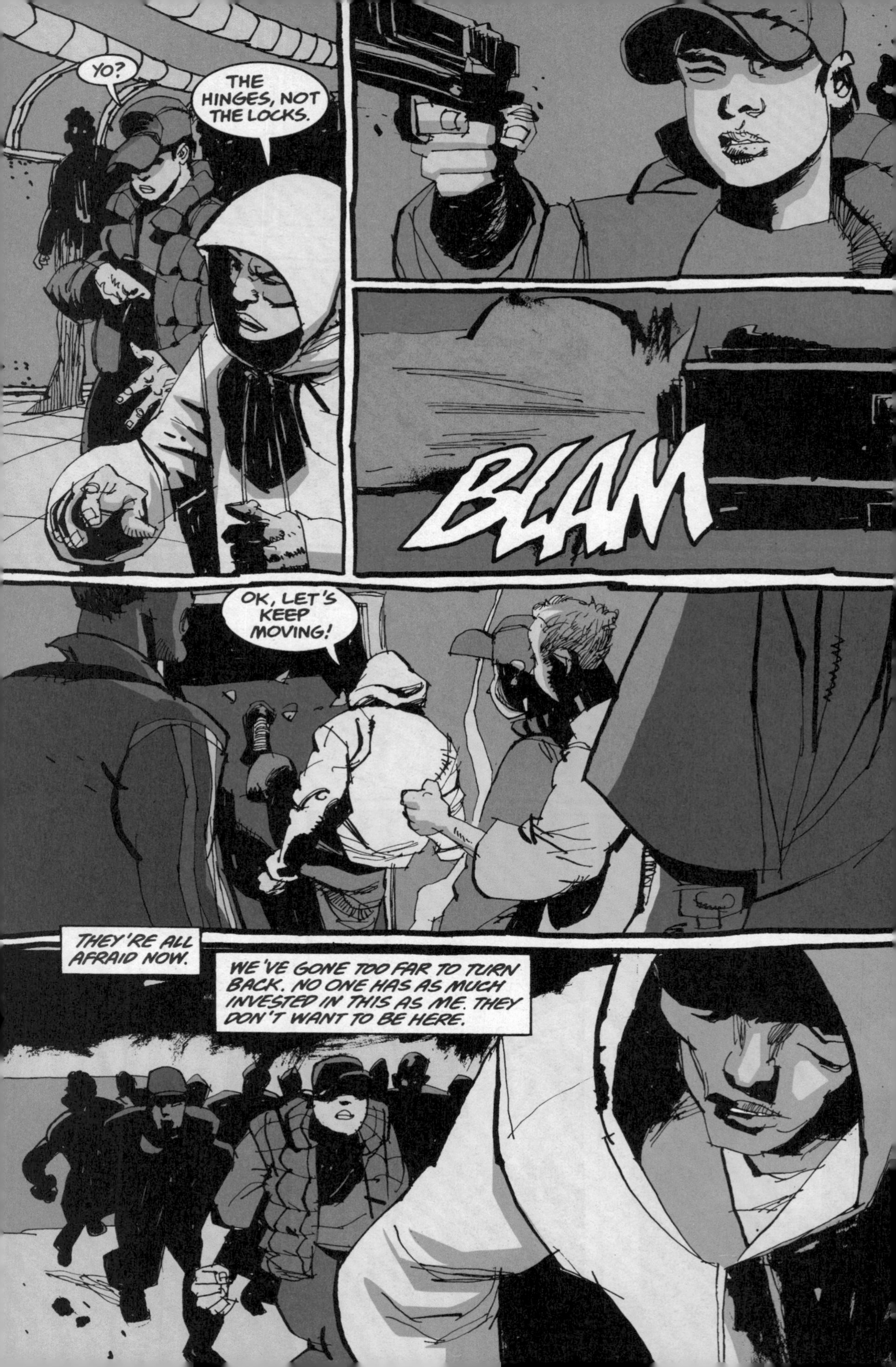
YO?
THE HINGES, NOT THE LOCKS.
BLAM
OK, LET'S KEEP MOVING!
THEY'RE ALL AFRAID NOW.
WE'VE GONE TOO FAR TO TURN BACK. NO ONE HAS AS MUCH INVESTED IN THIS AS ME. THEY DON'T WANT TO BE HERE.

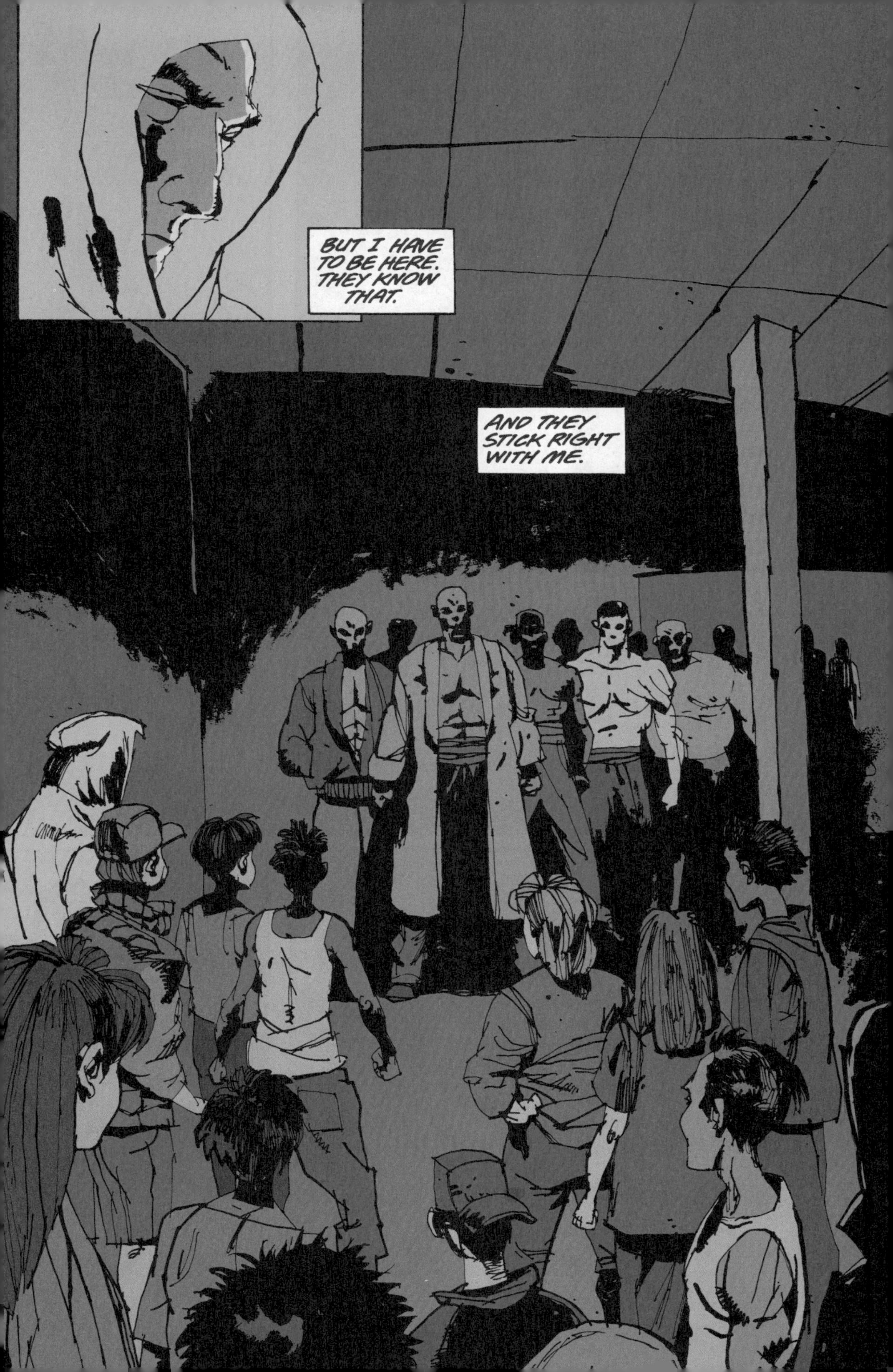
BUT I HAVE TO BE HERE. THEY KNOW THAT.
AND THEY STICK RIGHT WITH ME.

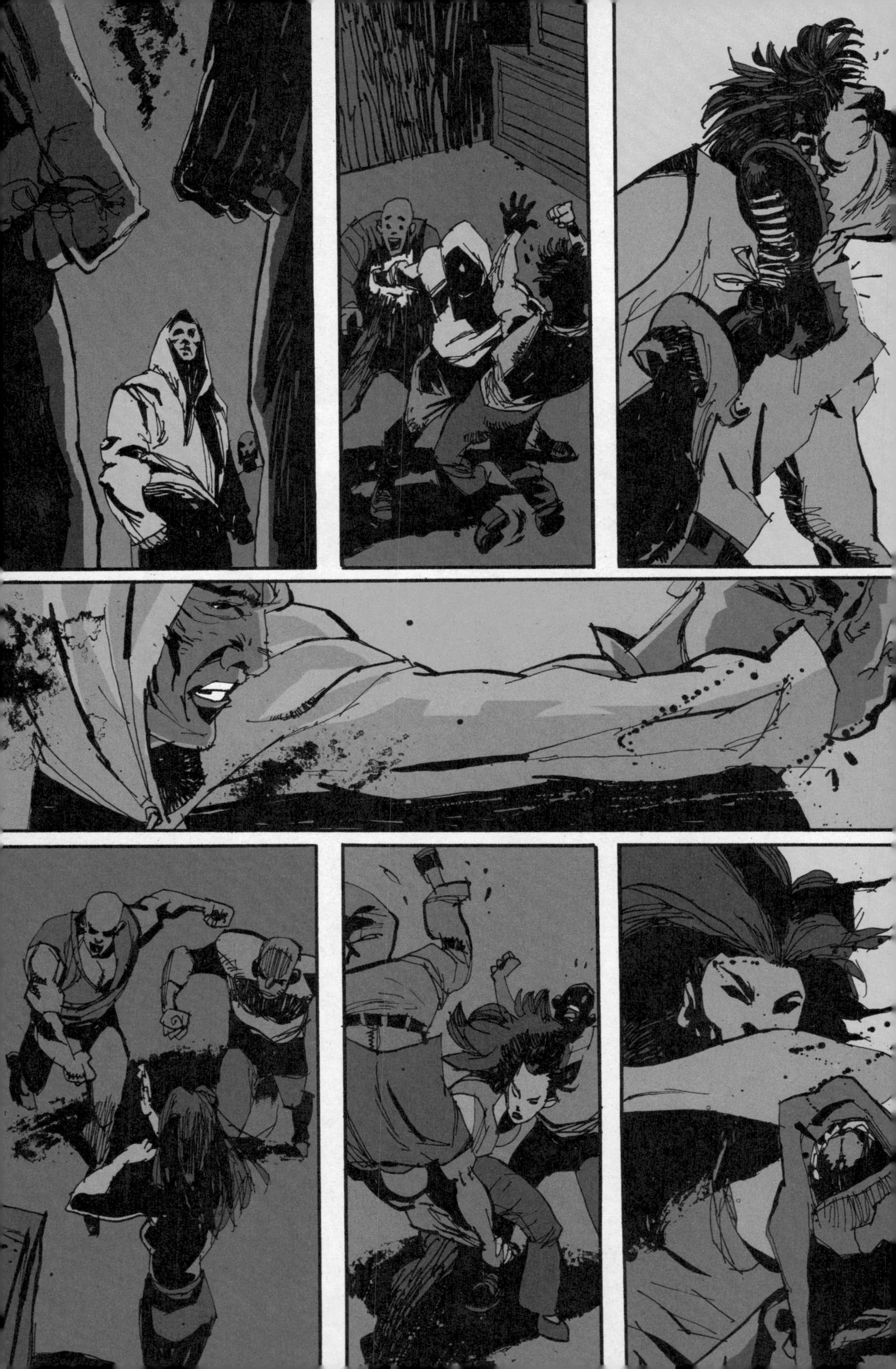

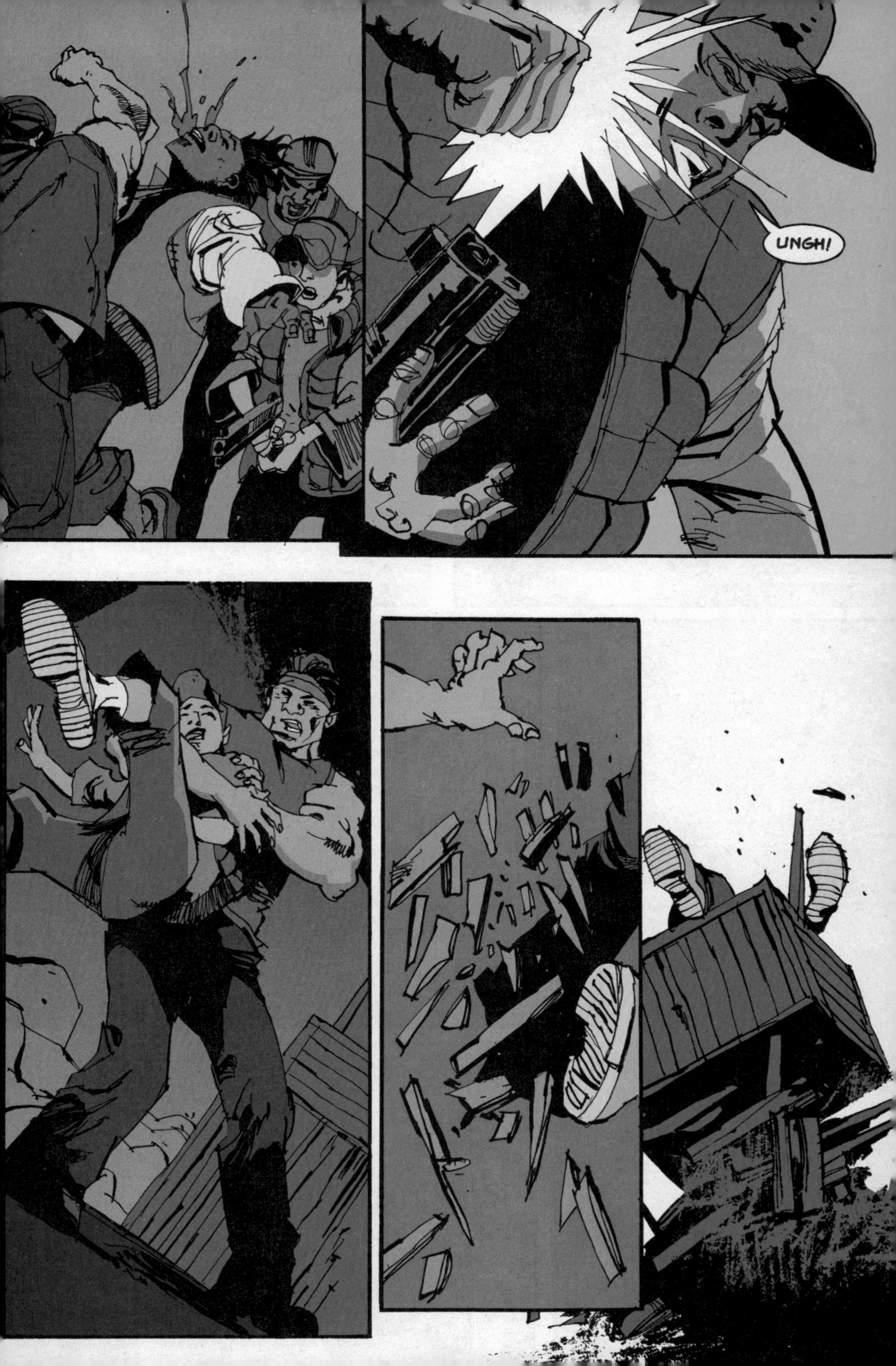
UNGH!

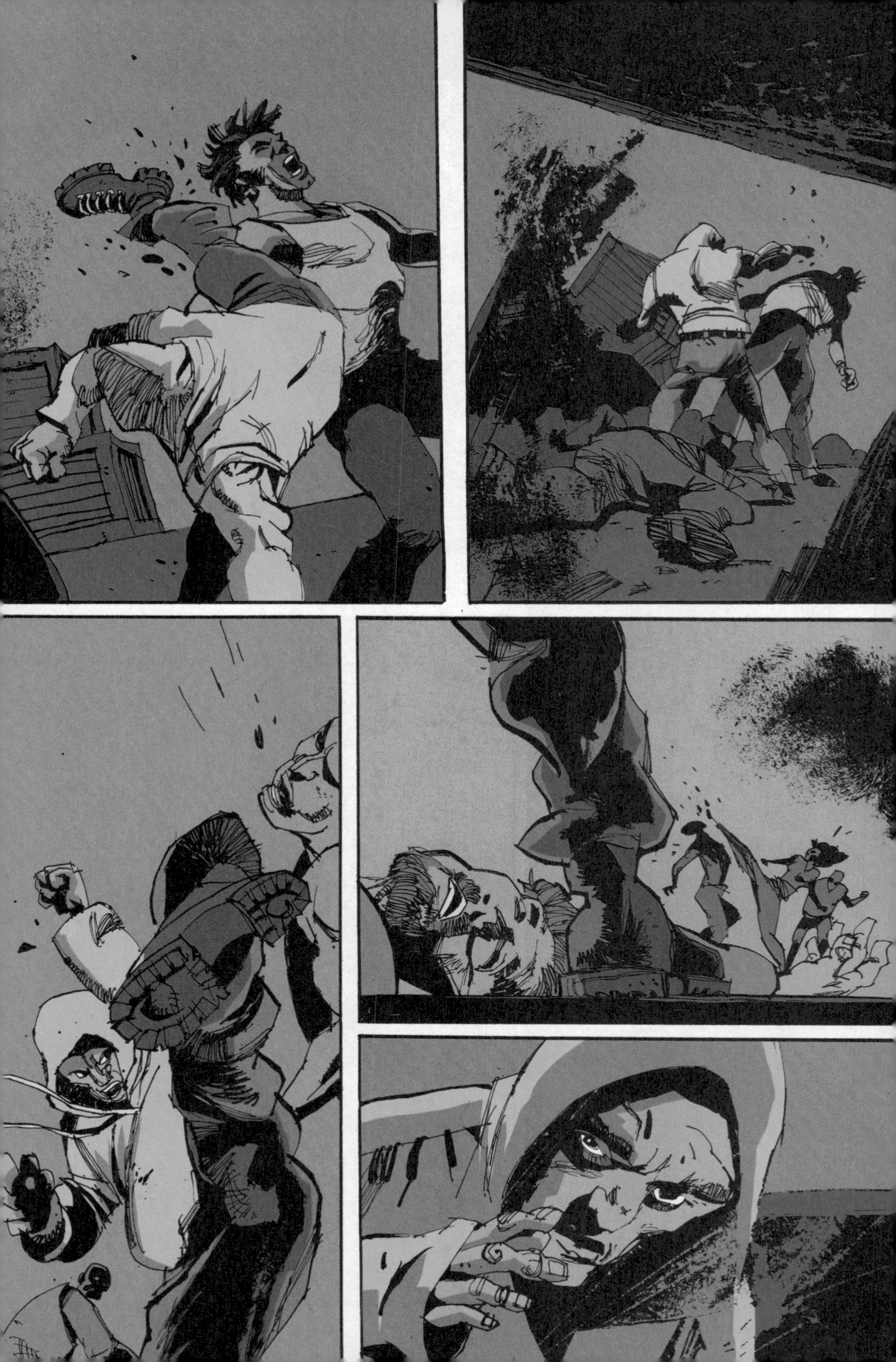

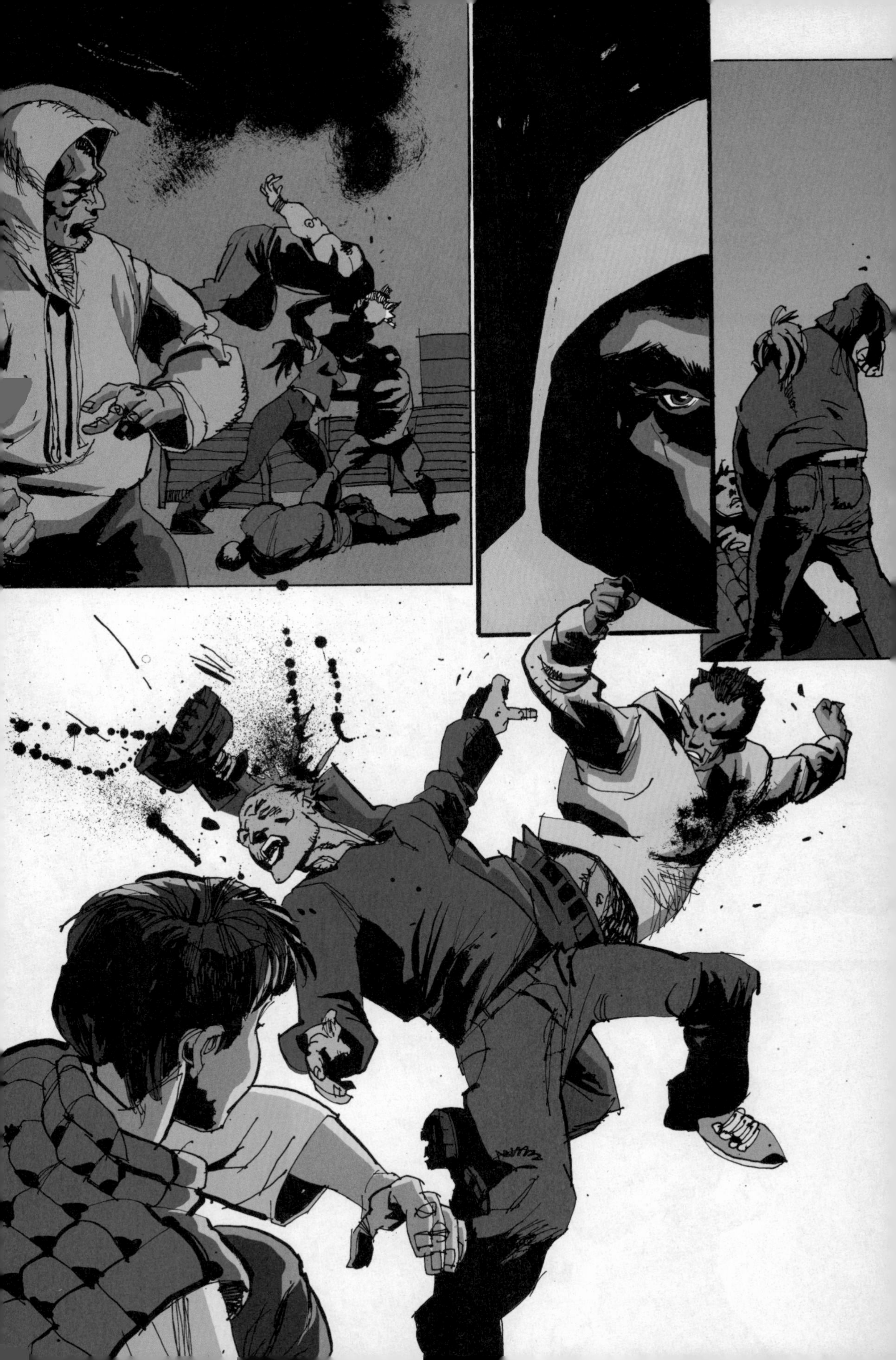

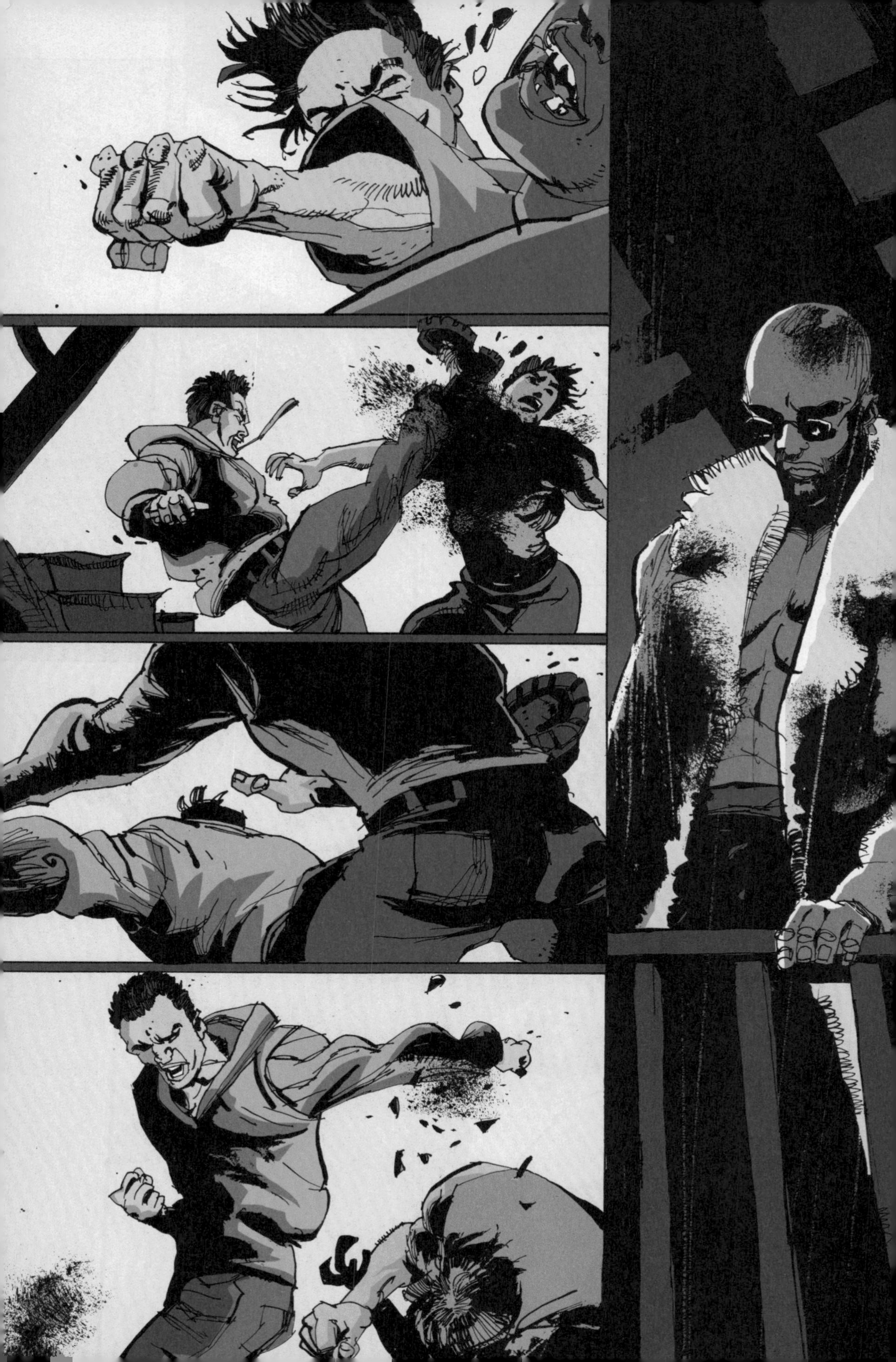

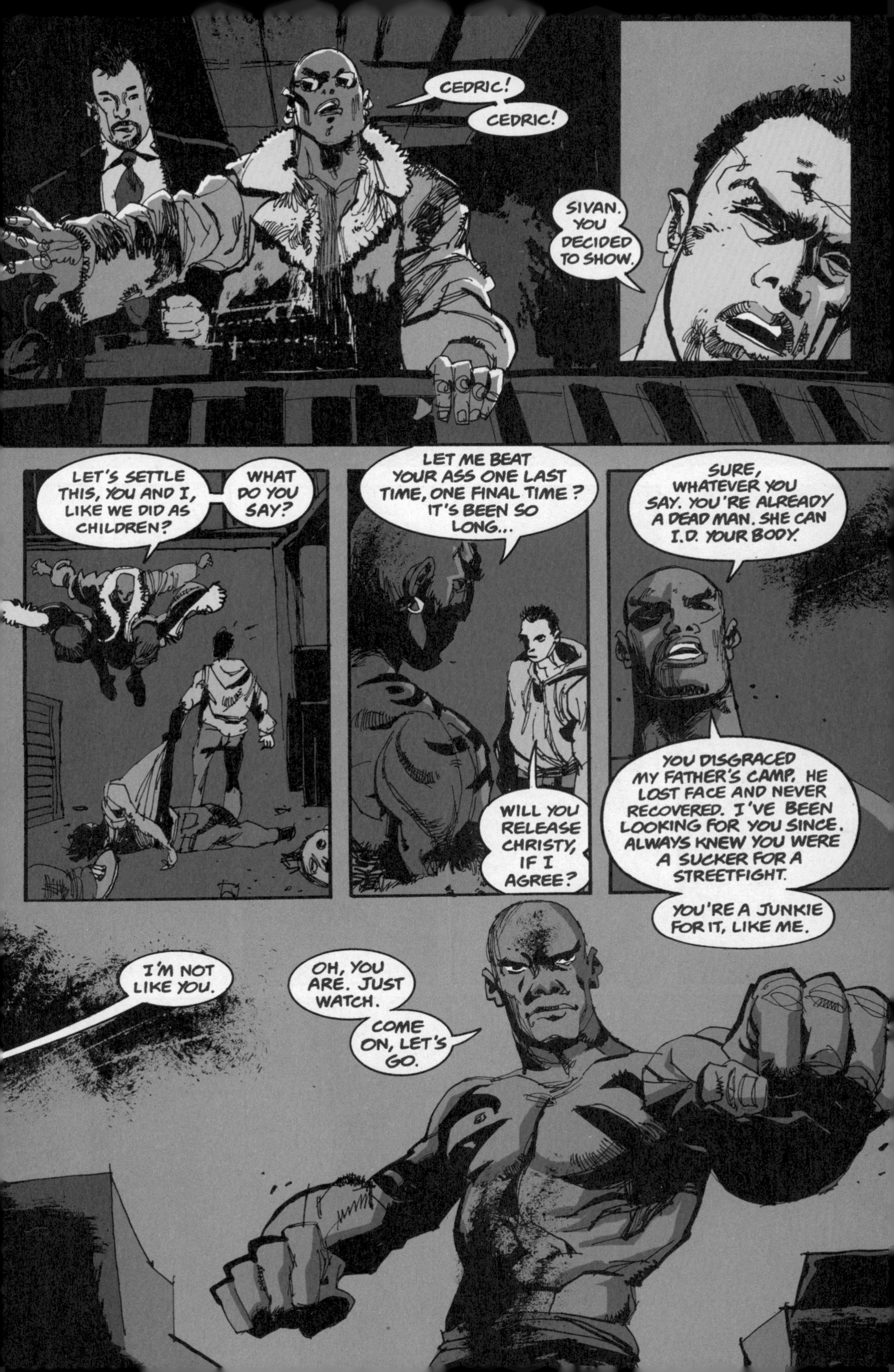
CEDRIC!
CEDRIC!
SIVAN. YOU DECIDED TO SHOW.
LET'S SETTLE THIS, YOU AND I, LIKE WE DID AS CHILDREN?
WHAT DO YOU SAY?
LET ME BEAT YOUR ASS ONE LAST TIME, ONE FINAL TIME? IT'S BEEN SO LONG...
WILL YOU RELEASE CHRISTY, IF I AGREE?
SURE, WHATEVER YOU SAY. YOU'RE ALREADY A DEAD MAN. SHE CAN I.D. YOUR BODY.
YOU DISGRACED MY FATHER'S CAMP. HE LOST FACE AND NEVER RECOVERED. I'VE BEEN LOOKING FOR YOU SINCE. ALWAYS KNEW YOU WERE A SUCKER FOR A STREETFIGHT.
YOU'RE A JUNKIE FOR IT, LIKE ME.
I'M NOT LIKE YOU.
OH, YOU ARE. JUST WATCH.
COME ON, LET'S GO.

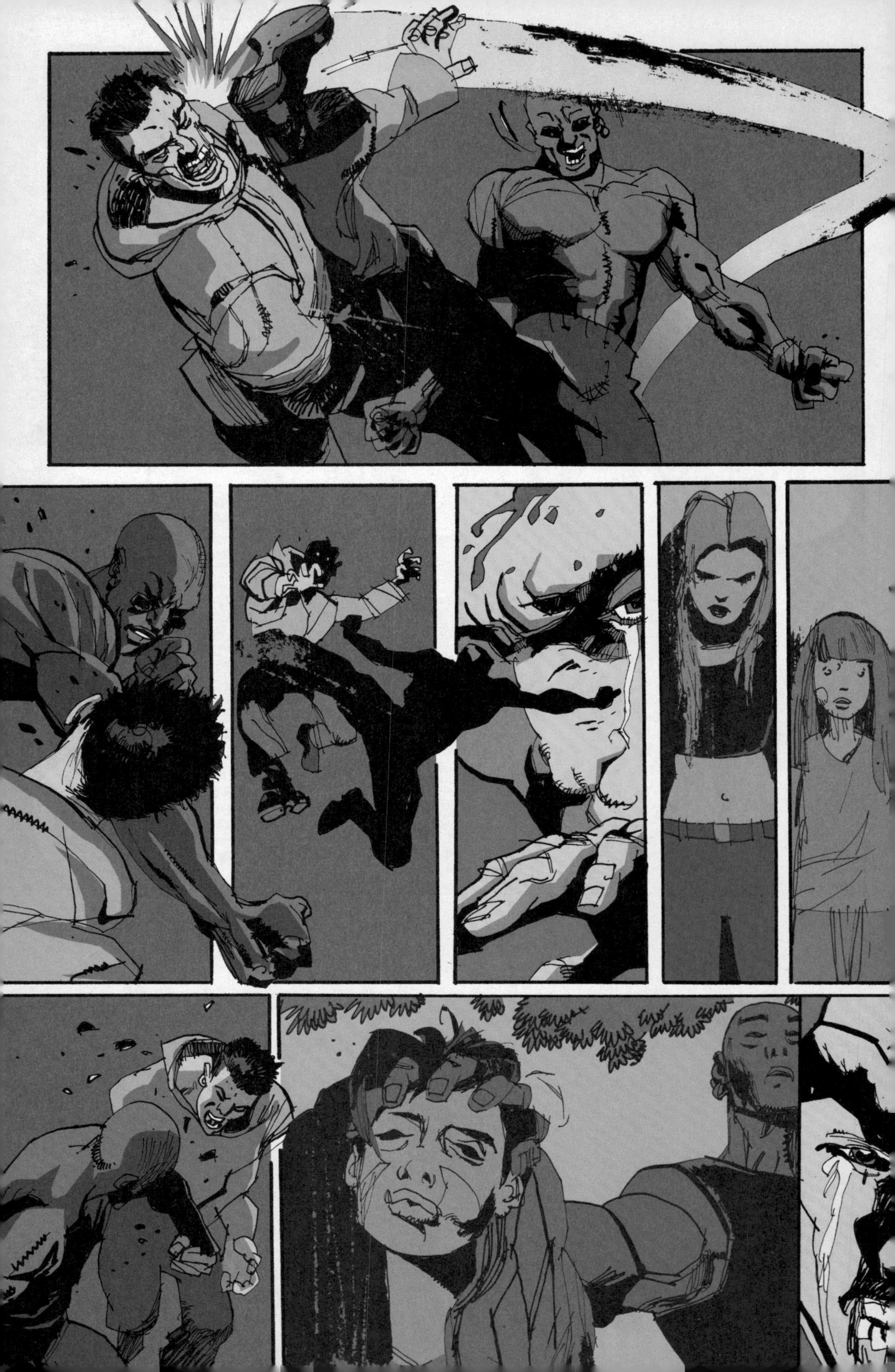

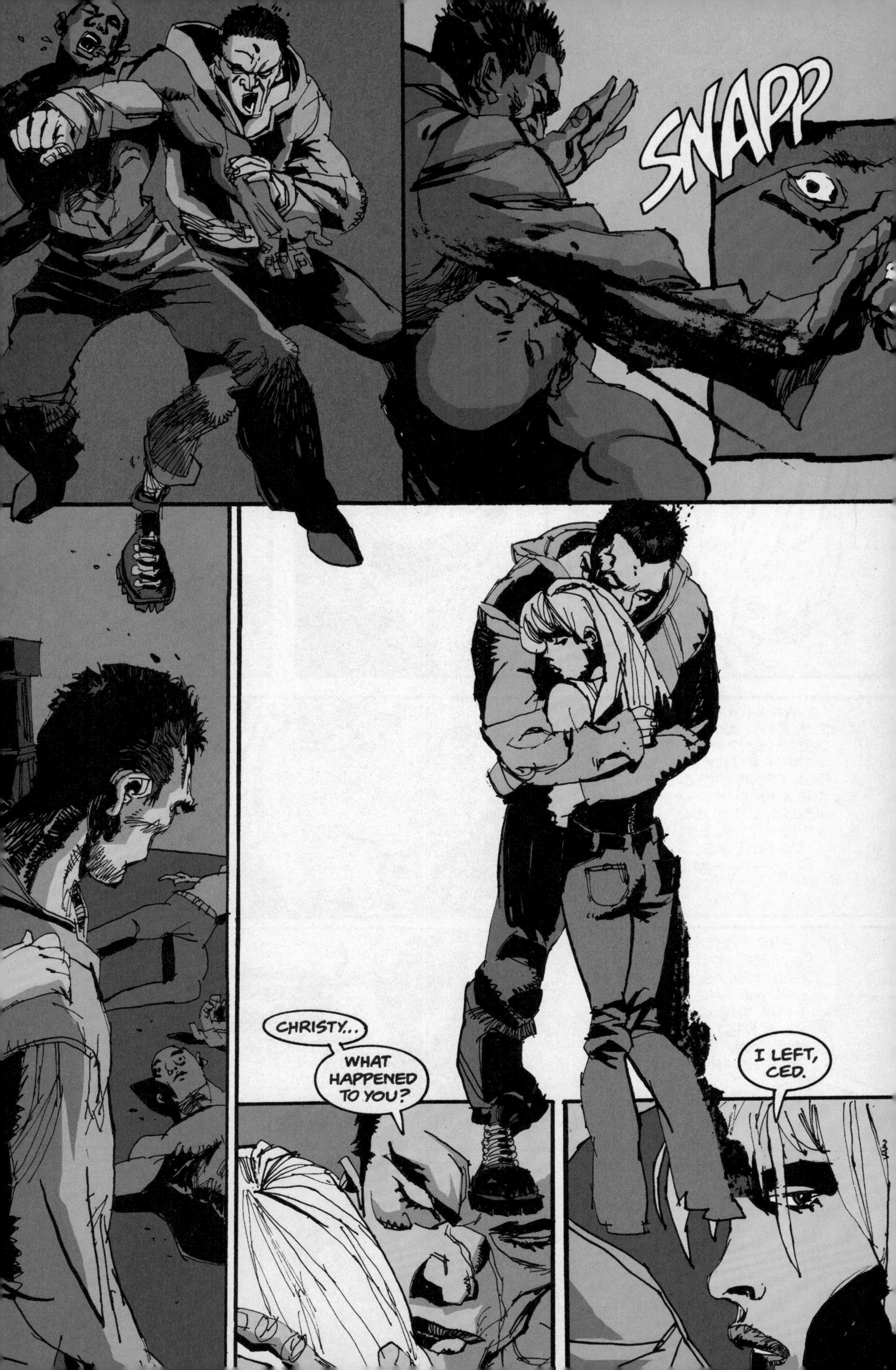
SNAPP
CHRISTY...
WHAT HAPPENED TO YOU?
I LEFT, CED.

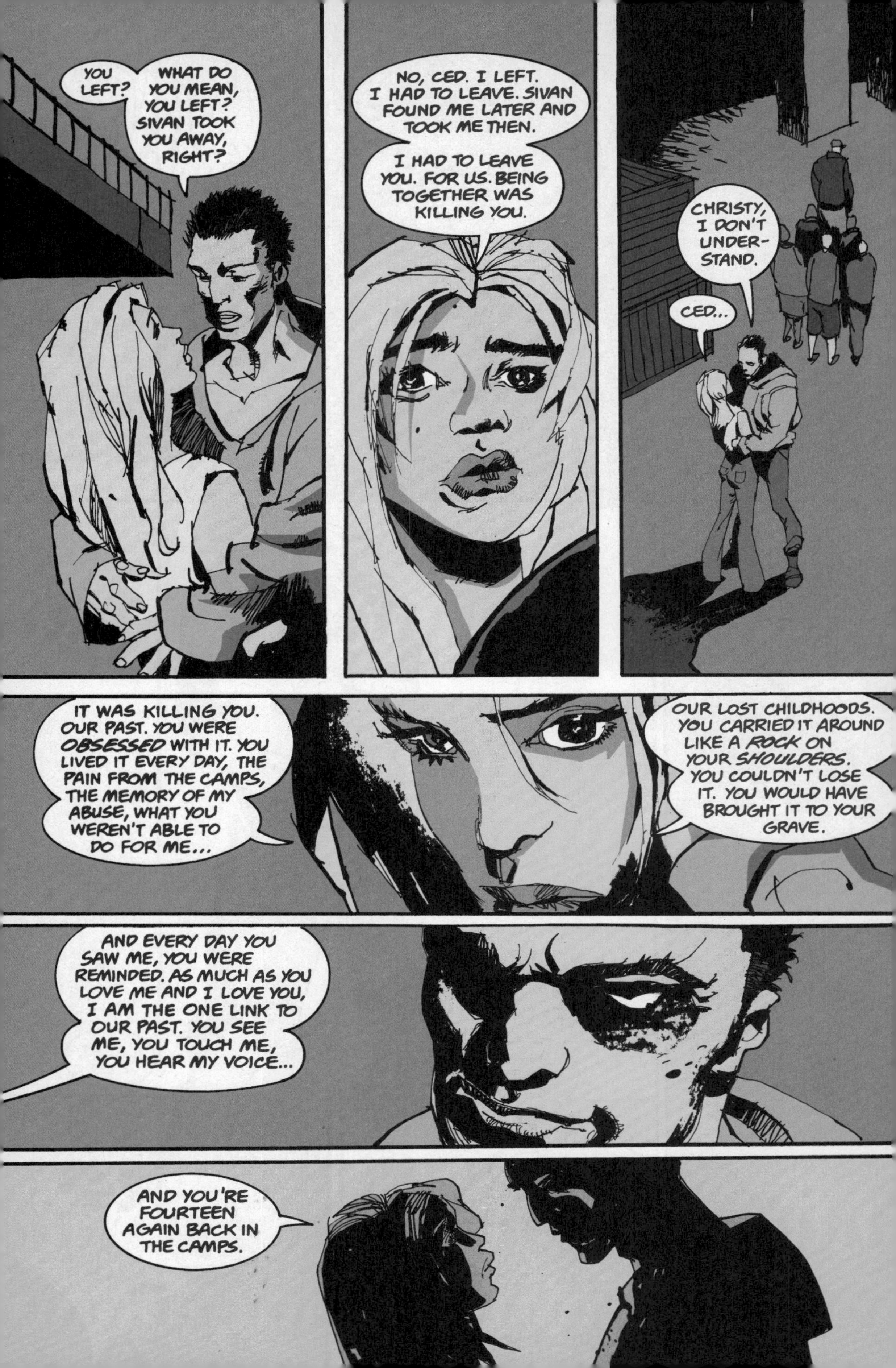
YOU LEFT?
WHAT DO YOU MEAN, YOU LEFT? SIVAN TOOK YOU AWAY, RIGHT?
NO, CED. I LEFT. I HAD TO LEAVE. SIVAN FOUND ME LATER AND TOOK ME THEN.
I HAD TO LEAVE YOU. FOR US. BEING TOGETHER WAS KILLING YOU.
CHRISTY, I DON'T UNDER-STAND.
CED...
IT WAS KILLING YOU. OUR PAST. YOU WERE OBSESSED WITH IT. YOU LIVED IT EVERY DAY, THE PAIN FROM THE CAMPS, THE MEMORY OF MY ABUSE, WHAT YOU WEREN'T ABLE TO DO FOR ME...
OUR LOST CHILDHOODS. YOU CARRIED IT AROUND LIKE A ROCK ON YOUR SHOULDERS. YOU COULDN'T LOSE IT. YOU WOULD HAVE BROUGHT IT TO YOUR GRAVE.
AND EVERY DAY YOU SAW ME, YOU WERE REMINDED. AS MUCH AS YOU LOVE ME AND I LOVE YOU, I AM THE ONE LINK TO OUR PAST. YOU SEE ME, YOU TOUCH ME, YOU HEAR MY VOICE...
AND YOU'RE FOURTEEN AGAIN BACK IN THE CAMPS.

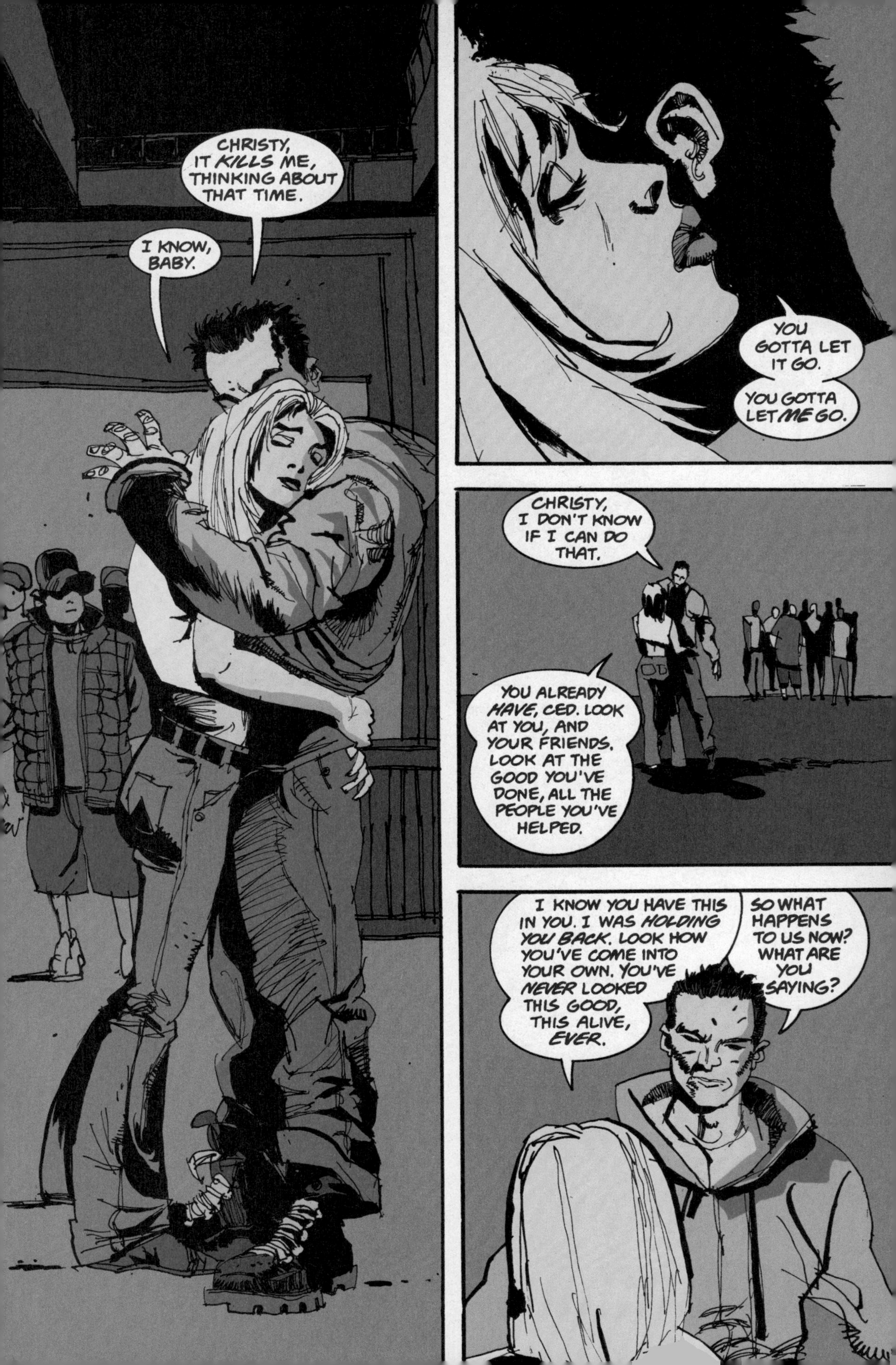
CHRISTY, IT KILLS ME, THINKING ABOUT THAT TIME.
I KNOW, BABY.
YOU GOTTA LET IT GO.
YOU GOTTA LET ME GO.
CHRISTY, I DON'T KNOW IF I CAN DO THAT.
YOU ALREADY HAVE, CED. LOOK AT YOU, AND YOUR FRIENDS. LOOK AT THE GOOD YOU'VE DONE, ALL THE PEOPLE YOU'VE HELPED.
I KNOW YOU HAVE THIS IN YOU. I WAS HOLDING YOU BACK. LOOK HOW YOU'VE COME INTO YOUR OWN. YOU'VE NEVER LOOKED THIS GOOD, THIS ALIVE, EVER.
SO WHAT HAPPENS TO US NOW? WHAT ARE YOU SAYING?

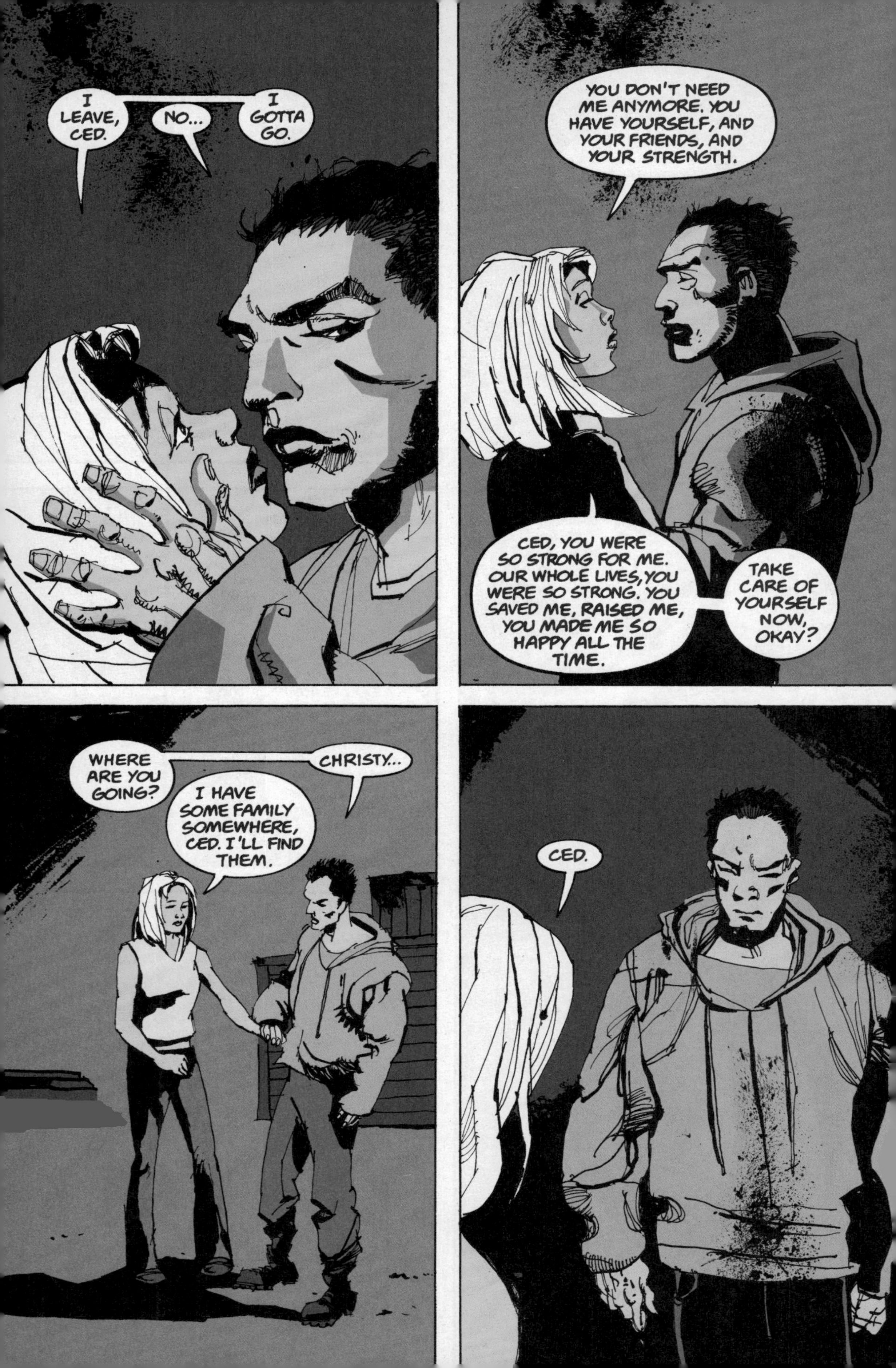
I LEAVE, CED.
NO...
I GOTTA GO.
YOU DON'T NEED ME ANYMORE. YOU HAVE YOURSELF, AND YOUR FRIENDS, AND YOUR STRENGTH.
CED, YOU WERE SO STRONG FOR ME. OUR WHOLE LIVES, YOU WERE SO STRONG. YOU SAVED ME, RAISED ME, YOU MADE ME SO HAPPY ALL THE TIME.
TAKE CARE OF YOURSELF NOW, OKAY?
WHERE ARE YOU GOING?
CHRISTY...
I HAVE SOME FAMILY SOMEWHERE, CED. I'LL FIND THEM.
CED.

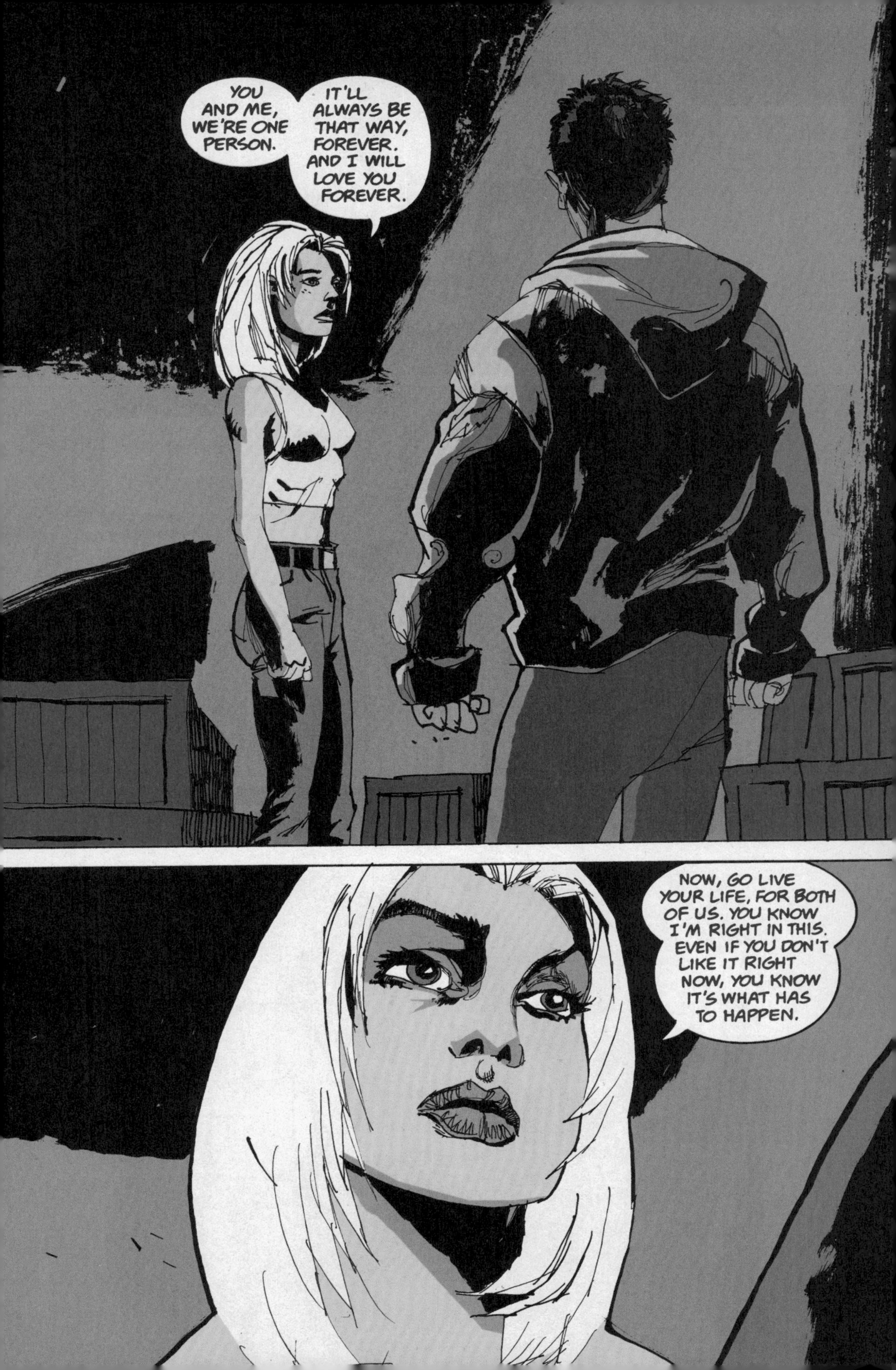

YOU AND ME, WE'RE ONE PERSON.
IT'LL ALWAYS BE THAT WAY, FOREVER. AND I WILL LOVE YOU FOREVER.
NOW, GO LIVE YOUR LIFE, FOR BOTH OF US. YOU KNOW I'M RIGHT IN THIS. EVEN IF YOU DON'T LIKE IT RIGHT NOW, YOU KNOW IT'S WHAT HAS TO HAPPEN.

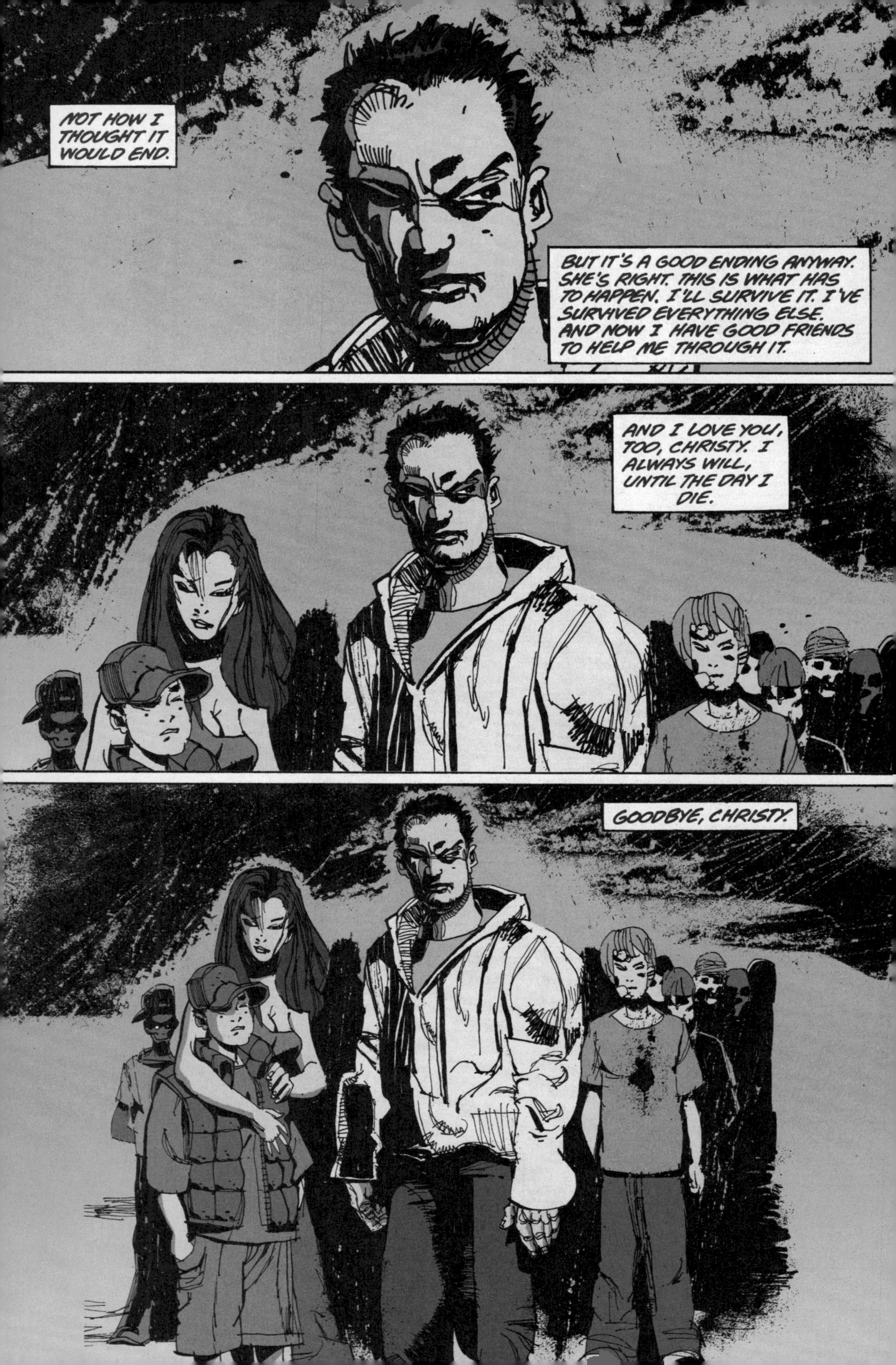
NOT HOW I THOUGHT IT WOULD END.
BUT IT'S A GOOD ENDING ANYWAY. SHE'S RIGHT. THIS IS WHAT HAS TO HAPPEN. I'LL SURVIVE IT. I'VE SURVIVED EVERYTHING ELSE. AND NOW I HAVE GOOD FRIENDS TO HELP ME THROUGH IT.
AND I LOVE YOU, TOO, CHRISTY. I ALWAYS WILL, UNTIL THE DAY I DIE.
GOODBYE, CHRISTY.

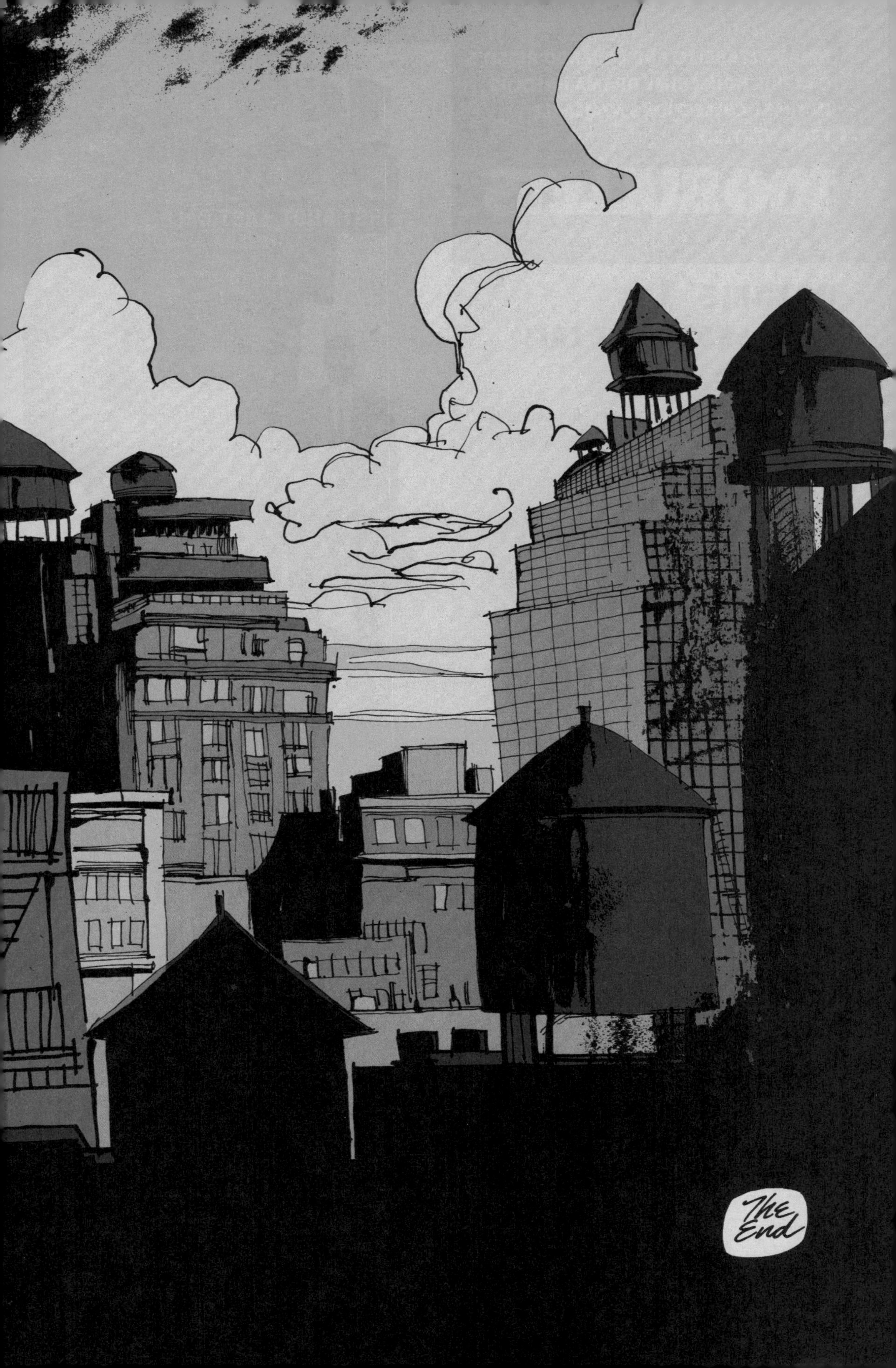
The End

BRIAN AZZARELLO AND EDUARDO RISSO'S GRAPHIC NOIR CRIME DRAMA UNFOLDS IN THESE COLLECTIONS AVAILABLE FROM VERTIGO.

100 BULLETS

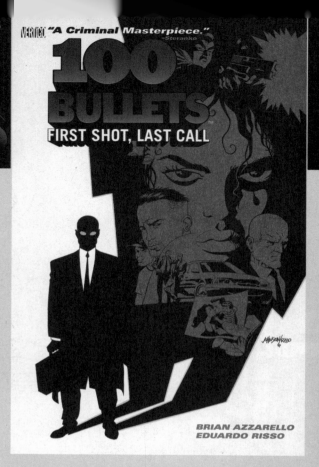

VERTIGO
"A Criminal Masterpiece."
-Steranko
100 BULLETS
FIRST SHOT, LAST CALL
BRIAN AZZARELLO
EDUARDO RISSO

VOLUME 1:
FIRST SHOT, LAST CALL

With one special briefcase, Agent Graves gives you the chance to kill without retribution. But what is the real price for this chance — and who is setting it?

ALSO AVAILABLE:
VOL. 2: SPLIT SECOND CHANCE
VOL. 3: HANG UP ON THE HANG LOW
VOL. 4: A FOREGONE TOMORROW
VOL. 5: THE COUNTERFIFTH DETECTIVE
VOL. 6: SIX FEET UNDER THE GUN
VOL. 7: SAMURAI
VOL. 8: THE HARD WAY
VOL. 9: STRYCHNINE LIVES

"AMAZING ARTWORK AND OVER-THE-TOP STORIES — REVENGE NEVER LOOKED SO SWEET."
—*TRANSWORLD STANCE*

VERTIGO
Brian Azzarello
Eduardo Risso
100 BULLETS
Winner of the 2001 Eisner Award for Best Serialized Story
HANG UP ON THE HANG LOW

VERTIGO
BRIAN AZZARELLO EDUARDO RISSO
100 BULLETS
SIX FEET UNDER THE GUN

BRIAN AZZARELLO EDUARDO RISSO
VERTIGO
100 BULLETS
SAMURAI

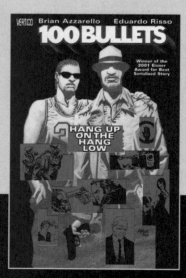

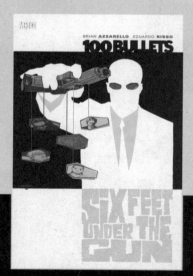

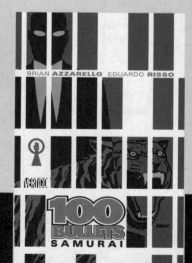

ALL TITLES ARE SUGGESTED FOR MATURE READERS.

SEARCH THE GRAPHIC NOVELS SECTION OF
www.VERTIGOCOMICS.com
FOR ART AND INFORMATION ON ALL OF OUR BOOKS!